PLAY IT LOUD

PLAY IT
LOUD

An Epic History of the Style, Sound, and Revolution of the Electric Guitar

BRAD TOLINSKI

and

ALAN DI PERNA

Doubleday

New York   London   Toronto   Sydney   Auckland

Book design by Maria Carella
Jacket composite image: Various electric guitars. Shutterstock
Jacket design by Michael J. Windsor

Library of Congress Cataloging-in-Publication Data
Names: Tolinski, Brad, author. Di Perna, Alan, [date], author.
Title: Play it loud : an epic history of the style, sound, and revolution of
the electric guitar / Brad Tolinski and Alan di Perna.
Description: First edition. New York, NY : Doubleday, 2016.
Includes bibliographical references and index.
Identifiers: LCCN 2016013874 ISBN 9780385540995 (hardcover)
ISBN 9780385541008 (ebook)
Subjects: LCSH: Electric guitar—History.
Classification: LCC ML1015.G9 T66 2016   DDC 787.8709—dc23 LC record
available at http://lccn.loc.gov/2016013874

MANUFACTURED IN THE UNITED STATES OF AMERICA

1 3 5 7 9 10 8 6 4 2

First Edition

CONTENTS

FOREWORD

Play It Loud is a dynamic history of the electric guitar, but more important, it's about the artists who painted the universal tones, colors, textures, and movements on the world canvas, through their fingertips, into a consciousness revolution to our hearts and minds. Brad and Alan get inside the note of the political and cultural significance of the guitar.

To me, the guitar symbolizes rebellion, liberation, and freedom of expression. It is a doorway through which we can profoundly touch people's hearts and souls and change lives. In the '60s we had the Black Panthers, Woodstock, and Vietnam, and the electric guitar became the iconic voice of our generation—from Dylan and the Beatles to Hendrix at Woodstock. Throughout the '70s we continued to question and shape the world around us through melody, rhythm, message, and song. The guitar helped open up the world. It broke down the racial barriers against black musicians who were our pioneers long before the British Invasion. Those musicians invaded us with music that was born here in the United States. B. B. King, Howlin' Wolf, Muddy Waters, Jimmy Reed, Buddy Guy, John Lee Hooker, and all the other greats survived because of their love for music. The guitar created a voice for the voiceless, bringing their lives to ours.

To be able to touch someone and change their molecular structure with just one note is very powerful. One note can bring someone back from the edge, make lovers come together, create life, end wars, and make you shed tears of joy and sorrow at the same time. It is called the universal tone, and for me it comes from six things I strive for every time I plug in my guitar: stay genuine, honest, sincere, true, authentic, and for real on every song. *Play It Loud* is all of these things, on every page.

—CARLOS SANTANA

PREFACE

Born in Roaring Twenties Southern California to a band of creative outsiders—transplants from the Dust Bowl, the Midwest, and Europe—the electric guitar very quickly grew into one of the defining symbols of our time. There are few greater, more prevalent modern icons. When used in advertising (as it often is), it is shorthand for freedom, danger, and unabashed hedonism. In the hands of a musician, it signifies artistry and rebellion. Its inventors' ambitions may have been modest, but the instrument they conceived—visually striking in appearance, utterly practical in its application—would leave an indelible imprint on our history.

Long before anyone thought to amplify it, the guitar proved a remarkably versatile musical instrument. Its six strings and wide four-octave range could be used for chordal accompaniment or melodic single-note soloing, in almost any style. Its biggest asset, however, was its remarkable portability. Unlike a piano, a guitar could be slung over your shoulder and played just about anywhere. The instrument was also democratic. Affordable models were available and relatively easy to play. (As Rolling Stones legend

Keith Richards once said, half in jest, "Guitar is easy. All it takes is five fingers, six strings, and one asshole.")

But electrified and amplified, the guitar became positively protean, infinitely malleable and amenable to each player's creative vision. In the hands of blues guitarist B.B. King, the instrument became an expressive solo voice that could sing, cry, and moan like a man in the pit of despair, or a woman in the throes of ecstasy. For the Beatles, it became a jangling orchestra that provided color, harmony, and heft to their timeless pop songs. Funk rhythm guitarist Jimmy Nolen used his axe almost like an amplified washboard, playing a Morse code of chicken scratches to power countless James Brown hits, such as "Papa's Got a Brand New Bag."

As players and instrument developed across the decades, a staggering sonic repertoire emerged. The resources of feedback and distortion allowed an electric guitar to evoke a nuclear meltdown, a dive-bombing aircraft, the ominous thrum of heavy machinery. But it is just as capable of producing crystalline tones and shimmering textures—the soundscapes of our most vivid dreams. This unprecedented range would allow the electric guitar to play a key role in a dazzling spectrum of musical idioms, from the hot jazz and Hawaiian music that formed the soundtrack of its creation to modern-day alternative rock, hard rock, heavy metal, contemporary country, and postmodern art music.

But the electric guitar would represent much more than just musical innovation. It would directly and indirectly impact the entertainment industry, politics, art, the economy, and many other facets of our cultural life. The instrument's burgeoning popularity played a small but nonetheless significant role in advancing the cause of racial integration. It became a symbol of the counterculture sixties, rallying opposition to the Vietnam War, as its urgent clangor pushed forward the sexual revolution and progress toward gender equality. The curvy contours and electronic appointments of the electric guitar were of a piece with the mid-century modernist movement in industrial, automotive, architectural, domestic, and fashion design, which was finding a voice just as electric guitar builders were hitting their stride. And its sound would become deeply embedded in the popular culture of the modern and postmodern eras. Its lineaments are a map of our progress through the twentieth century and into the digitized world of today.

The electric guitar's enshrinement in our cultural pantheon was cemented in 1977, when NASA launched two spacecraft whose missions were to explore the outer limits of our solar system and beyond. *Voyager 1* became the first human-made object to venture into interstellar space, and is currently about twelve billion miles from our sun, with *Voyager 2* on its heels. Packed away on each vessel is a twelve-inch gold-plated phonograph record containing 115 sounds and images, carefully curated to portray the diversity of life and culture on Earth. Each disc was encased in a protective aluminum jacket, together with a cartridge and a needle and instructions, in symbolic language, indicating how the record was to be played. A team led by the astrophysicist Carl Sagan chose a precious handful of musical selections, from different cultures and eras, to include along with a variety of natural sounds. There were pieces composed by Stravinsky, Bach, and Beethoven, as well as traditional songs from Peru, Zaire, and Senegal. Among this sonic panoply was "Johnny B. Goode," the stomping American rock-and-roll anthem written and performed by Chuck Berry. It was a controversial selection, but Sagan, a child of the modern era, understood there were few sounds in our world more exciting and life-affirming than the opening electric-guitar lick to Berry's classic song.

Before the electric guitar could be shared with the cosmos, though, it had to find its place at home. The story of how it did so is an epic tale of television stars, tinkerers, fugitive auto execs, motorcycle daredevils, cowboys, and MIT grads. It is a story of some of the world's most famous musicians, whose innovations pushed the electric six-string further. Some are household names—artists like

Les Paul, the Who's Pete Townshend, and Edward Van Halen, each of whom played a pivotal role in the evolution of the instrument. But there were countless others—figures just as fascinating and significant, if more obscure.

The story of this extraordinary musical instrument is ultimately our story—guitarists and nonguitarists alike. From rabid music fans to casual listeners, its siren call has touched us all.

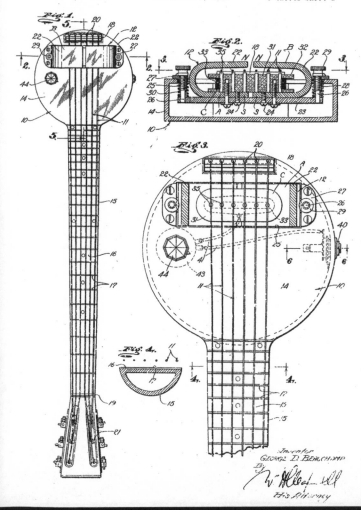

Patent drawing for the first
commercially produced electric guitar,
the Ro-Pat-In "Frying Pan"

PLAY IT LOUD

chapter 1

BROTHER MUSICIAN, LISTEN TO A MIRACLE!

For as long as there have been guitars, there have been young guitar players who have forsaken their rural hometowns for the bright lights of the big city, hoping that their six-string mastery will win them fame and fortune. This epic quest—a kind of latter-day pilgrimage—is no doubt what impelled George Delmetia Beauchamp to leave rural Texas and set himself up in Hollywood in the early years of the 1920s. Young Beauchamp (pronounced "Bee-chum") was in his mid-twenties at the time. And while he did all right for himself as a guitarist in the L.A. area, he is not at all remembered today among the guitar-playing immortals. We don't even have any recordings to give us an idea of what he sounded like.

Outside of a small circle of guitar obsessives, in fact, Beauchamp isn't even remembered for his most outstanding achievement— his pivotal role in the development of the electric guitar. His name may not resound through the decades like those of Les Paul, Leo Fender, or Charlie Christian, but the electric guitar may never have come into being without George Beauchamp. He not only invented the first fully functional guitar pickup, he also put it to work in his pioneering design for the world's first successful, commercially produced electric guitar.

The pickup can be regarded as the most important part of any electric guitar. It's what converts the guitar strings' vibrations into electrical signals that can be amplified. A pickup to an electric guitar is what wheels are to a car. Without that, you're going nowhere.

Beauchamp's friend and business partner Adolph Rickenbacker once described him as "a young Texas boy [who] got too fat to pick cotton." That wasn't entirely kind or accurate. Surviving photographs of Beauchamp show him to be a dapper (and rather trim) gent—a professional entertainer and entrepreneur with hair neatly slicked back and a sporty predilection for bow ties.

But he had indeed been born in Texas, on March 18, 1899, one of nine children brought into this world by Saybird and Fanny Beauchamp. George took violin lessons as a child but eventually switched to the guitar. When he grew to manhood and made his move to Los Angeles, he was accompanied by his brother Alton, also a guitar player. Not that the brothers Beauchamp immediately had all Hollywood at their feet. Like most musicians, they needed a day gig at first, so they found work as house painters.

It must have been an incredibly exciting time for a young man to land in a city like L.A. The film business had recently relocated there from New York; Hollywood had embarked on what would be known as its golden age. It was also well on the way toward acquiring a somewhat deserved reputation as a city of sin, Hollywood Babylon. Real estate was cheap and there was plenty of easy money around. People wanted to be entertained. It was a good place to make your mark as a musician.

George Beauchamp seems to have had little trouble fitting into Roaring Twenties Los Angeles. He was by all accounts affable and well liked, not at all averse to the occasional illicit drink, Prohibition being in effect at this time. George and Alton got work in vaudeville, the theatrical variety entertainment genre still going strong in the twenties. They secured booking representation by the William Morris Agency, then as now a major player in the entertainment world. As a guitar duo, the siblings performed Hawaiian music under the name Grasshopper and George. A promotional photo shows them with guitars in hand, wearing matching shirts and trousers, shoes immaculately polished, looking sharp in bow ties and with Hawaiian leis around their necks.

Hawaiian-style steel guitar was George's specialty. In this mode of playing, an acoustic guitar is held horizontally on the guitarist's lap, and notes are formed by sliding a metal bar, known as a "steel," across the strings. The style had originated in the 1880s, when Hawaiian guitarist Joseph Kekuku reportedly held the side of a metal spike gently against the strings of his guitar, producing a steely glissando (gliding) tonality, which quickly became an aural signifier of the Hawaiian Islands. To facilitate playing, the guitar would be tuned to an open chord (such that strumming without the steel would produce, say, a G major chord). In order to achieve some open tunings, the player must slacken, or reduce tension, on the strings by means of the guitar's tuning keys. For this reason the style is also called "slack key."

To accompany his brother, Alton Beauchamp played "Spanish style" guitar. This is the mode of playing most common today, in which the instrument is held vertically against the player's waist or torso and notes are formed by pressing the fingers of the left hand against the guitar's fingerboard (also called the fretboard). For some performances, George and Alton Beauchamp were joined by a third musician, Slim Harper (sometimes Hooper), on another popular Hawaiian instrument, the ukulele. On such occasions they were billed as the Boys from Dixie.

Some hundred years down the road, it's difficult to appreciate the immense popularity of Hawaiian music in the early decades of the twentieth century. Popular fascination with Hawaiian culture—or at least a romanticized version thereof—was first sparked by Broadway shows such as 1912's *Birds of Paradise*, and by the Hawaiian Pavilion at the 1915 Panama–Pacific International Exposition in San Francisco. Hit songs—including a 1917 recording of "My Waikiki Mermaid," written by Sonny Cunha, and 1925's "Ukulele Lady" by Gus Kahn and Richard Whiting—popularized a style known as "hapa haole" (literally "half white"), a Hawaiian song form with English lyrics. In the absence of recordings, we can only suppose that this is the musical style that the Beauchamp brothers played.

The nascent Hollywood film industry made its own contribution to the Hawaiian craze, with features like 1923's *The White Flower* and 1927's *Hula.* The latter starred movie idol and flapper icon Clara Bow, who dances in a grass skirt in one provocative scene. These idealized depictions of Hawaii in song and on the silver screen suggested a carefree, uninhibited way of life underneath the swaying palms, which played very well in the permissive Jazz Age.

Guitars had been integral to Hawaiian music ever since the first European settlers arrived there in the eighteenth century. Among them were Portuguese sailors who brought not only their guitars but also their *cavaquinhos,* a stringed instrument that the Hawaiians renamed the ukulele. With the advent of the steel guitar style in the nineteenth century, a uniquely Hawaiian guitar sensibility had taken shape and been drafted wholesale into the musical culture of 1920s America and Europe. As a result, a great deal of early electric guitar innovation was focused on the Hawaiian guitar.

An accomplished guitarist, George Beauchamp could play both Hawaiian and Spanish style. And in pursuing his art, he faced the dilemma shared by many guitarists of the 1920s—the need for greater volume. In a sense, the quest for increased amplitude had been part of the guitar's evolution ever since the instrument made its nineteenth-century journey out of the parlors and drawing rooms, where it was most frequently played as a polite accomplishment of well-bred young ladies, and into the dance halls and speakeasies of the Roaring Twenties.

In this period, the guitar eclipsed the banjo as the fretted string instrument of choice in jazz and dance bands. With more strings than a banjo, it was capable of more jazzy, chordal sophistication. But no matter how hard you strummed a guitar, it just couldn't achieve the same volume as a banjo.

AND SO IT was that George Beauchamp visited the shop of John Dopyera, a European-born instrument maker, sometime around 1926 and issued him a challenge: *Make this thing louder.* Together, they devised the idea of an acoustic resonator guitar. To understand how it works, you first have to consider the basic mechanics of the guitar. A guitar's strings are held in position by two small pieces of hardware: one at the lower part of the instrument's body and another at its head. The one near the head is called the nut and the one on the lower body is called the bridge. As the part of the guitar that absorbs much of the vibration of the strings, the bridge was often the focus of attempts to make the instrument louder. Beauchamp and Dopyera's acoustic resonator guitar, then, would be an instrument with one or more resonating cones made of spun aluminum and attached to the bridge. By affixing these cones to the bridge, the men attempted to amplify those vibrations the way an acoustic horn was used to amplify the sound of a phonograph.

While they are acoustic instruments, the resonator guitars that Beauchamp and Dopyera devised are important precursors of the electric guitar. Beauchamp's association with Dopyera, moreover, would allow Beauchamp to acquire both the guitar-building skills and a team of collaborators that would make possible his pioneering work in the years to come.

Six years Beauchamp's senior, John Dopyera—along with his brothers Rudy, Emil, Robert, and Louis—were part of the great wave of European immigrants, some ten million strong, who came to the United States at the close of the nineteenth century and early years of the twentieth. By 1924 more than thirteen million people living in the United States were foreign-born. Many of these immigrants would make significant contributions to American culture and industry—including the guitar business, as we'll see. The five Dopyera brothers, along with five more of their siblings, had emigrated from Slovakia to the United States early in the century. A skilled cabinetmaker and machinist, John had patented several inventions, including a machine for making picture frames. But he'd been trained as a violin maker by his father back in Slovakia, and he eventually returned to that pursuit in the New World. Working out of a shop in Los Angeles, he built and repaired violins, also collaborating with his brother Rudy on designing and building banjos.

Like many banjo makers at the time, the Dopyeras were aware of the guitar's encroachment on their market, and they were interested in turning their hand to guitar building. So John's meeting with George Beauchamp was fortuitous. Dopyera had the design and manufacturing skills; Beauchamp knew guitars intimately. Such partnerships, between players and makers, would prove key components in the electric guitar's evolution.

Beauchamp and Dopyera's first attempt at a resonator guitar was a hollow-bodied instrument with three spun cones attached to the bridge—a "tri-cone." It was a brilliant instrument, and one that would go on to have a role not only in Hawaiian music but also in blues and other pop genres. But it might not have gone anywhere had Beauchamp not leveraged his connections, both in the music world and within his own family. He placed a prototype resonator guitar in the hands of popular Hawaiian guitarist Sol Hoopii and then brought Hoopii's trio to play at a party hosted by Beauchamp's wild and wealthy playboy cousin-in-law, Ted E. Kleinmeyer.

Given Kleinmeyer's scapegrace reputation, the party was most likely a wild one. He's one of those figures who personify the excess of the Roaring Twenties, a time when the economy was booming and society was throwing off the moral constraints of the nineteenth century. The son of a well-heeled rancher with interests in oil and the stock market, Kleinmeyer inherited some $600,000 (the equivalent of over $8 million today) upon turning twenty-one, following the death of his father, Earnest. This was one-third of the total legacy, the balance to be issued upon his thirtieth birthday. The younger Kleinmeyer immediately set to work squandering the first installment of his inheritance, partying at a rate that put in some doubt the likelihood that he'd ever reach thirty. He was known to drive around L.A. roaring drunk in a Lincoln sedan equipped with a police siren that he wasn't shy about setting off.

So when the Sol Hoopii Trio, and the new resonator acoustic guitar they were showcasing, made a big hit at Teddy's party, it reflected well on cousin George. Kleinmeyer agreed to fund Beauchamp and Dopyera's new venture with a reported loan of $12,500, a sum more than adequate to launch a guitar manufacturing company at the time. The National String Instrument Corporation was certified by the State of California on January 26, 1928, with Ted E. Kleinmeyer as president. George Beauchamp became the company's general manager, John Dopyera was named factory superintendent, and Dopyera's cousin Paul Barth was designated assistant factory superintendent. Barth had skill in guitar making and would soon become one of Beauchamp's key design collaborators. Beauchamp was paid $55 per week, Dopyera received $50, and Barth $48.

All was fine at first. Well-capitalized, National came out with four Tricone resonator guitar models, Styles 1 through 4, each one more ornate and higher-priced than its predecessor in the product line. The guitars featured bodies made of cast aluminum, something brand new in the annals of guitar design. They were consummately flashy instruments for an extravagantly stylish time period, their gleaming aluminum surfaces adorned with slashing, angular sound holes and intricately etched curvilinear designs in floral and Hawaiian motifs. But it wasn't only about looks. The metal body, combined with the resonating cones, produced a distinctive, almost hornlike tone that could effectively "cut through" an ensemble of instruments.

Fabrication of the guitars' cast-aluminum bodies was outsourced to a machinist named Adolph Rickenbacker (or Rickenbacher, as it was spelled at the time). Like the Dopyeras, he had been part of the great late-nineteenth/early-twentieth-century wave of migration from Europe. Born Adolf Adam Riggenbacher in Basel, Switzerland, on April 1, 1887, he immigrated to New York with his family in 1891, while he was still quite young. From there he made his way to Ohio, where he married into money—his wife, Charlotte, being an heiress to the Standard Oil fortune. The couple lived in Illinois for a while, but in 1918 moved to California, where Adolph worked as an engineer/machinist for the Hotpoint oven company. There, he perfected an injection-molding process used to fashion the Bakelite knobs used on the company's products—this at a time when synthetic plastics such as Bakelite were an exciting new technology and profit center. But by the early 1920s, Rickenbacker had established his own machine shop, a tool-and-die business at 6701 South Western Avenue in Los Angeles, with Charlotte on the staff as a stenographer.

Rickenbacker assimilated himself into the culture of his new home. He was very successful at it, according to John Hall, the current chairman and CEO of the Rickenbacker guitar company. Hall was just a young boy when he knew Adolph Rickenbacker, who was by then a man of some years. But Rickenbacker left a vivid impression on the young Hall: "Adolph was a real character. He had a story for everything . . . He was in fact sort of like a Bakersfield [California] cowboy. He always wore a cowboy hat. And he was an inveterate tinkerer. He was always trying to figure out a way to make something better, or another way to make something more efficient."

Known as "Rick" to his friends, Rickenbacker wasn't a part of the National staff, but he became an integral part of their operation. Rickenbacker and his new collaborator George Beauchamp got along well from the start.

The same could not be said for Beauchamp and John Dopyera, whose partnership began to sour. Though their skills complemented each other well in the design room, the two had very different, one might even say antagonistic, personalities. Beauchamp was a good-time guy, "a jokester and a drunk," according to guitar historian Lynn Wheelwright. He was the kind of person, in short, who could run with Teddy Kleinmeyer. Beauchamp was also reportedly openhanded with money, a soft touch. John Dopyera, meanwhile, was a teetotaler, a vegetarian, and parsimonious, the kind of guy who prowled the National factory floor busting workers who'd thrown out a piece of sandpaper before it had been worn down to the last grain. Waste not, want not.

Dopyera had no small ego, either. He felt that Beauchamp was taking undue credit in the media for inventing the National Tricone guitar. Beauchamp then added insult to injury, as far as Dopyera was concerned, by patenting his own resonator guitar design, the National Style O, with a single cone rather than three. More affordable than Tricone models, the instruments based on Beauchamp's design were profitable for National, but Dopyera still claimed Beauchamp was wasting the company's money and resources on product development.

Not surprisingly, Dopyera also had problems with Kleinmeyer's spendthrift ways and louche management style. Indeed, by 1929 Kleinmeyer had burned through much of the money he'd inherited two years earlier, on his twenty-first birthday. He'd started to touch George Beauchamp for cash loans. It was the start of a sad personal decline that would last through the remainder of the onetime playboy's life.

And so Dopyera left National early in 1929. It turned out to be a singularly bad time to quit your day job. The catastrophic stock market crash of October 29, 1929, witnessed the start of an extended period of economic desperation in America and Europe. The Great Depression would see unemployment rates soar to nearly 25 percent in the United States.

But a determined man like John Dopyera wasn't about to let worldwide economic disaster stand in his way. Soon after leaving National in '29, Dopyera formed the Dobro Manufacturing Company with some of his brothers (the name presumably an abbreviation of "Dopyera Brothers"). When Dobro brought its own line of resonator guitars to the market, Beauchamp sued the Dopyeras for patent infringement, reportedly for $2 million. The siblings responded by countersuing and maneuvering Beauchamp out of National's board of directors. As guitar historian Matthew Hill observed, "The Dopyera brothers hated one another, but they hated everyone else even more."

THE RESONATOR GUITAR was a technical and commercial success, but George Beauchamp was far from done. While the instrument had achieved greater volume and a new tonality, he sensed that still more could be done to amplify the guitar. Independently of National, often working in his garage or at the dining room table at his home, he'd started to develop a new, altogether revolutionary concept.

The electric guitar was an idea whose time had arrived. By the early 1930s, a few factors had come together that made it all but an inevitability. The first was the widespread availability of electricity itself. This process had begun in America's large cities in the 1880s, the nation's first power generator being built in 1882 at Pearl Street in Lower Manhattan by Thomas Edison, with funding from J. P. Morgan. But it wasn't until the thirties that rural homes finally began to get wired up with electricity. This brought not only electric lighting but also an exciting emergent array of electrical appliances and gadgets into people's homes.

One of these, and foremost for the electric guitar, was radio. The radio that became commonplace in American homes in the early part of the twentieth century was itself the product of three important innovations. One was electricity, of course.

Second, there was the vacuum tube, which was developed by engineer Lee De Forest in 1907. The patent issued to De Forest describes the vacuum tube as "a device for amplifying feeble electrical currents." De Forest himself more poetically described it as "an Aladdin's lamp of our new world, a lamp by which one might hear instead of read."

De Forest's vacuum tube is indeed lamplike—a slender glass cylinder, sealed with no air inside (hence the term "vacuum"). An electrical signal is basically a stream of electrons flowing down a wire. This flow can be made more powerful via a system of small, heated metal plates positioned inside the vacuum tube. The strength of this increase is regulated in turn by a part of the vacuum tube called a "grid," which uses varying amounts of electrical voltage to control the flow of heated electrons. It operates much like a water faucet, which is why the British call a vacuum tube a "valve." When you crank up the volume knob on a tube guitar amp, you're basically goosing the grid voltage. This increases the flow of heated electrons, making the sound louder.

In 1911, four years after coming up with the vacuum tube, De Forest employed tube technology to devise and patent "an amplifier for radio frequency circuits." It was originally intended to help make Morse code transmissions more audible, but would soon find expression in commercial radio broadcasting—something that carried an aura of magic and mystery at the time: a technological marvel that enabled people to hear music and voices from clear across the country, or even the world.

But hear them through what, exactly? This is where we arrive at the third invention that made the electric guitar possible. In 1921, Chester W. Rice of the General Electric Corporation and Edward W. Kellogg of AT&T devised the first paper-coned speaker, the final ingredient in radio's ascent. At the time, the sound from early radio devices and windup Victrolas was conveyed through a cumbersome acoustic horn. Rice and Kellogg's speaker represented a substantial sonic improvement, and is essentially the same design used in the speakers we listen to today.

The difference, of course, was electricity. Kellogg and Rice's speaker employed an electromagnetic coil to convert electrical signals from a vacuum tube amplifier into sound vibrations that were then transferred to the device's resonating paper cone. The result was sound with a much fuller frequency range. Mounting the speaker in a wooden cabinet imparted a tone that was even richer still, with much more prominent bass frequencies in particular. The old acoustic horns sounded "tinny" in comparison (naturally enough, since they were fashioned out of metal).

The game-changing combination of vacuum-tube amplification and paper-coned speakers ushered in what's known as the golden age of Radio in 1920s America. Sales of vacuum tube–powered radio sets skyrocketed from an annual $60 million in 1922 to $843 million in 1929, as more and more homes became wired for electricity. In 1925 some five million American homes, accounting for 19.2 percent of the population, had radio receivers. By 1929 that figure had increased to 35 to 40 percent, reaching as high as 75 percent in more affluent areas. Powerful radio networks began broadcasting coast to coast, starting with the National Broadcasting Company (NBC) in 1926 and Columbia Broadcasting Company (CBS) in 1927.

The cultural impact of all this can very well be likened to the advent of the Internet in our own time. Suddenly people everywhere had access to substantially more of what we now call "content" than had ever been available at any prior period in history—news, weather, sports, serial dramas and comedies, quiz and game shows, advertisements (inevitably), and of course a much broader selection of music than had hitherto been available to the average person. The stylistic spectrum included classical music, Broadway melodies, the songs of New York's Tin Pan Alley tunesmiths, jazz, blues, gospel, Hawaiian, and country (or "hillbilly" music, as it was then known). Several of these genres would play a pivotal role in the development of the electric guitar, and vice versa.

Vacuum tube amplification also made possible the first public address (P.A.) systems, dramatically improved phonographs, and of course motion pictures with sound—the talkies. Inventor Lee De Forest led the way once again, introducing his Phono-film system for movie sound synchronization in 1923. But what really put the talkies on the map was Warner Bros.' blockbuster film *The Jazz Singer,* which debuted in New York on October 6, 1927, employing the Vitaphone sound-synchronization process. Once audiences heard the film's star, Al Jolson, sing "Mammy," while simultaneously witnessing his schmaltzy, tear-jerking performance, there was no turning back. Sound became an integral part of the cinematic experience.

"During long periods of history, the mode of human sense perception changes with humanity's entire mode of existence," the cultural critic Walter Benjamin wrote in his landmark 1936 essay "The Work of Art in the Age of Mechanical Reproduction." He was one of the first intellectuals to grasp the immensity of the changes being wrought by the era's technological advances. While many of his contemporaries saw the advent of mass media such as radio and movies as a triumph of vulgarity, Benjamin saw the dawn of a new era of populist art.

In the 1920s, for the first time ever, people found themselves living in an environment in which electrically amplified sound was everywhere. This constituted a major collective perceptual shift, a reorientation of the senses foregrounding the aural. It's what helped put the "roar" in the Roaring Twenties—one more factor that contributed to the amped-up excitement of the era. The electric guitar was very much the product of this zeitgeist, both technologically and culturally. Alongside the radio, P.A., and cinema sound, it was an innovation that would impact popular culture on an epic, unforeseeable scale.

IN A VERY real sense, then, the amplifier came before the electric guitar. The earliest guitar amps employed essentially the same circuitry as radio sets, P.A. systems, and other vacuum tube–driven technology. George Beauchamp, laboring in his California home, was among the first to see the potential in this, and to develop the electric guitar into an instrument that people would want to buy.

"If you can amplify radio waves," he is quoted as saying, "why not amplify vibration waves?"

But how to turn those vibrating strings into an electric signal capable of being amplified? This question had intrigued inventors for quite some time, and was by no means confined to the guitar. Some of the earliest attempts at electrical amplification were focused on violins and pianos, two instruments that were far more musically predominant and culturally significant than the guitar at that time.

Where guitars are concerned, attempts at electrification go back at least as far as a patent filed by U.S. naval officer George Breed in 1890 for an early electric guitar design. But it was never brought to market, and, according to what organologists and early guitar historians can surmise, it was more bizarre than functional. A design that came much closer to the modern electric guitar was the Stromberg-Voisinet Electro of 1928–29. This employed an electromagnetic pickup device mounted beneath the top of a conventional hollow-body guitar. As noted earlier, the pickup is the central element in any electric guitar, then as now. It was capable of transforming vibrations from the guitar's wooden top into an electrical signal that could be amplified. A small number of these instruments were brought out in 1928 but had disappeared from the market by mid-1929. No surviving examples are known to exist, but historians speculate that the Stromberg-Voisinet Electro was discontinued because it didn't work terribly well (which could explain why nobody thought to hand theirs down to future generations). George Beauchamp's developments in the late twenties and early thirties, on the other hand, would become the foundation of the modern electric guitar.

To the layperson, it might be hard at first to understand what the big deal is in all this. To electrify a guitar, why not just stick a microphone on it, or in front of it? That is in fact where Beauchamp started, as did many other early experimenters with guitar amplification. But there are limits as to how much additional volume can be attained this way before the howling sound of unwanted feedback becomes a problem. And besides, an acoustic guitar with a microphone in front of it isn't really an electric guitar. It's no different from a violin, a piano, or any other acoustic instrument exposed to a mic. The electric guitar as we know it today is a substantively different instrument from its acoustic counterpart. It has its own unique sonic and physical identity. You'd rarely, if ever, mistake the twang, jangle, and crunch of an electric guitar, let alone its svelte shape, for the classical bulk and organic warmth of an acoustic.

Not that Beauchamp gave up on the microphone approach right away. He tried taking apart a carbon button microphone—a forerunner of modern microphones, frequently used in telephone applications—and attaching the microphone's inner carbon element directly to a guitar. It was a little more effective. He was getting closer, but he still wasn't quite there.

Beauchamp next tried something else that had been attempted by other early electric guitar pioneers. He took apart a Brunswick phonograph, removing the pickup—the part that converts the vibrations of the phonograph's needle into electrical signals. He attached this and a single guitar string to a 2"x4" plank of wood, fashioning, in effect, a crude one-string electric guitar. The phonograph pickup consisted of an electromagnet and a small coil of wire. The role of the electromagnet was to transform the physical vibrations of the phonograph needle into an electrical signal suitable for amplification. Beauchamp mounted the pickup on his 2"x4" in such a way that it would sense vibrations from the guitar string rather than the phonograph needle, which he'd removed. While others had tried this kind of thing, only Beauchamp seems to have followed it through to its logical conclusion.

The insight he had was brilliant yet simple: *The string is the thing.* Where earlier efforts had attempted to amplify vibrations from the guitar's top or bridge, Beauchamp realized that the string itself is the best source of vibration. Everything else is just secondhand vibration, after all. The string is where any guitar sound begins. It's the direct source of contact with the player's fingers or guitar pick. Earlier experimenters had focused on the guitar's top (the surface of the guitar that usually faces the listener) because that's what traditional acoustic guitar design had always identified as the all-important source of tone. But all that becomes irrelevant when you're attempting to generate tone not with a wooden box, but electronically.

Moving beyond the phonograph pickup, Beauchamp next went on to fashion his own dedicated guitar pickups, more optimized for the way a guitar, rather than a phonograph needle, functions. He mounted some of these experimental guitar pickups on other 2"x4"s. Then he progressed to building full-guitar prototypes.

The one that has come down to us through the years is now enshrined in a case at the Rickenbacker corporate offices in Santa Ana, California. It's one of the holy grail instruments of guitar history—something that guitar-loving visitors to Rickenbacker HQ feel privileged to behold: the Frying Pan, also known as the Panhandle. (Adolph Rickenbacker and close friends of Beauchamp's are said to have also called it the Pancake.)

Beauchamp is thought to have assembled the instrument at home, with help from National shop foreman Harry Watson. John Dopyera's cousin Paul Barth and Adolph Rickenbacker may also have had input into either the design or building of the prototype. To bring this new instrument to market, the four joined together in the early thirties to form a new company, called Ro-Pat-In. (The name is assumed to be a shortened form of electRO-PATent-INstruments, or perhaps Rickenbacker-Original-PATent-INstruments. Nobody knows for sure.) The Frying Pan prototype was fashioned from a single solid piece of either maple or hemlock. There's a legend that the wood came from a fence post behind the National factory (not quite a piece of the True Cross, but more or less the equivalent in guitardom).

"Frying Pan," "Panhandle," and "Pancake" are of course all ludicrously prosaic names for a musical instrument that had so much to do with igniting the electric guitar revolution. But the first two offer a fairly accurate description of the instrument's shape—a small circular body with a long guitar neck protruding from it in the manner of a frying pan handle. It isn't known why Beauchamp and Watson opted for a circular body. Guitar historian Lynn Wheelwright strongly suspects that it was because they used a tin can, such as a coffee can, to trace out the body's shape.

Other elements of the Frying Pan prototype were clearly cannibalized from spare guitar parts. This isn't at all unusual for a prototype—especially one constructed during the Great Depression, when funds for parts would surely have been scarce. But the crucial DNA for what would become the electric guitar was all in place, particularly its electromagnetic pickup.

As with modern guitar pickups, the underlying principle is this: the vibrations of the guitar strings cause fluctuations in the magnetic field created by the pickup, which in turn generates an electrical signal that can be amplified. This is why you need steel strings on an electric guitar. It's necessary that the strings be made of a material that will interact with the magnet. Traditional gut or nylon strings won't work.

So what we have in the Frying Pan prototype is essentially

the first fully functional solid-body electric guitar. While primarily designed for Hawaiian-style steel playing (horizontally on the lap) it could also be adapted for Spanish-style playing (vertically against the torso). As this was a brand-new instrument, Beauchamp and his colleagues most likely wanted to cover all eventualities.

In converting Beauchamp's wooden prototypes into production models, the Ro-Pat-In company decided to manufacture the instruments with cast-aluminum bodies. Metalwork was an essential part of what Ro-Pat-In had inherited from National's legacy of cast-aluminum instruments. What's missing from the equation, however, is the Dopyeras' Old World guitar craftsmanship. There is no ornate engraving on the Frying Pan guitars. The body shape is unconventional. This was a completely new breed of instrument—clearly and unapologetically an industrial product rather than a finely crafted artifact. In this regard, it was a radical instrument—more so than most of the electric guitars that would come immediately after it.

Of course it wasn't the only card in Ro-Pat-In's hand. The company would also bring out a full line of more conventionally shaped electric Spanish and Hawaiian guitars. But all could be traced back to George Beauchamp and his string-focused pickup design.

THE FIRST PRODUCTION-MODEL Frying Pan, the A-25, hit the market in 1932. The letter A indicates that this was the new company's first product line. (The company's electric guitars made of Bakelite and released a few years down the road would carry a "B" designation.) The number 25 refers to the instrument's scale length, indicating that it was twenty-five inches from the bridge to the nut. The A-25 was soon joined by the A-22, essentially the same guitar but with a twenty-two-inch scale length. The A-22 would go on to outsell the A-25 substantially. Both were sold with an amplifier, also manufactured by Ro-Pat-In.

Early on, the guitar was variously marketed as the Ro-Pat-In Electro, the Rickenbacher Electro, and, ultimately, the Rickenbacker Electro. Why was Adolph Rickenbacker's name on the instrument rather than that of its inventor, George Beauchamp? No one knows for sure, although Adolph and his wife Charlotte's major financial stake in the new company likely played a part in the decision.

And the new company was in need of funding. By this point, Teddy Kleinmeyer's days as a deep-pocketed investor were over for good. A long streak of bad luck and bad checks would eventually reduce him to a pathetic figure. He served time on a chain gang and ended his days working as a school janitor in Temple City, California. Kleinmeyer died in poverty in the 1960s. Still, without his early financial support of Beauchamp's endeavors, the Frying Pan guitars might never have come into existence.

•

While the original Frying Pan prototype was made of wood, production models were made of cast aluminum.

SO WHO WERE the first customers for the A-25 and A-22 Frying Pan guitars? In answering this, it's useful to remember that the fledgling guitar market of the 1930s was very different from the guitar market today. Whereas a good deal of today's electric guitar sales are to beginners and garage band amateurs, the early electrics were bought pretty much exclusively by professional players. Not that there was a staggering number of these at first. The Frying Pan guitar hit the market during the height of the Great Depression, which had a dramatically negative effect on the music instrument business in general. And the guitar business wasn't that big to begin with. There were 106 string, wind, and percussion instrument companies in 1929, right before the stock market crash. By 1933, a third of them had gone out of business, leaving only 72. The workforce employed in this branch of the musical instrument industry dwindled from 4,000 to 2,000.

In this environment, it's not surprising that the Electro String Instrument Corporation started out slowly. It produced just 28 units in 1932, a number that includes both Hawaiian and Spanish electric guitar–and–amp sets as well as a few individual sales of guitars and amps. But by 1935 that number had increased to a total production count of 1,288. Even in the throes of the Great Depression there were a few adventurous players willing to take a chance on a strange new instrument.

The very first sale of an A-25 was to Wichita, Kansas, guitarist Gage Brewer, who made the purchase on September 21, 1932, along with one of Ro-Pat-In's hollow-body electric Spanish models. He also holds the distinction of having given the first-ever known public performance with these instruments—quite possibly the first electric guitar performance anywhere—on Halloween night, 1932. It took place at the Shadowland Pavilion in Wichita, a nightclub that Brewer also owned. A press release issued to promote the performance makes clear that novelty was one of the foremost attributes that distinguished the electric guitar in the eyes and ears of the general public:

In the orchestra we are at this time introducing the world's newest and most sensational instruments. A new invention which is startling to the music world, making possible a combination of natural personal technique and electrical perfection. We are indeed fortunate to be able to present these instruments to the public as they will not be on the market for several months, we assure you that if you've not already heard these remarkable instruments that we have a real treat in store for you.

In the early 1930s, electricity itself would still have been regarded with a certain mixture of awe and superstitious fear. The lightning bolt symbol used as a logo on many electrical products of that era—including the Rickenbacker Electro—is reminiscent of the lightning bolts wielded by the Norse god Thor, a signifier of immense, preternatural power. Quack advertisements at the time touted electrical devices purporting to do everything from enhancing sexual prowess to curing baldness. Electricity was seen as a mysterious force that could cure or kill. Some of these notions go back to the late-eighteenth-century work of scientist Luigi Galvani and his nephew Giovanni Aldini, who experimented with applying electrical currents to cadavers, both animal and human, producing spasmodic muscle movements in the lifeless flesh.

"And Galvanism has set some corpses grinning," the poet Lord Byron satirically wrote in the early nineteenth century. Byron's friend Mary Wollstonecraft Shelley dramatized the concept of electrically revivified human remains in her novel of 1818, *Frankenstein*. With the 1931 release of the Hollywood movie version of *Frankenstein* and the 1935 sequel, *Bride of Frankenstein,* the unnatural life-giving powers of massive sparking electrodes would have very much been a part of public imagination. These images might well have subliminally colored people's perceptions of the early electric guitar. More than just a musical instrument, it seemed a work of marvelous science.

Of course, people at the time were also keenly aware of electricity's power to take life. In the early twentieth century the electric chair had become the chief means of executing criminals in much of the United States. In 1928, photographer Tom Howard smuggled a camera into the execution of convicted murderer Ruth Snyder at Sing Sing prison. The New York *Daily News* published a gruesome front-page shot of the event shortly thereafter. It was one more occurrence that emblazoned the ominous power of electricity on the public's awareness right around the time the first electric guitars began to appear on the market.

Having such an awesome force readily available from electrical outlets and sockets in people's homes made some uneasy. In his comedic autobiography of 1933, *My Life and Hard Times,* author and cartoonist James Thurber wrote of his grandmother, who "lived the latter years of her life in the horrible suspicion that electricity was dripping invisibly all over the house. It leaked, she contended, out of empty sockets if the wall switch had been left on. She would go around screwing in bulbs, and if they lighted up she would hastily and fearfully turn off the wall switch."

Such attitudes were common at the time Thurber's book was published, just one year after the A-25 hit the market. So perhaps there was something fortuitous in Gage Brewer's choice of Halloween night for the electric guitar's debut performance. He did promise to "startle" the music world, after all. Even before the era of the rock-and-roll guitar god, the electric guitar seems to have possessed a mythic dimension. The Electro String Instrument Corporation itself didn't scruple to wax mystical with their 1933 marketing slogan: "Brother musician, listen to a MIRACLE!"

The second known purchaser of an A-25 was another professional musician, a Hollywood-based guitarist named Jack Miller, who is thought to have been a friend of George Beauchamp's. No less tireless a self-promoter than Brewer, Miller set himself up as an apostle for the miraculous new instrument, writing a column for *Down Beat* magazine extolling the electric guitar's virtues. Like Brewer, Miller seems to have regarded novelty as the key value of his investment in the instrument. After praising it for being loud, he goes on to proclaim, not quite accurately, "I own the FIRST of these instruments and used it in the Prologue at Grauman's Chinese Theater in Hollywood."

A smooth-looking character with sleekly pomaded hair and a slender Clark Gable mustache, Miller never paid in full for his Frying Pan guitar and amp, making him the first deadbeat on the new company's sales ledger. He also claims to have commissioned and owned the first seven-string version of the Frying Pan. (While a significant number of these were made—seventy-one in 1936 alone—and they would count as the world's first seven-string electrics, it is unclear whether Miller actually owned the first one.)

But by far the most notable early purchaser and player of the A-25 was pioneering electric guitar wizard Alvino Rey (Alvin McBurney), who at the time was playing steel and Spanish guitar with the popular dance band Horace Heidt and His Musical Knights. Himself an early experimenter with electric guitar and amplification technology, Rey was hired by the Gibson guitar company in 1935 to help develop a pickup that would be used on their landmark electric Spanish guitar, the ES-150 "Charlie Christian" model. It was during this period that Rey purchased his Rickenbacher Electro A-25, bearing the serial number 30, which indicates it was the thirtieth such instrument to be manufactured.

Rey somewhat famously built a wooden casing in the shape of a conventional Spanish guitar and mounted his frying pan–shaped A-25 inside it. He is said to have done so because he grew irritated with constant questions from audience members about the strange instrument he was playing—one more indication of just how peculiar the Frying Pan guitars seemed when they first appeared.

While Rey was a highly accomplished player and made many

serious contributions to the development of the electric guitar, he wasn't above milking the instrument's novelty to enhance his own public profile. He developed an early version of the talk box, a gadget that creates the illusion that an electric guitar is talking, decades before rock stars such as Peter Frampton and Jeff Beck employed a similar device on hit records of the seventies. Rey's talking guitar routine was a staple of his act with the King Sisters. The public's perception of the electric guitar as a novelty instrument would persist well into the 1940s. Its novelty began to subside when jazz musicians adopted the new instrument, but would only be fully laid to rest with the advent of rock and roll in the fifties.

ALMOST IMMEDIATELY AFTER the A-25 and A-22 became available, a host of other guitar companies began putting electric models on the market. Electro String's old rival Dobro was one of the first, in 1933. That same year saw the debut of electric models from Gibson and Vivi-Tone. They were followed in short order by electric guitars from Audiovox, Epiphone, and Volu-tone in 1935; Regal, Vega, and Slingerland in 1936; and Sound Projects in 1938. Many of these employed pickups closely modeled on Beauchamp's pioneering design. Because Beauchamp wasn't able to patent his pickup design successfully until 1937, a lot of companies were able to issue copycat products.

"When everybody started to make them, everybody started to buy them," Adolph Rickenbacker would later recall. He took a tolerant view of the competition. Although many of the newcomers were poaching Electro String designs, Rickenbacker and his company chose not to go after them in court.

Others weren't so liberal minded. Patent issues and threats of litigation were very common in the early days of the electric guitar. Once the instrument was seen to be a commercially viable commodity, everyone naturally wanted to corner the market. One of the most aggressive of these entrepreneurs was Benjamin

Franklin Miessner, who tried to establish a monopoly early in the instrument's life by threatening to sue every electric guitar maker for infringing on patents he'd filed in the early 1930s. A few significant companies, such as Epiphone, caved in at first. But Miessner's patent claims ultimately proved too flimsy to constitute much of a threat. By the early forties, he'd pretty much given up. Had he met with more success, he could have shut down the entire nascent electric guitar industry.

Amid a growing field of competitors, the Electro String Instrument Corporation continued to develop innovative electric guitars throughout the thirties, while also diversifying their product line to include electric violins, mandolins, and an electrified bass viol. They even accepted a 1933 commission to build a harp for the legendary film comedian and musician Harpo Marx. The A-25 and A-22 Frying Pan electrics continued to be available on a custom-order basis into the 1950s, and are still used by several of today's top steel players. In 1953, Adolph Rickenbacker sold the Electro String Instrument Corporation to F. C. Hall, father of the company's current CEO. With sleek new modernist guitar designs by German luthier Roger Rossmeisl, Rickenbacher would enter a new era, as we'll see.

Adolph Rickenbacker and Paul Barth, as well as John, Rudy, Louis, and Emil Dopyera, all lived to witness the electric guitar's ascendancy during the rock era. Many of them continued to make key contributions to the burgeoning field. Rickenbacker had the added satisfaction of seeing latter-day guitars bearing his name become some of the most hallowed instruments in rock music, owing to the Beatles' prominent and inspired use of them in the sixties.

Regrettably, George Beauchamp didn't make it that far. He retired from the Electro String Instrument Corporation in 1940, at the still-youthful age of forty-one. He apparently wished to devote himself to his other great passion in life, fishing. Perhaps he sensed he didn't have that much time left. On March 30, 1941, some six months after his retirement, he died of a heart attack while deep-sea fishing off the coast of California.

If any one man could lay claim for the electric guitar revolution, it was him. Beauchamp's groundbreaking work put the electric guitar on the map in the 1930s. Its time had indeed arrived. What was needed now was a guitarist with the vision and musical command to tap deeply into the new instrument's vast, unrealized potential. The world didn't know it yet, but it was awaiting the coming of the first guitar hero.

Jazz guitar pioneer Charlie Christian and his Gibson ES-150

chapter 2

THE CHRISTIAN CRUSADE

Before there was Michael Jackson, the Beatles, Elvis, or Frank Sinatra, there was Benny Goodman. With his horn-rimmed glasses and professorial air, the clarinet-playing bandleader from Chicago was perhaps an unlikely pop idol, but in 1939 he was an unstoppable force.

His meteoric rise to fame is often said to have begun on the night of August 21, 1935, at the Palomar Ballroom in Hollywood, California. After receiving a tepid response to the bland pop tunes and waltzes he thought his audience wanted to hear, Goodman and his fourteen-piece band decided to shake things up. Halfway through the night, Goodman called for his orchestra to perform "Sugar Foot Stomp," a hot arrangement written by the African American composer and bandleader Fletcher Henderson.

The band attacked the chart with a thundering ferocity rarely heard from white musicians. It was strong medicine, but the kids who had been prepped for it via Los Angeles's first celebrity disc jockey, Al Jarvis, and his radio show *The Make Believe Ballroom*, were ready and waiting. As the band exploded, so did the audience, who roared their approval. Goodman would later remember the response as "one of the sweetest sounds I ever heard in my life."

Emboldened by the enthusiastic reception to "Sugar Foot Stomp," Goodman and his band incorporated more Henderson material into their set, and by popular demand were invited to stay at the Palomar for an additional two months before traveling to Chicago, where they created a similar hysteria. The Windy City newspapers seized on the growing popularity of Goodman's sound, describing his edgy, black-influenced dance music as "swing."

After scoring fifteen Billboard Top 10 hits in 1936 alone, the mania reached a fever pitch in March 1937, when more than 21,000 young people came to New York's Paramount Theater to see Goodman and his band, dancing in the aisles and rushing the stage. While tame by today's mosh pit standards, the uninhibited outburst shocked parents of the day and inspired the *New York Times* to call it a "riot" (although the only evidence of real mayhem was at the refreshment stand, where Goodman set a Paramount record for the most nickel candy bars sold in a day).

By the end of the thirties, the media had crowned the clarinetist the King of Swing. But not all was well within the king's castle. In the wake of the swing frenzy, other formidable orchestras started threatening Goodman's domination. Additionally, in 1939 the bandleader lost three of his superstar sidemen in quick succession when trumpeter Harry James, drummer Gene Krupa, and pianist Teddy Wilson all jumped ship to start their own bands. For the first time since his rapid rise to fame, Benny felt threatened by the competition. He sent his talent scout and adviser, John Hammond, out in search of fresh new faces to fortify his big band—an ensemble that was growing smaller by the minute.

Hammond worked for Goodman, but the sharply dressed New Yorker—with a grin so generous it made his eyes squint and cheeks split in two—was no mere flunky. He was born to wealth, the great-grandson of railroad magnate William Henry Vanderbilt, and his role as producer and music executive would make him one of the most important figures in twentieth-century music. Among Hammond's early discoveries were jazz artists such as Count Basie and Billie Holiday, and later he would launch the careers of rock giants like Bob Dylan, Aretha Franklin, Bruce Springsteen, and Stevie Ray Vaughan.

But what really distinguished Hammond as a monumental figure in American culture was his work as a champion for African American musicians. He recognized that jazz was essentially a black art form and he preferred hiring black musicians over white ones, but racial integration in music, to say nothing of America's social institutions, was still decades away. He was determined to change that paradigm.

"To bring recognition to the Negro's supremacy in jazz was the most effective and constructive form of social protest I could think of," said Hammond years later.

Goodman's band was a perfect vehicle for his ambitions, and Hammond cannily used the clarinetist's popularity as a battering ram to break down color lines in popular music. His determination to introduce African American artists such as vibraphonist Lionel Hampton and Billie Holiday, who had her first hits with Benny's orchestra, to white mainstream audiences would not only lead to commercial success but also have far-reaching social consequences.

Despite Hammond's patrician background (and his posh enunciation of words like "mah-velous" and "ghah-stly"), he was one of the few white record executives trusted by the black music community. It was for this reason that Mary Lou Williams, a highly respected black jazz pianist and arranger, reached out to Hammond in 1939, urging him to take a look at Charlie Christian, a twenty-two-year-old guitarist from Oklahoma whose pioneering work on the electric guitar was knocking them dead in the Midwest.

The idea of a virtuoso electric guitarist sounded novel, so in his mission to find Goodman the next big thing, Hammond hopped a plane to Oklahoma City. He would later recall the guitarist's audition at Ruby's Grill, a local jazz hot spot, as "one of the most exciting days of my life." After hearing the skinny, six-foot-tall musician improvise more fluidly on his Gibson ES-150 than any guitarist he had ever encountered, he excitedly called Goodman to say he had found his next superstar.

The bandleader, who was not known for his patience, cut Hammond short. "Who the hell wants to hear an electric guitar player?"

"I don't know," Hammond said, "but you won't believe him until you hear him."

AS THE WORLD'S first electric guitar hero, Charlie Christian, one could argue, forged the tragic archetype for the many six-string revolutionaries that followed him, among them Jimi Hendrix, Randy Rhoads, Stevie Ray Vaughan, and Kurt Cobain, musicians who radically changed the face of music and died too soon.

Charles Henry Christian was born on July 29, 1916, in Bonham, Texas, to a family of musicians—including his parents and his two older brothers. His father, Clarence, was particularly gifted. It was said he could play almost any instrument he set his hands on, but he favored strings and his first love was the guitar. He encouraged his sons to play music, teaching his older boys to play violin and mandolin. It was assumed when Charlie was born that he'd complete the family band.

Soon after Charlie came into the world, Clarence contracted an illness that made him gradually go blind. After dealing with the initial shock and depression of his condition, Clarence rallied, turning to music for therapy and a way to feed his family. There weren't many formal jobs for musicians, black or otherwise, to be had in Bonham, so Clarence grabbed his sons, headed to the streets, and played in public places or door-to-door for change.

Unable to make ends meet, and with starvation a very real threat, the Christians left Texas in 1918 for Oklahoma City, where they found support in their extended family.

Locating a job that accommodated his blindness was no easy task. Clarence was eventually hired to do the physically demanding work of unloading railcars. He moved his family close to the northeast Second Street area, known as Deep Second or Deep Deuce, a narrow but lively downtown district that served as Oklahoma City's center of jazz music and black culture and commerce. Like Beale Street in Memphis or the French Quarter in New Orleans, Second Street was a buzzing hive of musical innovation and competition. It was the heart of black Oklahoma City, where respectable businessmen thrived by day and hustlers, pool sharks, and bootleggers ruled the noisy clubs at night.

One resident of the area and a childhood friend of Christian's, Ralph Ellison, whose 1952 novel *Invisible Man* made him the first black author listed on the *New York Times* best-seller list, remembered lying awake at night listening to the music and wild excitement drifting down from Second Street. "You couldn't escape it," he said. "That was one of the delights." In a more transcendent mood, Ellison, a lifelong jazz enthusiast, recalled standing on the street corner hearing a voice "miraculously unhindered by distance and earthbound things as is the body in youthful dreams of flying." For Ellison, the music of Second Street evoked the heavens.

For Clarence, however, the Deuce represented something a bit more terrestrial. As in Texas, he and his three boys hit the streets and started playing for extra money. While the two elder brothers didn't enjoy what amounted to panhandling, Charlie loved the music and action on Second Street, and soon became a fixture on the scene.

When Clarence passed away in 1926 at the age of thirty-six, he left his guitars to Charlie, who started seriously devoting himself to music. By the time he was thirteen he was studying theory with local jazz musicians and developing his signature sound: a sophisticated and idiosyncratic approach to soloing that, with its single-note melodies, owed more to local saxophonists Lester Young and Herschel Evans than to country blues guitarists such as Lonnie Johnson, or even the influential gypsy jazz guitarist Django Reinhardt.

During his teen years, Second Street became Charlie's second home: a place where he could skip school, play guitar, and make money as he honed his chops to a fine edge. There he became friendly with the then-unknown Aaron Thibeaux "T-Bone" Walker, a hotshot guitarist six years older than Charlie. The Texas-born guitarist regularly traveled through Oklahoma City as a member of a sixteen-piece band. But Walker knew a good side-hustle when he saw one; he and Christian shared an interest in guitar, were blues and jazz enthusiasts, and were avid dancers. Together they were a dynamite act on the street.

"We was really dropouts," Walker later recalled. "Because we were making money, we wouldn't go to school. We'd go dance and pass the hat and make money. Charlie would play guitar awhile, and I'd play bass, and then we'd change, and he'd play bass, and I'd play the guitar. And then we'd go into our little dance."

In many ways, the guitar was an unusual instrument for serious musicians to gravitate to. Still largely an acoustic instrument, it wasn't loud enough to compete with horns. It usually was overshadowed as a rhythm instrument by the piano. But as Charlie and Walker discovered, it was perfect for street entertaining. It was portable, you could play the chords to all the popular songs of the day on it, and you could dance while performing.

Despite realizing the seeming limitations of the guitar, Christian was determined to become a master like his father and elevate the instrument in the process. The guitar was in the early stages of becoming a lead instrument in popular music, and though there were no guidelines and few six-string role models available, one thing Oklahoma City had no shortage of was musical inspiration and innovation.

In the thirties, despite the Depression and the unprecedented Dust Bowl drought that sent thousands scurrying to other regions, Oklahoma City's music scene was thriving. The town played host to the Oklahoma City Blue Devils, an extraordinary Southwestern jazz band featuring future jazz giants such as Count Basie, drummer Jo Jones, and Charlie's hero, Lester Young. Equally important were Bob Wills and His Texas Playboys, one of the very first country bands to synthesize big-city swing jazz with folk instruments like fiddles and steel guitars.

Off the streets, inventions like the radio and phonograph filled the air with exciting new jazz, blues, and country sounds, and Charlie soaked it all in. By the time he was eighteen, in 1934, his talent was undeniable. He was performing in clubs and proper paying gigs, and the elder jazz community recognized his talent. Over the next four years he was allowed to sit in and learn from the best at clubs such as the Hole, the Goody-Goody Cafe, the Ritz, and on local radio stations like WXFR and KGFG.

The young man enjoyed his life as a professional musician, but what he most relished was being inducted into jazz's not-so-secret society: the exotic and intense world of the late-night jam session. Any musician visiting the area—black or white—knew that the only place to be after the clubs closed was Second Street, where musical showdowns erupted like knife fights almost every night in ballrooms, public halls, and even hotel rooms.

Most of the jamming was for fun—an opportunity for players to learn from each other, to stretch out and improvise without commercial restrictions. But just as often these midnight jams that lasted well into the morning were serious business: musicians clashed in order to win respect, local supremacy, and a chance to move up the club food chain. When a particularly hot battle broke out, word would spread like wildfire, drawing huge audiences who had no problem expressing their opinions by cheering or jeering.

If you ran out of ideas during a jam, you were a dead man. Steal them from your opponent and you were worse than dead. But if you could spin a new riff and twist it into something fresh over numerous choruses of a standard like "Sweet Georgia Brown," you'd become the talk of the town overnight. The bandstand was all well and good, but it was these nightly challenges of skill, technique, and intellectual rigor that turned Charlie Christian into the phenomenon he would become. In a cutting contest, he usually had the sharpest knife, and he had no problem sticking it to any musician with any instrument.

It was one of these jams in 1939 that would cement Christian's local hero status and set his trajectory toward world fame and fortune. Floyd Smith, who had a national reputation as a first-rate guitarist due to his hit "Floyd's Guitar Blues," was playing a one-nighter at the Oklahoma Ballroom when he was lured into a jam with Christian. Thinking he was facing off with a hick from the sticks, he burned through all of his best licks in his first couple of choruses, hoping to crush the young upstart at the outset.

Pianist Mary Lou Williams, an eyewitness to the event and the woman who later championed Christian to John Hammond, remembered: "For a while it was a close call, then Charlie decided to blow. He used his head on cutting sessions . . . taking it easy while other musicians played everything they knew, then cutting loose to blast them off the map. Never in my life had I heard such inspired and exciting music as Christian beat out of his guitar. Poor Floyd gave it up and walked off the stand. Charlie played for us till daybreak."

While improvising guitarists were still pretty rare in the thirties, Christian wasn't the only six-string gunslinger to come from Oklahoma City. The town—almost miraculously—would serve up two other giants who would eventually pioneer and revolutionize the use of the electric guitar in two completely different musical genres. Just as Charlie Christian would electrify jazz, his childhood friend "T-Bone" Walker would find fame by fusing blues and swing into his own highly polished sound (which would go on to influence B.B. King and rockers like Chuck Berry and the Allman Brothers). Eldon Shamblin, who starred in Bob Wills's swing band, would help introduce amplification to country music.

Together, these three men would put the electric guitar on the map. But before they could take over the musical world, they needed an instrument that was a match for their talents.

GIBSON'S ES-150 is regularly referred to as the world's first commercially successful Spanish-style electric guitar (the ES stood for Electric Spanish; 150 reflected an instrument/amplifier bundle priced at around $150). Designwise, it is a hollow-body guitar with two sound holes, each in the shape of a cursive "f" (known fittingly as f-holes) cut into its top. The top itself has a subtly arched contour, reaching its highest point where the strings pass over the body; this feature, along with the f-holes, came out of traditional violin design. The combination of features—the hollow body, the contoured top, the distinctive sound holes—came to constitute what is now collectively known as the "archtop" guitar. It would become the archetype for pretty much all jazz electrics to come.

Prior to the ES-150, Gibson had tried getting electric guitars onto the market as early as 1933. These initial attempts, however, were somewhat primitive, using pickups that relied on capturing vibrations off the top of the guitar rather than the strings. It was the introduction of George Beauchamp's revolutionary electromagnetic pickup for the Rickenbacker Electro that gave guitar makers their most essential piece of inspiration. In the spring of 1935, Gibson commissioned an amateur radio operator named Walter Fuller to develop an electromagnetic pickup that would better Beauchamp's. Remarkably, within a matter of weeks, Fuller had managed to create what is now commonly known as the "bar pickup" because of its long, hexagonal shape.

Destined to be known as the "Charlie Christian pickup," it was a definite improvement over Beauchamp's cumbersome pickup, which had a bulky magnet that arched over the strings and interfered with the picking hand. Instead, Fuller's pickup sat comfortably and discreetly beneath the strings. The outer portion of the pickup consisted of a coil of copper wire wrapped around a rectangular plastic spool known as a bobbin, both of which fit around a slim, chrome-plated steel blade.* Attached to this were two slender bar magnets. Fuller designed the pickup so that the two magnets were located beneath the top of the guitar, tucked inside the instrument's hollow body, like the bulk of an iceberg concealed under the surface. This design placed the magnets out of sight and, more important, out of the way of the player's picking hand. While the mechanics of Fuller's pickup were far from those of the compact version that would appear just a few short years later, the outward aesthetic set the tone for the way pickups would look throughout the modern era. The Fuller pickup was initially tested and installed in six-string lap steel guitars made of aluminum. While those instruments sounded just fine, Gibson was slow to deliver an equivalent Spanish model. It wasn't until retail giants Montgomery Ward and Spiegel, May, Stern began applying pressure on the manufacturer to deliver an electric Spanish guitar for their catalogs that Gibson started producing a genuine ES model.

In late 1936 and early 1937, Gibson delivered their first instruments to the large chains. The company was reluctant to put its name on the somewhat hastily constructed guitars, which were made from inferior pressed plywood rather than solid wood. In compliance, Ward called their Gibson-built model the "1270" while Spiegel dubbed theirs the "Old Kraftsman," and even though they were made with cheap materials, both guitars were genuine retail successes. Ward sold close to nine hundred of them through 1940.

---

* Owing to the coil of wire wrapped around the bobbin and pole piece, this style of pickup would become known as a "single-coil pickup." Later designs would feature two or more coil and bobbin assemblies, but the single-coil design has remained in use right up to the present day.

After that, there was no ignoring the burgeoning popularity of these new instruments. Gibson decided to put some real muscle into creating an electric guitar worthy of its name—which had by now become synonymous with innovative, quality instruments.

While the company saw the value in Beauchamp's developments, they had different ideas about what a guitar should look like and how it should be constructed (it should not resemble a frying pan, for one). Their first Gibson-branded electrics would be well-crafted acoustic instruments that could be played with or without an amplifier.

Before putting their name on the headstock, Gibson improved on the Ward/Spiegel model in almost every way. Their logo would be inlaid in pearl rather than stenciled on. The new ES-150 would have an adjustable truss rod (a steel rod running through the neck, used to adjust tension), a solid spruce arched top, solid maple back and sides, and tone and volume controls built into the guitar. Costing $72.50 with a cord, and $155 with a 15-watt amp and case (about $2,000 today), the revamped six-string would be, in Gibson's own words, "the perfect Spanish guitar."

Whether it was perfect is up for debate, but it was, and still is, a truly fine-sounding electric instrument. Gibson wisely decided to place the pickup toward the neck, away from the bridge, giving the guitar a rich, warm tone that blended well when accompanying other instruments, while still having enough "attack" that when played aggressively with a pick, it could hold its own against any horn or piano in a larger ensemble.

Charlie Christian had been searching for a bold guitar sound that would match the saxophone tones of players like Chu Berry and Dick Wilson, and the technology finally caught up to him. The ES-150 and Christian were a match made in heaven, and together they created a beautiful noise that changed the course of music and defined guitar jazz for years to come. Future greats such as Barney Kessel, Jim Hall, Wes Montgomery, and George

Benson would create their own signature sounds with the electric guitar, but they would all use Charlie's essential building blocks.

It's hard to say when Charlie first became aware of the ES-150, but it must have come as a revelation after years of struggling to be heard. Earlier accounts have him playing his acoustic guitars with a microphone balanced between his legs, or else fastened to his guitar with a network of rubber bands. With an ES-150 in his possession, it wasn't long before he started blowing everyone away, as he did with John Hammond at Ruby's Grill.

TWO ANXIOUS WEEKS after his audition with Hammond, Charlie finally received a telegram:

COME AT ONCE. HAVE POSITION WITH BENNY GOODMAN.

Upon receiving the news, Christian reportedly sat down and started laughing. When asked why, he replied, "That man's in Los Angeles. How in the hell am I going to make it to Los Angeles if I ain't got cab fare downtown?"

The problem was quickly resolved. Goodman had a weekly radio show, *Camel Caravan*, with a $300 budget for guest artists, and Hammond persuaded Benny to use the money to pay for Christian's flight to L.A.

The news sent huge ripples through Oklahoma's music community. *The Black Dispatch*, an Oklahoma City black newspaper, described Charlie's trip to the West Coast as "one of the biggest breaks ever received by a local musician."

And it was—Goodman was gigantic, after all. His popularity was often compared to President Franklin D. Roosevelt's. So when Christian walked in to perform for the bandleader in August of 1939, it was little wonder that he had a serious case of the jitters.

"I was so nervous and everything," Christian said to *Metronome* magazine. "Benny sent everyone home from rehearsal, and then asked me to play for him. So there we were, just the two of us, and I was so nervous with him just sittin' there and lookin' at me. I couldn't play hardly at all."

It probably didn't help that Benny was visibly irritated with the situation. He was still skeptical of the electric guitar, and he showed it by impatiently refusing to allow Christian time to plug his guitar into his amp. As the guitarist fumbled through a tepid version of "Tea for Two," an unimpressed Goodman excused himself and hightailed it out of the room. But the clarinetist must have felt some small twinge of sympathy for the poor Oklahoma musician who had traveled all the way to California, because before he left he extended an invitation for Charlie to come see his band play that night at Victor Hugo's, a swanky supper club.

Hammond was mortified by the news of Christian's botched audition, but he was not deterred. He knew Charlie was the new star Goodman was desperately looking for. That night, in a last-ditch effort, Hammond snuck Charlie onstage during a dinner break, hoping to give the guitarist one last shot at impressing Goodman. When Benny returned, he was not at all pleased to find Charlie on the bandstand. He called "Rose Room," a song he was certain the guitarist wouldn't know. To Goodman's surprise, it was a favorite of Christian's, and he devoured the song, playing with the passion and innovation he reserved for his fiercest Second Street showdowns. Goodman was so mesmerized by Charlie's ability to build long, complex hornlike lines that slid, bent, and slurred into sophisticated bluesy shapes that he allowed the guitarist to solo over an astounding twenty choruses. When the song finally ended, Christian had earned his spot in the band.

Within three weeks—largely due to Goodman's full touring schedule and his high-profile radio show—Christian had become a star. And five months later he became one of music's most respected names when *Down Beat* magazine, America's most influential jazz publication, voted him #1 in their Best Guitarist poll. Christian dominated with 2,665 votes, compared to Django Reinhardt's paltry 55 and Les Paul's positively anemic 12.

As Charlie's fame exploded, so did the electric guitar's. Soon Epiphone, Kay Musical Instruments, Vega, Harmony, and Gretsch all introduced competing electrics. Gibson unabashedly promoted the ES-150 as having "Charlie Christian pickups."

Goodman's estimation of Charlie also grew. In a 1982 interview conducted a few years before the bandleader's death, he remembered the guitarist as being rather shy and reserved. "But, by gosh, when he sat down and played the guitar, he was something! He was way ahead of his time and a joy to listen to."

But not everybody was a Christian convert. Adding yet another black musician to the Goodman band (the other two having been vibraphonist Lionel Hampton and pianist Teddy Wilson) rankled some observers; segregation was still a matter of state and local law in the South in the 1940s, and violations were punishable by imprisonment and death by hanging. But a combination of artistic integrity and arrogance (not to mention witnessing the band's commercial success) made Goodman stand his ground.

"Benny didn't have to have us in his band, and he put up with a lot," said Hampton about his early days with Goodman.

> Theater managers would tell him they were getting a lot of mail protesting Teddy and me, but Benny wouldn't back down. He once bopped a guy in the head with his clarinet when the guy told him he should "get those niggers off his show." Meanwhile, he was getting flak from some critics in the black community who accused him of using blacks. That was nonsense. He didn't have to hire Teddy or me; he hired us because we made his kind of music. And this was in the North! Benny knew he was going to have to make some serious advance plans when we went south.

Goodman's commitment to the African Americans in his band had been put to severe test in the summer of 1937, two years before Christian joined the band, when he was invited to perform at the Pan American Casino in Dallas. He knew it was going to be a rough gig for an integrated band; no integrated orchestra had ever played in the Deep South before, and Goodman planned his visit like a military campaign.

First, he made it a part of the orchestra's contract that his black musicians would be able to stay with the rest of the band in the Statler Hotel in downtown Dallas, and that they would also be able to use the same entrance and elevators. While the hotel's management wasn't thrilled, they were willing to relent since it meant delivering the country's biggest name in music.

To further guarantee the safety and dignity of his musicians, he had his own car, a Packard, sent down to Dallas by train so they wouldn't have to worry about taxi drivers refusing to pick them up. He also hired an escort to accompany the musicians from the hotel entrance to their rooms and back.

"I wasn't worried about going south with Benny," said Hampton. "People said to me, 'Why you goin' down south? Those white folks will kill you.' And I'd say, 'They'll have to kill Benny Goodman first.'"

As it turned out, when it came to music, fans were often willing to look past color, a phenomenon that would recur many times throughout the decades—with the guitar playing a surprising role in softening racist attitudes.

For Charlie, playing for Goodman was life altering. He went from making $7.50 to $200 a week. He became one of Goodman's favorite soloists, given ample room to blow on hits like "Flying Home," "Six Appeal (My Daddy Rocks Me)," and "Good Enough to Keep (Air Mail Special)." But even with his newfound fame, the guitarist spent most of his time playing, practicing, and searching for the next after-hours jam session.

For years, Goodman had been plagued by terrible back pain,

and in July 1940 he decided to have major surgery performed on his lower spine. When he returned to playing in October, the band was reassembled in New York City. This was both a blessing and a curse for Christian. Manhattan was the heaviest town in the world for a musician with his voracious appetites. The guitarist rarely turned down an opportunity to hang out and jam after gigs with Goodman, and he soon found his home away from home in a dingy club on 118th Street in Harlem called Minton's Playhouse. It was there he made friends with club bandleader Kenny Clarke and house pianist Thelonious Monk, two of the founding fathers of modern jazz.

Soon the guitarist was the star attraction of Minton's truly legendary after-hours jam sessions, where he presided over and helped fan the flames of the next revolutionary movement in jazz: bebop. The style was characterized by small ensembles playing at lightning-fast tempos with new levels of virtuosity and harmonic complexity, and this non-danceable music was a younger genera- tion's direct counter to big band swing like Benny Goodman's. While Charlie by no means rejected Goodman's influence, he simply could not resist the challenge of learning a new musical language and beating those Young Turks at their own game. He astonished cocky newcomers like Monk and Charlie Parker with his dexterity and deep understanding of chords and harmony.

But Goodman's demanding schedule combined with Chris- tian's late-night activities started to take a toll on the guitarist's health. Back in March of 1940, he had been hospitalized for exhaustion and doctors discovered scars on his lungs from tuber- culosis. He was told to slow down and get rest, but that had never been his style. If anything, the excitement at Minton's accelerated his pace.

On March 4, 1941, he recorded "Solo Flight," a track that many aficionados consider his finest hour with Goodman. But that June, Charlie collapsed during a tour of the Midwest and was rushed back to New York, where he was admitted to Bellevue Hospital. His tuberculosis had returned.

Christian's health continued to deteriorate. Well-meaning friends didn't help matters much, sneaking girls and marijuana into his room when he was supposed to be recovering. In January of 1942, stuck in the ward at Sea View Hospital on Staten Island, he received news that he had won the *Down Beat* poll for the third straight year, gathering over 40 percent of the vote. It was probably the last good news he would hear. On March 3, at the young age of twenty-five, Christian contracted pneumonia and died.

IF IT TOOK a technological wizard like George Beauchamp to give the electric guitar legs, it took an artistic genius like Charlie Christian to give it meaning and purpose.

But what would happen if ingenuity and virtuosity could be found in the same person? Into what new and fantastic realms could the embryonic idea of the electric guitar be taken if you could marry the demands of a player with the problem-solving imagination of an engineer?

World War II slowed the evolution of the electric guitar. The government would order instrument companies to alter their production processes to focus on the war effort. But the electric guitar was an idea with its own momentum now, and its future lay around the corner. It would take the shape of a onetime child prodigy and prodigious showman from Wisconsin, a man who'd adopted the stage name Les Paul.

Les Paul holding a Rickenbacker
SPC-1948 (top) and four-string tenor
guitar (bottom). Other instruments (left
to right): Gibson L-12 (on chair), Les
Paul's "Clunker," headless aluminum
guitar, the "Log," Gibson L-2,
Kalamazoo mandolin, Rickenbacker
Bakelite ES

THE WIZARD
FROM WAUKESHA

In the late 1940s, the house that once stood at 1514 North Curson Avenue in West Hollywood wouldn't have attracted much notice. In all its external details, the dwelling typified the cozy domesticity and middle-class comfort of American life in the years immediately following World War II. A trim, unassuming single-story structure, the house had a modest patch of front lawn that was adorned with palm trees and verdant Southern California foliage. A straight concrete pathway led up to four steps flanked by white columns, beyond which lay the front door.

The house was just around the corner from the stretch of Sunset Boulevard known as Sunset Strip—then, as now, a thoroughfare associated with showbiz glamour. The golden age of Hollywood filmmaking was in full swing, and the town's movie studios were turning out box-office smashes and instant classics such as *The Big Sleep, Notorious, Gilda,* and *Mildred Pierce.* Sunset was the playground of movie moguls, mobsters, stars, and starlets who would dine and dance at the Trocadero, the Mocambo, Ciro's, and other exotic *boîtes de nuit.* Strolling down Sunset, you could get a fine suit at Michael's Exclusive Haberdashery—a front for the notorious gangster Mickey Cohen—or have an ice cream at Schwab's drugstore soda fountain, where film star Lana Turner was said to have been discovered. Celebrities and would-be celebs resided at the Garden of Allah, Sunset Tower, Chateau Marmont, or one of the area's tropically themed garden apartment complexes.

But L.A. has always been a place where you could turn off a busy main drag like Sunset and find yourself on a tree-lined, distinctly suburban side street, with rows of well-kept homes. The house on North Curson was just such a place, and its owner was something of a celebrity in his own right. Then in his thirties, Les Paul had established himself as one of America's foremost guitarists through frequent radio appearances, live performances, and recordings with his own Les Paul Trio and top singers of the day, such as Bing Crosby and the Andrews Sisters. Audiences appreciated his homespun good humor as much as they enjoyed his supple guitar work.

In the late 1940s, Les would sometimes play host to two other men with more than a glancing interest in the guitar. They'd sit on the back patio at Les's place, drinking beer and exchanging ideas. Unlike Les, they weren't at all famous at the time—just humble tradesmen and fellow tinkerers from down in Orange County, south of L.A. and appreciably less fabulous than West Hollywood.

Leo Fender was a bit older than Les Paul, pushing forty at the time. Unlike Les, he was a native Californian, born and raised in Fullerton, where his parents had an orange grove. To a certain extent, Fender was the kind of guy that people would later call a nerd—a bespectacled man quietly obsessed with the mechanical and electrical workings of things, invariably equipped with a few pens and pencils protruding from the front of his shirt in a plastic pocket protector. He had recently parlayed his radio repair business into the Fender Electric Instrument Company, manufacturing lap steel guitars and amplifiers in a smallish way.

Les's other guest on those Sunset nights was a more rough-and-tumble figure by the name of Paul A. Bigsby. The eldest of the three men on the patio, he'd certainly done his share of living. A Midwesterner like Les, he was born in Illinois and had moved to California, where he took a few hard knocks and epic spills as a motorcycle racing champion before turning his hand to designing and building them. A skilled machinist, he had eventually gravitated from building motorcycles to lap steel guitars on a custom basis for western swing musicians like Speedy West, Joaquin Murphey, and Noel Boggs. Bigsby was louder than Leo Fender and less suave—if no less outgoing—than Les Paul. A man of action with a big, booming voice and towering presence, he liked to describe himself as a guy who could build anything.

Given their relatively minor stake in the guitar business at the time, Fender and Bigsby were more than happy to travel north to Curson Avenue and pay a call on Les Paul. And they were warmly welcomed. Although the youngest of the three men, Les possessed an innate gift for putting people at ease while slyly making himself the center of attention. He was charismatic, if slightly avuncular, and a natural-born raconteur.

His studio-cum-workshop, out in the garage, was also a big draw. It was here that Les Paul did some of his most significant design work. The garage was cluttered with bulky, arcane, and frequently homemade pieces of electronic gear perched atop assorted items of household furniture. But it was a fully functional studio where Les would do commercial sessions—often with hillbilly and western swing ensembles—as well as record his own music. Leo Fender and Paul Bigsby were more than a little keen to find out what Les was up to in that garage.

"We enjoyed sharing our likes and dislikes in life generally," Les would later recall of those nights. They'd listen to the group that was currently recording, to the amplifier and the guitar, and talk about what changes they were going to make. "We used to spend hours after a recording session with some hillbillies—you know, country players. We'd sit in the back yard on the patio by the fire for hours and discuss sound."

To a nosy neighbor peering into the backyard, it may not have looked like much. Just three guys settling into middle age, sitting around and talking shop. But the trio was quietly fomenting a revolution. They'd all been developing an idea that had been in the air for quite a while but had never quite come together until then. The upshot of their work would dramatically affect the sound of pop music, and indeed the tone, tenor, and trajectory of all popular culture in the latter half of the twentieth century and beyond. Each man, in his own way, was laboring to make the solid-body electric Spanish, or standard, guitar a reality. The instrument would become the mainstay of modern rock music and many other popular musical genres.

These days, the Mocambo, the Trocadero, and other hot spots of 1940s Hollywood have long since disappeared from the Sunset Strip. But their place has been taken by equally historic nightclubs like the Roxy and the Whisky a Go Go, where bands such as the Doors, the Byrds, Van Halen, and Guns N' Roses made rock history for decades, and where today's and tomorrow's rock stars still strut their stuff. The stretch of Sunset right around Curson is home to a panoply of guitar shops where rock guitarists and other six-string aficionados flock in search of their dream axe. More often than not, they're seeking gear that bears the name Fender, Bigsby, or Les Paul.

IT'S A POPULAR misconception that Les Paul single-handedly invented the electric guitar, or at least the solid-body electric guitar. While he contributed substantially to the instrument's development, Les Paul most certainly did not invent the solid-body electric guitar, much less the electric guitar itself. George Beauchamp, Adolph Rickenbacker, Paul Barth, Harry Watson, and Walter Fuller's enormous contributions to the electric guitar's early development have been discussed. These men and others—

including Lloyd Loar, Paul Tutmarc, and Victor Smith—had made significant progress with the new instrument, both technologically and commercially, well before Les did anything notable with it.

So where did we get this myth of Les Paul's single-handed creation of the electric guitar, ex nihilo, like Yahweh summoning the cosmos into existence? All too often the source of this creation story was Les himself. He did have a talent for embellishing the truth and rewriting key chapters of musical history with himself as the sole hero. Among his many other gifts, Les Paul possessed that of gab. His easygoing charm and folksy way with a tall tale made people just want to believe anything he said. Maybe it was an artifact of that Depression-era determination to get over by any possible means—to make do, to improvise, to invent if necessary.

Born Lester William Polsfuss in Waukesha, Wisconsin, on June 9, 1915, he displayed both musical and mechanical inclinations from an early age. As a boy, he altered the player piano rolls at home, adding notes that weren't meant to be there. There's a story, probably coined by Les himself, that, at around age twelve, he fashioned a homemade electric guitar, amp, and P.A. system using a record player pickup, telephone mouthpiece, and parts from the family radio. "Looking back over my life," Les said in 1999, "I think I probably spent a little more time tinkering with electronics than I did playing music."

He played plenty of music as well, first hitting the road at the tender age of thirteen with a cowboy band during a summer break from school. "They were short on hats," he recalled. "So when it came time to feature me, one of the other guys would give me his cowboy hat and boots. Of course they were way too big. When I went out there to sing my songs, pretty much all you could see was a big hat and a pair of boots."

Hillbilly and western music were two kindred genres that the golden age of Radio had helped to popularize throughout the twenties. Launched in 1922, WSB in Atlanta was perhaps the first radio station to broadcast this style of music, followed by WBAP out of Fort Worth, Texas, in 1923. The *National Barn Dance* program, which began broadcasting in 1924 on WLS in Chicago, brought down-home music to millions of listeners. Nashville's *WSM Barn Dance* got under way in 1925, and two years later would be renamed the *Grand Ole Opry*.

By the early 1930s, as Les reached his late teens, he had made his own way onto the airwaves, singing and strumming the guitar under the cheerfully countrified name of Rhubarb Red. Early in the history of broadcast, he appears to have had a keen sense of the new medium's power, not only to reach a wider audience than a touring musician could ever hope to, but also as a platform for a savvy performer to craft a persona and sell himself as a larger-than-life character.

Rhubarb Red started out on Missouri radio stations KMOX and KWTO, playing sometimes on his own and sometimes in a duo with Sunny Joe Wolverton known as the Ozark Apple Knockers. The Knockers performed on Chicago's WBBM for several months, as well, before going their separate ways in 1934.

It was as Rhubarb Red that Les Paul made his recording debut on the Montgomery Ward label, in 1937, with a series of sides that included the jaunty "Just Because" and "Deep Elem Blues." Both tracks adhere to the same old-timey formula—a briskly strummed acoustic guitar accompaniment to verses that alternate melodic harmonica passages with Les's reedy vocalizing. With the possible exception of a few jazzy passing chords, there's little indication here of the more uptown musical approach Les would develop in just a few years, although an element of Rhubarb Red's cornball humor would remain part of his personal style, even after he moved on to slicker musical genres and newer media.

It was during his time in Chicago in the 1930s that Les made one of his first serious forays into electric guitar design. He had teamed up with Carl and August Larson, a Swedish-born fraternal guitar-building team active from the 1890s through the 1940s. Their handmade guitars were marketed under a variety of brand names, including Maurer, Prairie State, Euphonon, Stahl, and Dyer, and are still highly regarded today.

"In 1934 the Cumberland Ridge Runners were working at the same radio station I was at, WJJD," Les recollected. "I saw that their guitarist Doc Hopkins, and several other country players, were playing a brand of guitar that I'd never seen before. It wasn't a [C. F.] Martin [& Company brand] or anything familiar. I said, 'What is that thing?' 'Oh, it's the Larson brothers,' was the reply. So I had to get my butt over there. To my amazement they were in a barn out in the country, outside Chicago."

Once he'd tracked down the barn, Les found a sign on the front entrance that simply said PULL THE STRING. He did as instructed. The string triggered a bell in a loft at the top of the barn where the Larsons had their workshop. A man, presumably one of the siblings, stuck his head out of a top window demanding that the visitor state his business. On announcing he wanted to talk about building a guitar, Les was admitted to the premises.

> The guy pulls the latch up with a long string. You had to quickly leap in there and the door locks after you. I walk up two flights of stairs, up to the top of the barn. And one of the Larson brothers, I guess it was August or Carl, says, "What do you want?"
>
> "Well, I'd like to have you make a guitar for me."
>
> "Well, I'm a busy man. Tell me specifically what you want."
>
> "I'd like one that has a solid top on it. No f-holes in it, and additional frets."

On describing his concept, Les was asked if he was a player himself. "Oh I play pretty good," he demurred, picking up a guitar that was lying around and offering a small sample of his technique.

"You're pretty good," Larson conceded, "but not as good as Rhubarb Red."

"You think so?"

"I *know* so. You ever hear of him?"

"They didn't even know I *was* Rhubarb Red!" Les marveled. "I had to explain to them that I used two different names. They didn't get it anyway, but they made the guitar for me. They made two for me. One I gave to Chet Atkins. The other one, I don't know what happened to it. Maybe I gave it away when I went to New York later on. But the Larson brothers were just great. I had a lot of fun working with them."

Les had asked the siblings to build him two or three guitars (accounts vary), each hollow-bodied but with a solid maple top approximately an inch thick, with no sound holes and two pickups. The thick, solid top marks a significant early step in his eventual evolution toward a completely solid-body guitar design. Traditional guitar craft had long favored making the top as thin as possible, supported by the slenderest practicable bracing underneath. (A thinner top will vibrate more, thus creating greater natural resonance.) And guitar tops had always contained one or more sound holes to maximize projection from the hollow body. The instruments the Larsons built for Les took a different tack—minimizing the natural vibration of the wooden top, thus allowing the electronic pickups to do more of the work of generating the instrument's tone.

It also was during this time in Chicago that Les began to move away from the hillbilly-inflected sound of his Rhubarb Red persona, in favor of a more sophisticated jazz guitar style that was gathering momentum. And so Lester Polsfuss rechristened himself yet again—now as Les Paul—creating a more sophisticated persona to complement his new musical direction. There was, however, a transitional period when the guitarist's two identities coexisted, somewhat schizophrenically, side by side.

"In the daytime, I made money playing country music on the radio," Les would later explain. "At night, I played jazz. You didn't make much money playing jazz but you learned so much. That's when I had the privilege of learning from Coleman Hawkins, Art Tatum . . . all the greats. Chicago was the place to lock into jazz."

Chicago, in 1937, was where the first of many Les Paul Trios was formed, with upright bassist Ernie Newton and rhythm guitarist/vocalist Jimmy Atkins (elder half brother of guitar legend Chet Atkins). Subsequent lineups and instrumentation would vary, but Les Paul was always heavily featured on electric guitar—playing either one of the many commercially available hollow-body electric guitars then available, or various instruments he had built or modified over the years. The small-ensemble format seemed to suit Les as a player. It was also a harbinger of things to come; small combos would eventually eclipse the big bands of the day. That was, in part, a result of the increased capacity for volume and wider tonal range of the guitar in its emergent, electrically amplified form. In fact, the New York chapter of the American Federation of Musicians came out against the electric guitar in the 1930s, for fear that it would put horn players and other musicians out of work. But ultimately there was no stopping the electric guitar's rise to prominence.

WITH ITS THRIVING jazz scene and vibrant nightlife, mid-thirties Chicago may have been exciting to a young musician, but Les soon had his eyes on a destination that promised even greater thrills. On the strength of his ambition and a tall tale to his bandmates, Les Paul persuaded his trio to try their luck in New York.

"I told them, 'I know all kinds of people in New York.' I was lying like hell. I didn't know anyone, but I didn't want to tell that to the other guys."

So, in 1938, the trio relocated. It didn't take long for Les to make good on his promise, wangling a regular thrice-weekly spot for the trio on bandleader Fred Waring's radio program, *The Chesterfield Hour* (sponsored by a leading cigarette brand of the day). Fred Waring and His Pennsylvanians were one of the top orchestras of the era, and the show's presenter, the National Broadcasting Company (NBC), was not only America's first coast-to-coast radio network, launched in 1926, but also one of only three major networks at the time.

Not all listeners responded favorably to the new act coming across NBC's airwaves. Some wrote in to complain about the strange and, to their ears, unpleasant sound of the newfangled electric guitar Les Paul was playing. There were demands to fire him, or at least rein him in. But Waring stuck by him, and slowly but surely the radio audience adjusted to the hollow-body electric guitar's timbres. Some may have persisted in their complaints, but others wrote in to say they liked what they heard.

Les Paul had hit the big time. Then as now, New York was a fertile environment for new ideas in music, and Les found himself hobnobbing with Charlie Christian and Django Reinhardt. He and his fellow guitar players would gather at the Epiphone guitar showroom on Fourteenth Street, or Eddie Bell's New York Band & Instrument Company on Sixth Avenue and Forty-sixth Street, where they could exchange ideas and play the newest guitar gear.

While Les may have enjoyed the company, he found that the new equipment just didn't suit his needs as a player. The archtops typically favored by jazz guitarists—those hollow-body guitars that took inspiration from violin making—came with their own inherent set of liabilities. Stated in the simplest terms, they resonated too much. Resonance—natural vibration of the instrument's wooden body—is a good thing in unamplified guitars. But with the addition of electronic amplification, all that resonance can create a "woofy" tone that's hard to control or subdue as volume increases. At higher volume levels, hollow-body guitars are highly prone to feedback—the "howling" sound that results when the pickups start interacting with the amplifier's speakers, setting up what's called a transduction loop. In future generations, guitarists like Pete Townshend and Jimi Hendrix would find creative musical uses for feedback. But to players in the late thirties and early forties, it was still very much to be avoided.

So Les decided to push forward with the concept he'd been exploring with the Larsons, and which had been incubating among guitarists and builders for more than a decade—an electric Spanish guitar with a partially or completely solid body.

"When I started fooling with guitars back in the 1920s it was all about, 'What if we could hear the string all by itself?'" Les said.

> We know that a hollow-body guitar has an acoustic chamber that is resonating at different frequencies. But what if we could isolate the string from that? If you could take the string all by its lonesome, with nothing sustaining it but the nut and the bridge, what would this honest-to-God string sound like? Is it something we would want to hear? Could the sound be manipulated electronically in some way? That was the challenge: to take a string that was completely divorced from the body and make it sound better, or at least just as good.

And so, starting sometime in 1939, Les decided to put his theory into practice. He got hold of a solid, 4"x4" slab of pine, roughly the length of a conventional archtop guitar body (about 20 to 22 inches). To this he attached a bridge, two wood-covered pickups that he made himself and, also of his own making, a crudely wrought vibrato tailpiece (which anchored the strings and allowed for bending the pitches of notes). To the upper portion of the pine slab he affixed a Spanish guitar neck.

Attachable to either side of the pine block were two "wings" of an Epiphone hollow-body archtop guitar—an instrument whose body he had sawed in half the long way, in the direction that the strings run. These may have been added to the instrument as an afterthought, to make it look more like a conventional guitar, and also perhaps to make it easier to hold in the seated playing position.

The "Log," as it came to be known, is a true work of bricolage—a folk-art assemblage of spare parts and found guitar artifacts. It was a testament to Les's resourcefulness and creativity, and one of his most important inventions. But the most important question still remained: Would it play? Les strung it up and plugged it into one of the amps that was in use for his hollow-body guitars, and he found, much to his satisfaction: the thing actually sounded pretty good. It can be heard on several of his classic recordings, including "Lover" and "Lady of Spain."

Les would later recall the reaction his homemade guitar elicited when he brought it to a jam session prior to adding the body "wings." "I took it to a bar out in Sunnyside [Queens, New York]," he told *Guitar Magazine,* "and when I sat in with just the four-by-four they laughed at me! When I put the wings on, they thought it was a guitar and everything was fine."

In a way, the Log was a successor to the guitar made by the celebrated nineteenth-century luthier Antonio de Torres, who fashioned his instrument's back and sides out of papier-mâché in order to demonstrate the effectiveness of the thin wooden top and bracing pattern he'd devised. The back and sides of a hollow guitar are superfluous, Torres was, in effect, saying. You can make them out of anything. It was the vibrational qualities of the top of the guitar, the part that faces a guitar's audience, and its bracing that created the instrument's beautiful tone.

Les's Log, like Torres's papier-mâché guitar, is a demonstration instrument, although it demonstrates a different acoustical principle. In an amplified setting, the traditional guitar's hollow body and thin, resonant top become superfluous—or, even worse, a liability. In other words, the vibrational qualities—or the relative lack of vibration—exhibited by a solid chunk of wood lend themselves to amplification better than those of a hollow box.

And if you get rid of the box, then why couldn't your electric guitar be shaped like pretty much anything? The elongated rectangle of the Log's central body-block eloquently—if somewhat inelegantly—demonstrates this. The traditional guitar shape can be discarded. (Luthiers in subsequent decades would run wild with this idea, as we'll see.)

Though Les didn't go out of his way to dispel the notion that he was the first electric guitar builder, the truth is that his Log had its predecessors. George Beauchamp had attached a guitar string and a very primitive pickup to a solid chunk of 2"x4" wood, way back in the late twenties. But his prototype didn't work very well, and he had been aiming to create an electrified Hawaiian steel guitar, not an electric Spanish guitar like the Log.

The Log, in contrast, became one of Les Paul's main working instruments for years to come. Of course, if he had not gone on to lend his name to a Gibson electric guitar—an instrument, incidentally, that he did *not* design, but that would become hugely popular in subsequent decades—the Log might have been a mere footnote in musical history. But as it is, that prototype is regarded as a major milestone in the development of the solid-body electric Spanish guitar. As an indicator of the Log's historic importance, it is now enshrined in the Country Music Hall of Fame's collection of iconic musical instruments.

NOT THAT THE world instantly recognized Les's genius. He had been doing some of his work on the Log at the Epiphone guitar factory in Lower Manhattan. Noted for its stylish jazz archtops, Epiphone was one of the top guitar manufacturers and a major rival of Gibson. Les would later remember Epiphone chief Epi Stathopoulo's less-than-enthusiastic reaction to his new instrument:

"Epi looked at me and said, 'What in the hell are you doing?' I spent a few Sundays at the Epiphone factory making that thing. They were all curious to see what I was up to. And when I got done making it, the only ones who liked it were the night watchman and me. No one was very impressed with it."

Nor was Gibson interested in the Log when Les brought it to the company's Kalamazoo, Michigan, headquarters at some point in the forties, hoping to partner with them on a commercially produced solid-body electric. Gibson was then enjoying huge success with its hollow-body archtop electrics and saw no reason to take a chance on a solid-body contraption. Les was reportedly dismissed by Gibson president Maurice H. Berlin as "that character with the broomstick with a pickup on it." Years later, Berlin would confide to him, "We laughed at you for ten years."

While accounts vary—as they often do in Les's case—Les claimed that he first brought the Log to Gibson in 1941, which would have been a singularly bad moment to embark on a risky new business venture. It was the year that the United States entered World War II. Wartime shortages of materials curtailed productivity for many manufacturing industries. Factories were commandeered and converted into manufacturers of war supplies. As a result, a number of guitar companies were forced to fold. Even a major player like Gibson would emerge from the war years seriously hobbled. The solid-body electric guitar would have to wait nearly another decade to take flight.

Fortunately, Les Paul had other fish to fry. While passionately interested in the idea of a solid-body electric guitar, his creativity had further avenues to explore. It was also in 1941 that he acquired another electric guitar—a hollow-body this time—that would become a key element in his recorded sound during this period. He was in Chicago doing some radio work when a man approached him with an Epiphone guitar and an amp.

"The guy told me that he'd got his hand caught in a bread

wrapping machine at work and he'd mangled it badly," Les recalled.

> He said, "I can't play guitar anymore, and I'd like you to have this guitar and amp." Well, that guitar and amp were to become history. I said to myself, "I can operate on this guitar. I can cut it all up. It's a guitar I don't care about. I'll make it different than any other guitar I got, and I'll do some of the things I always wanted to do but couldn't." This one had a hole in the back of it, so I could go in there and do a hysterectomy. It was called the Clunker.

This guitar would be the first of several "Clunkers," hollow-body electrics that became platforms for design experimentation. Les Paul was a key originator of the concept that an electric guitarist could—and should—make modifications to his instrument in pursuit of a sound uniquely his own. Seen from this perspective, electrical and mechanical engineering of both the guitar and amplifier are an integral part of the electric guitarist's art—a creative resource to be pursued just as avidly as playing technique or any other traditional musician's skill. Following in Les's wake, many of the greatest electric guitarists, from Pete Townshend to Eddie Van Halen, would become not only virtuosos but technical innovators of the instrument and its amplifier.

Like most of Les's guitars, the Log and the Clunker would undergo a process of constant rewiring, revamping, and revision as their owner experimented with new sonic ideas. And those ideas weren't flourishing in isolation. His thoughts on the electric guitar were starting to converge with those of others. The instrument's dramatic moment of cultural ascendancy was right around the corner.

•

THE LOG AND the Clunker served Les well in his new home: Hollywood. He and his trio relocated there in 1942, and the city proved to be just as good to the guitarist as New York had been. Before long, the Les Paul Trio was backing Bing Crosby. A well-groomed, personable singer, film actor, and all-around entertainer with a massive fan base, Crosby was one of the first true pop stars of the modern era, and Les's work with him brought only greater attention to the guitarist.

"Bing just loved the guitar," Les would later recall. "He would lay down on the floor and put his head right near [the guitar amp] speaker. And there was eight hundred people in the audience, and they'd watch Bing."

The Les Paul Trio's first recording with Crosby, "It's Been a Long, Long Time," became a hit for Decca Records in 1945. The record showcases Les's considerable talents as an accompanist, his lyrical electric guitar lines echoing and answering Crosby's wistful baritone voice in graceful counterpoint. It was the start of a long and successful relationship with both Crosby and Decca.

Les also recorded with the popular singer Helen Forrest and "America's Sweethearts," the Andrews Sisters. He toured with Crosby and the Andrews Sisters as well, and was also quite active in radio during this period. NBC placed him in charge of several shows, some featuring jazz and others country. Searching for a singer for one of his country spots, he was introduced to Colleen Summers. The two hit it off and would later marry and record together as Les Paul and Mary Ford. (The latter name is one that Les found in a phone book and subsequently copyrighted. Stage names mattered a lot to him.)

The Les Paul Trio would also cut many instrumental recordings of their own for Decca. These included jazzy arrangements of such standards as Cole Porter's "Begin the Beguine" and Irving Berlin's "Blue Skies," as well as a selection of Hawaiian and country music. A number of the Decca sides, such as 1947's "Guitar Boogie," "Steel Guitar Rag," "Caravan," and "Somebody Loves Me," feature another innovative electric guitar that Les designed—a headless aluminum model. Tonally, the guitar didn't sound much different from other electrics he played at the time— clean and crisp, a little lacking in low-end warmth, perhaps all the better to articulate Les's extremely nimble and inventive playing style on these tracks. The fact that this aluminum guitar sounded so similar to ones made of wood only served to underscore Les's central premise that the sound of an electric guitar comes principally from the electronics rather than the body. The metallic instrument worked well in the studio but not onstage, where hot theatrical lighting caused the aluminum to expand, thus throwing the guitar out of tune.

Always a staunch supporter of Les's experiments with music technology, Bing Crosby offered to set him up in his own recording studio and music school, Les Paul's House of Sound. But the guitarist declined, preferring to put together a studio in the detached garage of his home on Curson Avenue. Musicians today commonly have their own home recording studios; Les Paul was an early pioneer of the practice.

Curson Avenue is also where he began to make some of the earliest known experiments with multitrack recording, using not tape but a disc-cutting lathe he built with the flywheel from a Cadillac and outfitted with multiple cutting heads. Les says he was playing around with "disc multiples" (his term for what we call multitracking) as early as the thirties, but by 1946 all the pieces were in place for him to exploit these technological innovations in a major way. He discovered, for instance, how to create echo effects using the record and playback heads of his recording machine, thus pioneering the use of what is now called slapback echo. This is the "hiccupping" sound later to become a mainstay of rockabilly and other early rock and roll, created as the audio signal is reproduced by the playback and recording heads in rapid succession.

The catalyst that led Les to deploy all these developments in a single recording was a comment made by his mother—and frequent career advisor—Evelyn Polsfuss:

> She said, "Lester, I heard you playing on the radio this afternoon and you were great." I said, "Maw, I wasn't on the radio this afternoon." And she says, "Well, you better do something because everybody else is getting to sound like you!" So I went back to Hollywood, got in that studio and said, "I'm not gonna come out of here until I got a sound that's so different that my mother can tell me from anybody else on the radio."

The result was "Lover," a tour de force of glycerin guitar work performed on the Log and the Clunker. A tipsy waltz-time intro gives way to a frenetic up-tempo reading of the old Rodgers and Hart standard that might have been beamed in from another galaxy. The arrangement's giddy, high-pitched arpeggios and crazy chromatic runs sound as if Les's guitars had inhaled a massive breath of helium. The track still comes across as delightfully bizarre today. One can only imagine how strangely it must have struck listeners in the forties. "Lover" introduced the world at large to the wondrous array of sounds that could be generated by the creative manipulation of recording technology. In addition to echo, there was varispeeding—the helium effect produced by increasing the speed at which the tape passes over the playback head—and overdubbing, the process of piling one sound on top of another by means of multiple tape tracks.

This was the principle of musique concrète—the tape-manipulated art music developed by composers such as Pierre Schaeffer and Karlheinz Stockhausen—applied to pop music. "Lover" also gave birth to the concept of the electric guitarist as studio auteur, manipulating guitar effects and the multitrack resources of the studio itself to build a beguiling sonic landscape.

Les Paul was one of the first musical artists to intuit that the best use of a recording studio might not be simply to document a live performance but rather to serve as a workshop for building audio collages track by track. And because the electric guitar, by its very nature, produces an electrical signal rather than an acoustic sound, it made for an ideal and infinitely malleable input device for the studio's array of magical effects.

This insight would go on to provide tremendous inspiration for Jimi Hendrix, Brian May of the band Queen, and a host of other classic rock guitarists who employed the recording studio in this painterly way. One of these six-string titans, Jeff Beck, was just six years old when he heard Les Paul recordings such as "Lover" and its follow-up, "How High the Moon," for the first time on BBC Radio.

"I remember the sound was fantastic, especially the slap echo and the trebly guitar," Beck told *Guitar World* magazine in 2009.

> I had never heard an instrument like that before. Up to that point, all I listened to were marching bands from World War II and dance orchestras that played music to entertain housewives. All of a sudden this scatty guitar came over the airwaves. To a kid like me, who had been around music all of the time, it sounded so different. It still sounds fresh today compared to contemporary music, so imagine what it sounded like compared to a bunch of trombones. It just leapt out of the speakers.

"Lover" seemed sufficiently weird to Decca that they refused to put the track out, which led Les to sign a new deal with Capitol Records. Released in 1947, "Lover" was billed as introducing "Les Paul's New Sound." It did much to foster public perception of Les as the high-tech Svengali of the electric guitar—"The Wizard from Waukesha," as he became known. It also inaugurated a long string of Les Paul and Mary Ford hits for Capitol. Mary served as a highly accomplished rhythm guitarist as well as lead vocalist on many of these recordings. She and Les seemed the ideal duo, musically as well as romantically.

"She was a very fine musician," Les said of Mary. "A very fine singer. Had a great ear, too. Tremendously talented gal. I had all the luck in the world."

But this run of good fortune came perilously close to a premature and permanent end. Les was involved in a serious auto accident in 1948. His right arm was broken in such a way that the elbow joint was rendered incapable of motion. At one point, the doctors thought they would have to amputate the arm. Les later claimed that he started working on ideas for a guitar synthesizer at this time, searching for a way to be able to continue making music with just one arm.

"That wouldn't have fell together had they not said they were gonna amputate my arm. After the automobile accident, they said, 'Sorry.' I said, 'Don't feel sorry. I've already thought of an idea.' So I got a pencil and paper and with my left hand started to draw out a synthesizer."

Luckily, Les got to keep his right arm. With characteristic determination, Les had the doctors set his broken bones in such a manner that his partially immobilized arm would always be in position to pick a guitar. He later claimed that he'd abandoned the guitar synth idea because his hands were full with other commitments and inventions. Was the whole thing another one of his tall tales? It's hard to say.

Meanwhile, Les's old friends Leo Fender and Paul Bigsby were starting to come into their own. They too were making discoveries about pickup design and the other topics of discussion on those late-forties Hollywood nights, out on the patio at Les's Curson Avenue house. Fender and Bigsby were poised to take center stage as the forties gave way to the fifties. But Les wasn't about to let them hog the spotlight for too long. The world hadn't heard the last of Les Paul.

IT'S NEWS
THE ORIGINAL

Fender

ELECTRIC
STANDARD GUITAR

1. Fine fast action.
2. True intonation.
3. Wide range tone effects.
4. Steel re-enforced adjustable neck.
5. Strings adjustable for length and height from fret board.
6. Pickups adjustable for tone response.
7. No feedback.
8. Last fret position accessable.
9. Modern design.
10. Single and double pickup models available.

"Telecaster"
Dual Pick-Up Model

"Esquire"
Single Pick-Up Model

VISIT OUR EXHIBIT
IN
ROOM
795
AT THE
PALMER HOUSE, CHICAGO
All models come equipped with a beautiful top grain leather strap.

Distributed Exclusively By

RADIO & TELEVISION EQUIPMENT CO.
207 OAK STREET   SANTA ANA, CALIF.

*A trade ad for the Fender
Telecaster and Esquire*

chapter 4

THE MODEL T

In the years between 1957 and the early '60s, American teenagers and preteens tuned in excitedly to a weekly television sitcom called *The Adventures of Ozzie and Harriet*. Not that they were particularly interested in the tepid domestic mishaps and misunderstandings of bandleader Ozzie Nelson and his on-screen family (which was also his real-life family). What younger viewers really wanted to see were the musical segments at the conclusion of many of the episodes. These were devoted to performances by the Nelsons' teenage son, Ricky, and his rock-and-roll band. For kids in more conservative homes, this was a rare chance to experience the excitement of rock-and-roll music, which had become a national sensation with the outbreak of Elvis Presley mania in 1956.

No other sitcom in those early days of television featured rock and roll. Ricky Nelson was well on his way to becoming a significant recording artist, a position that the television show helped him to secure. Strikingly handsome in a more or less Presleyesque manner, he performed in an engaging but less frenetic style than Presley, eschewing stage moves such as the pelvic gyrations that had gotten Elvis into trouble with censors and self-appointed guardians of public morality.

Nelson nonetheless lit up the black-and-white TV screen (color television was still a relative rarity at the time), singing and playing rhythm guitar on a flashy instrument, a Martin brand acoustic housed in a hand-tooled leather casing emblazoned with his name. But perceptive viewers might also have noticed another pompadoured young guitarist off to Nelson's left, grinning from ear to ear while ripping snaky lead lines and blast-off solos from what was still a new and quite revolutionary electric guitar at the time—a Fender Telecaster. It was smaller than the guitar Nelson played, and certainly nowhere near as ornate. But it sure had a big sound.

The beaming youth was James Burton, a hero and role model among guitarists but a name perhaps not as well known to the general public as it should be. Burton was one of the very first players to embrace the Telecaster, and few guitarists, if any, have accomplished more with the instrument. Burton would come to be known as "the Master of the Telecaster." His style—an amalgam of steely country twang and gritty, bluesy string bends—encapsulates the essence of early rock and roll, and indeed of all American roots music, not to mention the unique tonal qualities of the Telecaster itself. The Tele he played on many *Ozzie and Harriet* episodes and countless landmark recordings was a model from 1952, which was only the second year that Telecasters had been produced.

Burton was just thirteen when his parents purchased the guitar for him. But just a year later, he and his Telecaster were already working professionally as part of the house band for the influential country music radio show *Louisiana Hayride*, the same program that had first brought Elvis Presley to fame. Burton had also written and performed the lead guitar lick on early rock-and-roll singer Dale Hawkins's seminal 1957 hit "Susie Q." Employing the guitarist's trademark style of "combination picking"—combining a flat pick and bare fingers—was an approach for which the Telecaster seemed ideally suited.

So Burton was already a seasoned pro by age sixteen when he left his parental home in Shreveport, Louisiana, to go to work on the *Ozzie and Harriet* show. But he was really still just a kid—a teenager playing a brash new style of teenage music. The guitarist was so young, in fact, that he lived with the Nelson family in their cozy West Hollywood home, which was also used for exterior shots in the show.

"Ozzie said, 'I know what it's like being away from home at such a young age. You're part of the family; so we'd like you to live with us,'" Burton recalled. "I was like the third son. It was Ricky, David, and James."

The sound of Burton's Telecaster is deeply ingrained in the fabric of American popular culture. He has backed legendary performers such as Elvis Presley, Johnny Cash, Glen Campbell, John Denver, Emmylou Harris, Roy Orbison, Elvis Costello, and many others on countless recordings and live dates. But he's also always had a special relationship with television and the movies. In 1957, the same year he started on the *Ozzie and Harriet* show, he'd performed in the early rock-and-roll film *Carnival Rock*. Following his tenure with Nelson, Burton would go on to be a member of the Shindogs, house band on America's premier mid-sixties rock-and-roll TV show, *Shindig!* And as a session player, Burton's guitar can be heard on hits by the Monkees, the world's first made-for-television rock act. (Second, perhaps, if you count Ricky Nelson.)

As we'll see, it was a random set of circumstances that led Clarence Leonidas Fender—better known simply as Leo Fender—to name the world's first commercially produced solid-body electric guitar after another great innovation of the day, television. But the name is an apt one. TV and the Tele were both the result of electronic advances that had been gestating for decades. They both came to fruition during America's mid-twentieth-century golden age, a time of big-finned Cadillacs, sporty T-Birds, sleek modernist furniture, tiki exoticism, and unprecedented middle- and working-class prosperity.

Urban apartment dwellers who'd barely managed to survive the lean years of the Great Depression and World War II were now moving out to the suburbs to start their own personal *Ozzie and Harriet* family lives. And they were hungry for entertainment. The small screen and Leo Fender's game-changing electric guitar would both play key roles in fostering a new era in American popular music—the age of rock and roll. But rock and roll was the furthest thing from Fender's mind when he began designing the guitar that would become the Telecaster.

I. COWBOY COOL: LEO FENDER AND THE BIRTH OF THE TELECASTER

A good head for business ran in Leo Fender's family. His parents, Clarence and Harriet, owned a thriving orange grove on what, in the early decades of the twentieth century, was a verdant stretch of land between the Southern California towns of Anaheim and Fullerton. Leo's uncle had done all right for himself, too, with his own automotive electronics business. Sometime around 1922, when Leo was thirteen, his uncle bestowed upon him a box of spare car radio parts, along with a battery. Experimenting with ways to connect the random bits of electric junk he'd inherited, the lad stumbled upon his destiny—one that would lead him to be acclaimed as the Henry Ford of the electric guitar.

It's not just that Leo Fender was good with electronics—although he definitely was, and at a time when electronics was a hot new profession, not unlike software engineering in our own era. But Fender was also gifted at finding ways to make the most of minimal resources. He possessed the kind of pragmatism that the Great Depression tended to foster. Give him a box of reject electronic components and he'd figure out how to make something useful of them.

This ability would serve Fender well when his first serious job, as an accountant for the California Highway Department, fell victim to the Great Depression. By this point he was a married man, having wed Esther Klosky in 1934. Losing the accounting gig was a bad break for a young man just starting out in life. Fortunately, Leo had already been moonlighting as an electronics wiz for hire, building P.A. systems for local musicians he'd befriended. Although he couldn't play a musical instrument himself, Fender had a great love for western swing and the music that would come to be known as country. He'd gotten to know some of the local players and was starting to see ways in which his skill with electronics might be of service to them.

Not that he plunged right into the music business. The Depression was still in full cry, and Fender needed to find an enterprise with a wider client base than just a small coterie of musicians barely eking out a living in the local honky-tonks. Managing to borrow $600, Leo launched his own radio shop, Fender Radio Service, in 1938, in Fullerton. It was a very practical move.

Radio was the great source of entertainment and escapism that helped people get through the Great Depression. At a time when the price of a movie ticket or phonograph record was beyond the means of many, the family radio was often the last household item to go to the repo man. And if the thing broke, many folks couldn't afford a new one. They needed a guy like Leo Fender to fix their old one up. And if they were so fortunate as to have the purchase price of a new radio, Fender's shop could sell them one of those as well.

As we've seen, radio circuitry was very much the parent of electric guitar amplifier circuitry. It was all the progeny of Lee De Forest and his seminal vacuum tube. Leo was as familiar with those circuit paths as he was with the streets of Fullerton. And during the years of World War II, he'd met a man who was just as intimate with the device at the other end of the patch cord—the electric guitar. Thus it was that Fender began to start building and selling lap steel guitars and amplifiers in partnership with one Clayton Orr "Doc" Kauffman.

Kauffman was a lap steel player who had worked for Rick-enbacker. While there, in 1935, he had invented the Vibrola, an important precursor of the "whammy bar" that would play a large role in much guitar rock. It became standard equipment on many early electric guitars, including some of Rickenbacker's pioneering electric Spanish models.

Fender and Kauffman launched the K&F Manufacturing Company in the mid-1940s, designing, fabricating, and selling lap steel guitars and amplifiers. It was strictly a sideline at first. They worked out of their houses, and later in back of Leo's radio shop in Fullerton. Doc was the guitar guy and Leo was more the electron-ics guy. From the start, there was an emphasis on selling guitars and amps in paired sets. Other early electric guitar manufacturers did this as well, but a special magic would quickly manifest itself in the way Leo's pickup designs worked in tandem with his amplifier circuitry. All those years spent mucking around with busted radios would pay a big dividend.

In light of what was to come from Fender, surviving exam-ples of Leo and Doc's earliest work are surprisingly crude. The nascent company nonetheless grew quickly, and soon the garage out behind Fender's radio shop, which had been the original K&F atelier, started to feel cramped. K&F's rate of growth was perhaps a little too rapid for Doc Kauffman, who bailed out of the business in 1946.

"Leo wanted to move the workshop and build a larger area, and Doc didn't want to invest any more money in it," recalled longtime Leo Fender associate George Fullerton in 1999. "I guess after Doc went through the Depression, with his family and things, he was afraid he might lose everything he had put into [the busi-ness], including his home."

Undaunted, Leo expanded and rebranded, launching the Fender Electric Instrument Company in 1946, taking possession of two small sheet-metal buildings on Santa Fe Avenue in Fuller-ton, not far from the radio shop. It was a major step for the small

Southern California businessman, as future Fender vice president Forrest White recounted in his memoir, *Fender: The Inside Story*: "Leo said that when he moved into those two buildings he had never seen so much space before in his life. They seemed absolutely huge to him. The facilities within the new buildings were not the best, however. Everyone had to walk across the street and then up a block or two to the Santa Fe Railroad Station to use the restrooms. That certainly was not very pleasant during the winter rainy season."

The Fender Electric Instrument Company's early years were far from easy. Without heat or air-conditioning, the factory buildings were freezing in the winter and sweltering in the summer. Toxic fumes from acetate varnish filled the air, something that would be highly illegal today. Leo was unhappy with his distributor, the Radio and Television Equipment Company (Radio-Tel), disparagingly calling the company's chief, F. C. Hall, a "former shipping clerk" who didn't understand the power of advertising. Leo had been buying electrical parts from Radio-Tel for years, but he felt they weren't doing enough to promote Fender products.

Taking on established electric guitar giants like Gibson and the equally significant Gretsch was a feisty move, and sometimes Leo must have wondered if he'd bitten off more than he could chew. F. C. Hall, for his part, wasn't entirely in love with the early Fender products his company had to distribute. He would later complain that guitars shipped to Radio-Tel for distribution had to be sent back to the Fender factory to correct faulty wiring and other manufacturing defects.

"Those years were absolute hell," Fender later told White. "I think I worked from six in the morning till midnight every day of the week. A new trademark is a hard thing to get accepted. With no advertising, no one knew who we were and there was nothing to pep up sales. It took every penny I could get my hands on to keep things together."

Fender managed not only to hang on but to move forward. Among the first new employees that he recruited, in 1948, was the aforementioned George Fullerton, a guitarist and electronics repairman whose ancestors had founded the town where Fender's business was located. Fullerton had known Fender since the early forties—he used to buy phonograph records at the Fender radio shop—but became a full-time Fender employee on February 28, 1948. The two men promptly started work on a prototype solid-body electric Spanish guitar, an archetypal design that would soon morph into the Fender Telecaster.

IN COMING UP with his electric Spanish model, Fender was aiming at the same core market he'd targeted with his lap steels—the proliferation of western swing bands that enjoyed immense popularity in the region stretching from Texas and Oklahoma out to the West Coast. A lively hybrid of old-timey country sounds and big band dance music, western swing was especially popular in Leo Fender's Southern California backyard. Severe droughts and economic hardships had driven a wave of migrant farm families from the Texas and Oklahoma Dust Bowl into California during the Depression years of the 1930s—an exodus movingly depicted in John Steinbeck's 1939 novel *The Grapes of Wrath* and the songs of folk minstrel Woody Guthrie.

The migrant "Okies" had brought their music with them. As a result, western swing could be heard all over the Southern California airwaves. And there was an abundance of dance halls, bars, and honky-tonks devoted to the music all across the L.A. Basin—venues such as the Los Angeles Country Barn Dance at the Venice Pier Ballroom, the Baldwin Park Ballroom, Riverside Rancho, the Painted Post, Cowtown, the Cowshed Club, and, perhaps the most legendary of them all, the Palomino in North Hollywood. The clubs, radio broadcasts, and recording sessions fostered a wide-ranging community of country and western swing musicians, all of whom needed instruments to play.

These were not only Leo Fender's customers, they were the men and women making the music that he personally loved most. He enjoyed going to the honky-tonks and dance halls to hang out with the players. The instruments and amps he created were voiced with them and their music in mind.

Among the kindred spirits Fender met on the circuit was guitar builder Paul Bigsby. The big man with the wild, brownish gray hair, commanding voice, and daredevil motorcycle racing past was also a technically accomplished industrial pattern maker and designer. And after a few too many perilous crack-ups on the racing circuit, he'd decided to turn his attention to producing parts for the Crocker Motorcycle Company.

But Bigsby—known as "P.A." to his friends and associates—was also a passionate devotee of western swing music. He'd played a bit of guitar and upright bass in local bands, but his real musical talent was for designing and building guitars. Exposure to the instruments available on the still nascent electric guitar market reportedly led him to exclaim, "This is junk! I can make something better myself."

And so he did, starting in the mid-1940s with lap steel guitars that he built for top players such as Joaquin Murphey and Speedy West. From there he moved on to pioneering designs for a more sophisticated kind of steel guitar, the "pedal steel." With his flair for mechanical engineering, Bigsby was ideally suited to devise an elaborate system of pedals, levers, and pulleys in order to change the pitch of strings mounted on two or three different steel guitar necks. Like many of his designs, these mechanisms would be much imitated later on, becoming industry standards.

Bigsby's background in motorcycle and industrial design is handsomely evident in his steel guitars. They are elegantly modernist masterpieces in contoured cast aluminum and blond wood.

Like a luxury sedan, some even came equipped with onboard ashtrays. The time-honored link between automotive and guitar design can be traced back to some of these remarkable instruments.

And while steels gave him his start, Bigsby soon turned his hand to solid-body electric Spanish designs as well. One of the earliest, dating from 1944, was a guitar he made for none other than Les Paul. But the Bigsby creation that marked a significant milestone in the solid-body electric guitar's evolution was the instrument that he created for legendary country picker Merle Travis. Like Les Paul, Travis had begun to think about the tonal advantages a solid guitar body could provide.

"I kept wondering why steel guitars would sustain the sound so long, when a hollow-body electric guitar like mine would fade out real quick," Travis wrote in his memoir "Recollections of Merle Travis: 1944–1955." "I came to the conclusion it was all because the steel guitar was solid."

Travis first met Bigsby in 1947 and soon thereafter commissioned him to build an instrument that would realize Merle's dream of an electric Spanish guitar with the singing sustain of a steel. Travis sketched out the shape of the body, historically regarded as the first to resemble the general silhouette of the solid-body electric guitar as we know it today. It was also his idea to mount all six of the guitar's tuning pegs on one side of the head of the guitar (rather than three on one side and three on the other, as many guitars, acoustic and electric, continue to feature). This was hardly a new idea. "Six-on-a-side" headstocks can be found on instruments made by Austrian luthier Johann Stauffer (1778–1853) and early guitars by his apprentice Christian Frederick Martin (1796–1873), not to mention traditional Croatian folk instruments of the tamburica family. But it was something new in the emergent realm of electric guitars.

The pickups on the Travis solid-body were Bigsby's own creation—a design that leading guitarists such as Les Paul and

Chet Atkins had already installed on their guitars. The instrument's cast-aluminum bridge was also Bigsby's handiwork. Completed on May 25, 1948, the Travis-Bigsby guitar is loaded with features that foretold the future of electric guitars. In addition to the singular body shape Travis had sketched out and six-on-a-side headstock, there was the way the strings anchored directly *in* the body rather than to an affixed tailpiece. This would become a defining feature of Fender electric guitars. And the way the neck and central portion of the body are fashioned from a single piece of maple on the Travis-Bigsby electric—what is known as "neck-thru" construction—is an idea that wouldn't really catch on until the seventies.

But like pretty much all of Bigsby's instruments, the Travis guitar was unmistakably a hand-built custom creation—the idiosyncratic work of an individual, and a fiercely individualistic, craftsman. The same big, blustery personality and obsessive perfectionism that made Bigsby a larger-than-life figure also rendered it somewhat difficult for him to work with other people. He had a hard time delegating. He even did his own bookkeeping. It would fall to others to bring some of Bigsby's innovative ideas to the mass market. Perhaps the most notable of these fellow guitar builders was Leo Fender.

How much does the guitar that would become Fender's legendary Telecaster owe to the solid-body electric guitar that Bigsby made for Merle Travis? Did Fender just rip Bigsby off? The two men certainly both moved in the same world of Southern California western swing and country bands. Like Bigsby, Fender was designing electric guitars, both steel and Spanish, for country players, beta-testing prototype models by placing them in the hands of countrified SoCal talent like Jimmy Bryant, Roy Watkins, Bill Carson, and others. These were essentially the same guys with whom Bigsby was rubbing shoulders.

Fender was friendly with Merle Travis as well. And Travis later claimed that he loaned his Bigsby solid-body electric to Leo for a week sometime in 1949, right when Fender and Fullerton were working on their prototype solid-body electric Spanish guitar. Fender, for his part, always maintained that he did not borrow the Travis-Bigsby guitar. This would become a sore point of contention between Fender and Travis for years. In fact, Bigsby would later attempt, unsuccessfully, to sue Fender for purloining his six-on-a-side headstock design. And as the man who made the initial sketches for the instrument Bigsby built, Travis felt he deserved more credit for the solid-body electric than either Bigsby or Fender. In later years, Travis would reportedly approach young Fender players, demanding, "How do you like the guitar I designed?"

At the time, nobody had the slightest idea that the electric guitar would go on to become the most important musical instrument of the twentieth century. Once it did, everyone who'd been involved wanted to claim primary credit. But great inventions are often the product of multiple minds—a zeitgeist rather than any individual's genius. The Fender and Travis-Bigsby instruments are both products of the same era, region, and musical milieu. Given this close proximity, it's fair to surmise that a certain amount of cross-pollination would have been inevitable.

THE FIRST FENDER and Fullerton solid-body electric guitar prototype, completed in 1949, is a somewhat primitively wrought instrument, obviously never intended for production. But it embodies most of the design principles that would make the Telecaster a radical instrument that would revolutionize the embryonic electric guitar market. The distinctive single-coil voicing of the Telecaster's bridge pickup would become a prime signifier of the Fender sound, even as other builders began to experiment with double coils. Fender's implementation of the single-coil pickup design is a key factor in the Telecaster's unmistakable steely tone, beloved of country players as well as rock guitarists looking for a lead tone to cut through even the densest of instrumental mixes. Long after the steel guitar itself had passed out of fashion, the crisp twang of the Telecaster bridge pickup would carry some high, lonesome steel guitar DNA into a new musical era.

On the '49 prototype, the basic lineaments of the Telecaster's simple slab body are also in place. It's like an abbreviated, one-dimensional silhouette of a traditional guitar shape. Even the "cutaway," a feature of the guitar body's shape allowing the player easy access to the highest frets, is in the time-honored tradition of classic guitar design. Like everything about the instrument that would become the Telecaster, its contours are executed in the most basic, minimalist way possible.

"We used to draw up different shapes and things," Fullerton recalled. "We kind of decided to make it resemble a guitar at least a little bit. We put a cutaway on it so you could get at all the frets. We had to make [the guitar body] small enough, since it was solid wood, so that it would be light enough that the player could hold it."

Perhaps the single most radical thing about the Telecaster is the way the neck is attached to the body by means of four common bolts. This essentially disrupts several centuries of guitar-making tradition, which stipulated that the only way to attach a guitar neck to the body was via an age-old woodworking technique known as a dovetail joint. Many established guitar makers sneered at the Telecaster at first for just this reason. It looked like something a working-class guy had put together in his basement woodshop. Which is basically what it was—and why it's so revolutionary. The Telecaster is a proudly populist, working-class instrument. In traditional acoustic guitar making, a dovetail joint allows the instrument's neck and body to vibrate uniformly, almost as a single piece of wood, which enhances tone. Seen in this light, the bolt-on neck is all wrong. But there's no such thing as wrong when you're inventing a new musical instrument—an instrument, moreover, that was destined to create hitherto undreamed-of forms of music.

Often compared with Henry Ford and his Model T automobile, Fender's Telecaster is a pragmatic instrument for the working musician—affordable and easily repaired. With just a little skill, a guitarist could easily replace a flawed or damaged neck by him- or herself. In a sense, Fender's modular approach to guitar building in the middle years of the twentieth century set the stage for the guitar hot-rodding craze that would take shape in the seventies, which saw guitarists readily swapping out guitar pickups, necks, bridges, and other components in quest of the perfect tone and high-performance playability.

One feature of the Telecaster was missing from the original 1949 prototype. It had its tuning pegs on either side of the head, three-and-three rather than six-on-a-side. The second proto-type that Fender and Fullerton built, also in 1949, would include this iconic feature. It was a subtle change, but a meaningful one. The Fender six-on-a-side headstock would become one of the com-pany's most widely recognized design features, often imitated and closely associated with the rock-and-roll era.

AMONG THEIR OTHER virtues, the design simplicity of Fender's 1949 prototypes made the instruments ideally suited for mass pro-duction. Long before he built his first guitar, Leo Fender had been an accountant. He knew how to make the numbers work, just as he knew how to make a guitar work. The basic slab body and bolt-on neck designs that Fender and Fullerton had come up with meant that the guitars could be fabricated quickly and relatively inexpen-sively with just basic machinery and materials. Yet the end result was still a good-quality instrument.

And so, by 1950, Fender had its first electric Spanish pro-duction model, the single-pickup Fender Esquire, on the market, introduced at a list price of $139.95. This was followed by a small number of two-pickup Esquires. The second pickup, mounted in the guitar's body very near where it joins with the neck, was able to produce a warmer tone than the pickup nearer to the bridge, a tone not unlike that of an acoustic guitar and thus eminently suitable for rhythm playing. But because so few two-pickup Esquires were ever made, they're extremely rare and collectible today. By the fall of 1950, the two-pickup iteration of Fender's design had been renamed the Broadcaster, carrying a list price of $169.95.

And that might have remained the guitar's name for all time, had history not intervened. In 1951, a somewhat disturbing telegram from the Gretsch company reached Don Randall, general manager of Fender's distributor, Radio-Tel. In its entirety, the Western Union message read:

YOUR USE OF TRADEMARK BROADKASTER ON
YOUR ELECTRIC GUITAR IS INFRINGEMENT OF OUR
TRADEMARK BROADKASTER U.S. PATENT OFFICE
REGISTRATION 347505 OF 29 JUNE 1937. WE REQUEST
IMMEDIATE ASSURANCE THAT YOU ARE ABANDONING
THE USE OF THIS NAME.

THE FRED GRETSCH MFG CO.

Gretsch had been marketing a drum set bearing the similar name "Broadkaster." The company had been around since 1883 and had become a significant force in both the drum and guitar markets. Fender was still a relatively new company—a much smaller fish just barely managing to survive in the big pond of musical instrument sales.

The cease-and-desist order from Gretsch was one more setback in what had been a difficult product launch. There had been earlier problems with necks warping on the first Esquires, requiring Fender to revamp, retool, and add a truss rod—a reinforcing metal brace long used in guitar building—to all subsequent Esquire and Broadcaster necks. And now there was the Gretsch problem to be resolved.

Reluctantly, Randall and the Fender leadership conceded that

Gretsch were "fair in their request." Randall wrote to Fender's nationwide sales force, advising them to stop using the name Broadcaster and to inform their customers that the name would be changed.

"It is a shame that our efforts in both selling and advertising are lost," Randall wrote. "But I am sure we can change over with little if any detrimental effects. If any of you have a good name in mind I would welcome hearing from you immediately."

Until that new name was finalized, Fender had to do something to protect themselves from a potential lawsuit, while still managing to sell some of their new guitars. Les Fender was a pragmatic man who had witnessed shortages of building materials during World War II—not to mention the Korean War, which was then under way—and his initial response to Gretsch's demand was simply to snip the name BROADCASTER from the headstock decals. And so a very few guitars came out with no model name at all. (These are known as "No-casters," and routinely fetch five-figure prices on the auction market today. A '51 No-caster that had formerly belonged to Les Paul sold for $225,000 at a Julien's Auctions sale in 2012.)

Before 1951 was finished, however, Randall had come up with a new name for the guitar, one that Leo Fender approved. "Telecaster" proved to be a much more apt name. Born of a simple marketing dispute between rival brands, the change was nonetheless reflective of a momentous cultural shift taking place contemporaneously.

WHILE THE ROOTS of television go all the way back to experiments in the late nineteenth century, the technology gained substantial momentum in the twenties and thirties. But TV only really got under way in America with the advent of national network broadcasting in 1948. It would prove to be a major force in the cultural

life of America and much of the rest of the world in the latter
half of the twentieth century. By 1951, some six million TV sets
were already in people's homes, and an additional five million new
units would be produced by the end of the year. The Packard-Bell
company had even marketed a television set with the name "Tele
Caster," but, for reasons unknown, the company never challenged
Fender's right to use the name. And so, at Randall's suggestion,
Fender affixed the buzzworthy "Tele" on a musical instrument
whose impact on popular culture would prove to be nearly as profound as that of the small screen.

Both television and the Telecaster, moreover, were part of a
larger cultural trend taking shape in the prosperous economy of
post–World War II America. As working- and middle-class people
were acquiring more disposable income and upward social mobility, an inspired new breed of industrial designers and architects
was getting creative with mass-production techniques and inexpensive materials to come up with affordable yet stylish consumer
goods that would make life more comfortable and gracious for this
growing new body of consumers.

Rather than aping Old World craftsmanship, the mid-century
modernists sought to find a kind of practical beauty in industrial building materials. The bolts that held chairs together, for
instance, were left visible, proudly proclaiming the structural principles that held the chair together, rather than hidden beneath a
wooden veneer in an effort to make the object look like it had been
fashioned in 1850 rather than in 1950.

Which is to say, the Telecaster fits neatly within the context of
the mid-century-modernist movement in design and architecture.
The simple lineaments of the Telecaster find a close parallel in
the iconic molded-plywood chairs designed by Charles and Ray
Eames in 1946, and the spare, angular functionality of Southern
Californian Case Study Houses designed by architects like the
Eameses, Richard Neutra, and Eero Saarinen in the years between

1945 and 1966. The blond wood finish of many early Teles is also quintessentially mid-century modernist, particularly echoing the finishes found on furniture by the Heywood-Wakefield Company.

Charles Eames, one of mid-century modernism's chief theorists, summed up the movement's goals. Although he was speaking about furniture, it's easy to see how his words are equally applicable to the new kind of electric guitar that Fender was building: "The idea was to do a piece of furniture that would be simple yet comfortable. It would be a chair on which mass production would not have anything but a positive influence. It would have in its appearance the essence of the method that produced it. It would have an inherent rightness about it, and it would be produced by people working in a dignified way."

Which is precisely what Leo Fender was striving for in his own way. His goals were identical to Eames's stated ambition "to make the best for the most for the least," that is, the best possible guitar, accessible to a great many players at the lowest possible price. And, as much of the energy and activity of mid-century modernism was centered in Southern California, its stylistic principles were very much in the air as Leo Fender was working on his early electric guitar designs. In these contexts the Fender aesthetic can be regarded as essentially SoCal modernist in spirit—casual, informal, populist; effortlessly and elegantly discarding the fussy, hidebound traditions and restrictions of the prewar world order, not to mention the greater formality of America's Midwest and East Coast.

The Telecaster and Esquire more than exceeded Leo Fender's initial design goals, quickly becoming the quintessential country music electric guitars. The deep talkin', percussive chug of early Johnny Cash hits like "Folsom Prison Blues" and "I Walk the Line" is the sound of Cash's lead guitarist Luther Perkins and his Esquire. The plaintive Bakersfield sound of Buck Owens and his co-guitarist Don Rich is also pure Telecaster tone. And such country music icons as Merle Haggard, Willie Nelson, and Waylon Jennings have all been conspicuous Tele players, a tradition continued by contemporary country pickers such as Marty Stuart and Brad Paisley.

But the Telecaster is an amazingly versatile guitar. Its tonalities seem to lend themselves readily to numerous musical genres. This, combined with the instrument's affordable pricing, made it fairly ubiquitous in the popular guitar music of the 1950s and beyond. Bluesmen like Clarence "Gatemouth" Brown, Albert Collins, and Muddy Waters all adopted the Telecaster or the Esquire. As did early rock and rollers such as Nathaniel Douglas in Little Richard's band and Paul Burlison of the Johnny Burnette Rock 'n' Roll Trio, whose lead work on Burnette tracks like "The Train Kept a Rollin'" inspired a youthful Jeff Beck to pick up an Esquire and play it during his mid-sixties tenure with the Yardbirds. And in R&B, Memphis guitarist Steve Cropper's Telecaster stylings were an essential ingredient in hits by Otis Redding, Wilson Pickett, Sam & Dave, and other legendary artists on the Stax Records label.

In the seventies and beyond, the instrument even spawned a special breed of Telecaster virtuoso, guitarists such as Roy Buchanan, Danny Gatton, and the Hellecasters. And among the most iconic rock stars, the Telecaster has been closely associated with Keith Richards, Bruce Springsteen, and Joe Strummer. True to Leo Fender's original intention, the guitar has become a signifier for a kind of working man's credibility and plainspoken honesty.

If bringing the Telecaster to market had been Leo Fender's sole achievement, his place of honor in electric guitar history would still be assured. But, as it turns out, the Telecaster was just the start of a dynasty of solid-body, single-coil-pickup, bolt-on-neck Fender electric guitars. In 1951 Fender introduced the seminal electric bass guitar, the Precision Bass. Prior to its introduction, the bass instrument of choice in almost all genres had been the large, bulky double bass or bass fiddle—also sometimes known as the "doghouse" bass, for being nearly as large as its titular canine dwelling. The advent of the Precision Bass revolutionized the lives of working bands, making it much easier and economical to travel to and from gigs, and changing the sound of the music they played.

The magic, of course, was electricity. In the purely acoustic realm, you need a large-bodied instrument to produce the large sound waves that create low frequencies. This is why a double bass, for instance, is so large. Or a tuba, for that matter. These are not the kinds of musical instruments you'd want to carry around or try to fit into the trunk of a car. But electronic amplification made it possible to produce very low frequencies without a large resonating body cavity or brass bell.

Electric amplification also afforded better control of volume than the double bass could offer. The Precision Bass—or P-Bass, as it came to be known—could get much louder than the old doghouse and didn't need to be miked. It's also considerably easier to play. The double bass, like most members of the violin family, has a fretless fingerboard. It takes a fair amount of technique to sound notes accurately on this type of playing surface. Just a slight variation in finger position can result in a pitch too sharp or flat. In contrast, the Precision Bass's fretted fingerboard made it much easier for players to sound notes with precision. (Hence the instrument's name.) A metal fret, rather than the player's finger, is what produces the pitch of each note played. And the frets are all located in exactly the right places.

Perhaps even more important, the P-Bass made possible a whole new range of playing techniques and tonalities. A doghouse bass is essentially a fiddle; you can bow it or pluck it pizzicato-style. The P-Bass is a guitar. It can be played with a pick like a guitar for a bright, crisp attack that can be further accentuated by muting the strings with the palm of the picking hand—something that isn't possible on a double bass. Or, for a more traditional tone, it can still be plucked with the fingers like a double bass. In a sense, it offers the best of both worlds.

It would be hard to overemphasize the importance of the Fender Precision Bass in the evolution of popular music in the twentieth century. Even after bass guitars by other manufacturers entered the market, for a long time any electric bass guitar was generically known as a "Fender bass." The instrument's 1951 introduction provides a subtle but distinct line of demarcation between the popular music of the first half of the twentieth century and that of the second half.

With a growing line of electric instruments and amplifiers, the Fender company had evolved beyond the early days of employees sweltering or freezing in the company's twin steel shacks on Santa Fe Avenue. By gradual degrees, Fender had moved into larger, more comfortable and modern facilities, settling by 1953 into four buildings at 500 South Raymond Avenue in Fullerton. The staff had grown from fifteen employees in 1947 to about fifty by 1955. And none of them had to exit the building and walk several blocks to use the restroom.

II. SURF'S UP: THE STRATOCASTER MAKES THE SCENE

The year 1953 brought the guitarist and designer Freddie Tavares to the Fender staff. An accomplished steel player, Tavares had performed one of the most frequently heard electric guitar recordings in the world—the steel guitar glissando heard at the beginning of the Looney Tunes cartoon shorts that Warner Bros. began producing in the thirties. The Hawaiian-born guitarist was playing a regular gig with Wade Ray and His Ozark Mountain Boys at the Los Angeles–area club Cowtown when he was introduced to Leo Fender by the steel player Noel Boggs from Bob Wills and His Texas Playboys. Leo was impressed with an amplification setup Tavares had devised for the group's violinist. After chatting for a while about amp design, Fender decided to hire Tavares.

Once onboard, the newcomer immediately went to work with

Leo on a new guitar design that would prove as revolutionary as the Telecaster, if not even more so—the Fender Stratocaster. By '53 Fender knew that he had to up his game if he wanted to stay in it. The guitar establishment had laughed at the Telecaster when it first came out. But once everyone saw how well the instrument was selling, companies started rushing to market with their own solid-body electrics—perhaps most notably the Gibson Les Paul, which debuted in 1952. Some of these new models were appreciably sexier than the homespun Tele. For players in search of a solid-body electric, Fender was no longer the only—or even the most attractive—option.

So Fender and Tavares got to work on a new design that would take the quintessential Fender solid-body guitar style to a new plateau. A key collaborator in the process was SoCal guitarist Bill Carson, who at the time was playing with country honky-tonk legend Hank Thompson, then riding high on the momentum of his 1952 hit "The Wild Side of Life." Early in the process, Carson succinctly summed up the chief design goal for the new instrument.

"The guitar should fit like a good shirt," he declared.

Which the Fender Stratocaster does. This is perhaps why the Strat has been a great fit for a broad range of legendary guitarists, including Buddy Holly, Ritchie Valens, Buddy Guy, Jimi Hendrix, Eric Clapton, Jeff Beck, and Stevie Ray Vaughan, among many others. A great deal of thought went into the Stratocaster body contours. Balance was a key consideration. With the solid-body electric's reinvention of traditional guitar dimensions, it was vital to find a new shape that would hang evenly on a strap or cradle snugly into the lap of a seated player. Fender came up with a design that would be frequently imitated in years to come.

Where the Telecaster was a single-cutaway guitar, the Strat boasted a radically curvy double-cutaway design, affording unprecedented ease of access to the highest notes on the fingerboard. The Strat body is stylishly—one might say sexily—asymmetrical in shape. The upper-body "horn," which supports one end of the guitar strap, is appreciably larger than the lower one. The other innovative feature of the upper-body "bout," as it's known, is that it is contoured in back to fit comfortably against the player's rib cage. This is thought to have been the suggestion of another guitarist who consulted on the project, Rex Gallion, who complained that the right-angle edge of the Telecaster body had been digging into his ribs.

When initially envisioning the guitar, Bill Carson called for it to have four pickups. But in the end, the designers settled on three—one more than the Telecaster.

"Two is good," Leo Fender is reported to have said. "But three will kill them!"

The Stratocaster's bridge pickup possessed a bright, steely tone similar to that of the Tele. And the neck pickup was similarly warm in timbre. But the addition of a third pickup, midway between the bridge and neck pickups, opened up a broad range of new tonal possibilities. Any of the three pickups could be used on its own. But players quickly discovered that by placing the instrument's three-way pickup switch in between the three standard positions, it was possible to activate two pickups at once—either the bridge and the middle or the neck and the middle. Either of these combinations produces a sweet, lyrical sound heard in much of Mark Knopfler's guitar work, for instance, or in the more gentle, ballad side of Jimi Hendrix's recordings. Eventually Fender would replace the original three-position switch with a five-position selector, making these coveted tonalities more easily obtainable.

Everything about the Stratocaster's hardware configuration is fine-tuned and superbly well-thought-out. Six individual "saddles" serve as the guitar's bridge, with each adjustable for string height and string length, allowing the guitarist to tweak the instrument's playability and intonation to the smallest degree. (Intonation refers to the guitar's ability to play perfectly in tune all up and down the neck.) Fender also devised a spring-operated vibrato bridge system that was significantly more advanced than the Kauffman Vibrola or any other similar system available at the time. About the only thing on the Stratocaster that looks back to an earlier design—the Travis-Bigsby guitar—is the headstock, which is more bulky and shapely than the Telecaster's. In time, it would come to be thought of as a key signifier of the Fender design aesthetic.

If the Telecaster exemplifies the pragmatic, minimalist side of mid-century modernism, the Stratocaster is a sterling example of the curvy, parabolic elegance that could be wrought from industrial mass-production techniques. Even the Strat's bullet-shaped, angled, chrome patch-chord receptacle is a fashion statement, boldly and conspicuously mounted on the guitar's top rather than hidden on the lower side like that of most guitars.

The guitar's name derives from "stratosphere." The space race between the United States and the Soviet Union would officially begin in 1955, both nations vying to be the first to launch a satellite into orbit around the earth. So, just as Fender had moved forward in time and technological sophistication—from radio to television—in rebranding the Broadcaster as the Telecaster, they'd ventured into the brave new world of outer space in christening the Stratocaster.

The Fender Stratocaster is an addictively comfortable instrument to play. The volume and tone controls, the pickup selector switch, and the slender vibrato arm are all located within easy reach of the player's picking hand. Of all the iconic rock guitar virtuosos, Jeff Beck has perhaps made the most creative use of this aspect of the Strat, building a whole style around expressive volume swells and dramatic vibrato arm histrionics.

Which is to say that, like the Telecaster, the Strat quickly transcended Leo Fender's initial cowboy-centric vision for the instrument, finding a welcome across a broad range of musical styles. In this context, it's fortuitous that the Stratocaster's contoured body also bears an uncanny resemblance to the sleek curves of a surfboard. One of the instrument's early champions was the guitarist born Richard Anthony Monsour, who took the stage name

Dick Dale, and would ultimately be crowned "King of the Surf Guitar."

Just as the country-and-western musical aesthetic was central to Fender's earliest years, surf music became an essential part of the Fender vibe in the late fifties and early sixties. Surf music is the great bridge between the early days of rock and roll and mad-mod guitar sounds of the British Invasion. It became the soundtrack for an early-sixties Southern California youth culture based around hot-rod cars, sunny beaches, and the aquatic sport of riding the massive waves on well-waxed, precision-engineered planks of wood. Originally a free-spirited outsider cult, the surf scene became a national obsession through "youthsploitation" feature films such as *Ride the Wild Surf, Girls on the Beach, Beach Party, Bikini Beach,* and *Beach Blanket Bingo,* many starring the perky brunette and former *Mickey Mouse Club* television star Annette Funicello along with teen heartthrob Frankie Avalon. While the visuals focused on cars, surfboards, and teens in beachwear, the soundtrack music heavily featured the twangy cadences of electric guitars.

A key surf music architect, Dick Dale was an actual surfer and a true iconoclast—a left-handed guitarist who nonetheless played guitars strung in the conventional right-hand manner, forging a style based around rapid staccato runs on the guitar's lower strings and a reverby tonality that became one of the chief sonic signifiers of the surf scene. Based in El Segundo, California, as a teenager, Dale took to the water early. And his hometown was just a stone's throw from Fullerton, where he first made Leo Fender's acquaintance at some point in the late fifties or early sixties.

"I went to him and said, 'My name is Dick Dale. I'm a surfer. I've got no money and I really need a guitar. Can you help me?'" Dale recalled. "Me and my dad looked him up. I was getting ready to go play the Rendezvous Ballroom [in nearby Balboa, California]. Leo said, 'Take this guitar and tell me what you think about it.'"

Despite a difference in age and background, Dale and Fender

turned out to be kindred spirits. Both loved country music and shared an obsession with boats, each maintaining his own craft in the nearby harbors of the Pacific shore. Dale related an anecdote illuminating the nature of their friendship and working relationship:

> I'm interested in how everything is built, and so was Leo. When I brought my Rolls-Royce around, Leo would sit in the backseat of the car and just keep opening the picnic tray, looking at the hinge. He'd call and say, "Freddie, Freddie [Tavares], come here and look at this! Look how this hinge activates itself!" He was like that. Leo took a liking to me because I was blowing up everything he was making. He was going, "How are you doing that!"

Dale became a key consultant, working with both Fender and Tavares on new product designs, particularly in the area of guitar amplification. Among other things, Dale encouraged Fender to begin incorporating spring reverb units into the company's amplifiers. The splashy "spring reverb" sound would become one of the sonic common denominators in electric guitar music, integral to country, surf music, rockabilly, psychedelic rock, and many other genres.

In search of a louder sound to accommodate his growing audiences at the Rendezvous, Dale also goaded Fender to produce larger and more powerful amplifiers, particularly the 100-watt Fender Showman. Its fifteen-inch JBL loudspeaker was built to withstand the rigors of Dale's extreme playing techniques.

"When I plugged that speaker into the Showman amp," Dale later recalled, "the world of pansy-ass electronics came to an end. It was like Einstein splitting the atom."

Early Dick Dale singles such as 1961's "Let's Go Trippin'" and '62's "Miserlou" touched off an explosion of surf guitar instrumental hits in the early years of the 1960s. These included the

Chantays' "Pipeline," the Surfaris' "Wipe Out," the Ventures' "Walk Don't Run," "Penetration" by the Pyramids, "Out of Limits" by the Marketts, and "Torture" by the Fendermen. As the latter band name clearly suggests, the sound was generally very Fender-centric—bright, trebly single-coil pickup tones and tons of reverb. Many of these groups became Fender endorsers, their photos featured in Fender product catalogs of the era.

The surf guitar hits of the early sixties were part of an even greater wave of popular guitar instrumental music that had begun a few years earlier with hit songs such as "Tequila" by the Champs and "Rumble" by Link Wray and His Raymen. The latter is often credited as one of the first records to employ guitar power chords and distortion. Legend has it that Wray poked holes in his amp's loudspeaker to achieve a more raunchy sound. The tonality would go on to have a huge influence on British Invasion groups such as the Kinks and the Who. But even before then, the guitar instrumental craze had reached British shores, as can be heard on hits by English groups such as the Shadows' 1960 track "Apache," and the Tornados' 1962 smash "Telstar," which got all the way to #1 on the U.S. charts. These U.K. recordings would also prove to be a major inspiration for the British Invaders soon to arrive on U.S. shores in the Beatles' wake.

But surf music proper wasn't confined to just instrumental music. The genre developed a vocal harmony branch as well, with groups such as the Beach Boys, Jan & Dean, the Hondells, and the Rip Chords. Along with the allure of the wild surf and the inevitable romances on sunny beaches, the songs celebrated Southern California hot-rod culture. The lyrics were packed with references to Cobras, Stingrays, XKEs, 409s, and other objects of automotive desire that were just coming onto the market at that time.

But it was the surf guitar instrumentals that launched thousands of garage bands across the United States and indeed worldwide in the early to mid-1960s. These hit records provided a ready-made repertoire.

Fender gear was in high demand by these fledgling ensembles, and the company had a growing line of guitars and amps to offer. The Fender Jazzmaster, introduced in 1958, boasted an elaborate array of pickup selection switches and a slightly warmer tone than previous Fenders. Leo had entertained hopes that it would appeal to archtop jazz players; instead it became another iconic surf music guitar, as did the flashy, chrome-surfaced Jaguar, which debuted in 1962. To counterbalance these upscale Fender models, there was a growing range of more affordable "student model" guitars and basses, including the Musicmaster and Duo-Sonic lines, both introduced in 1956, and the Mustangs, which first appeared in '64.

Fender was at the vanguard of marketing guitar gear to the younger musicians who were playing surf music and other forms of rock and roll. By the early sixties, Fender guitars were available in fourteen different custom colors, many of which were stock DuPont Duco automotive hues such as Fiesta Red and Burgundy Mist. This marked a significant departure from the sunbursts and blond finishes of traditional guitar making. As such, it reflects a key shift in how electric guitars were perceived and marketed. They became more fun and sexy—like fast sports cars—rather than staid musical instruments in rich wood tones worthy of enshrinement alongside violins, clarinets, pianos, and other instruments kids were forced to study in school.

In the early sixties, graphic designer Robert Perine devised a series of ads for Fender, photographing the company's instruments in beach scenes alongside surfboards and young girls in bikinis, in automotive settings (a Fender Jaguar guitar alongside a Jaguar XKE auto), or in wild scenarios that had people jumping out of airplanes or climbing onto city buses with Fender guitars slung around their necks. YOU WON'T PART WITH YOURS EITHER the accompanying headline read.

"The teenage market was of vital importance because kids

in every major city were being encouraged by dealers to take guitar lessons," Perine later recalled. "So I slanted many of the ads towards them, going to teenage fairs in southern California, finding teen models, putting them in situations where the guitars looked user-friendly."

BY 1964, FENDER'S workforce had grown to about six hundred employees operating out of some twenty-seven buildings in Fullerton. But those who collaborated most closely with Leo had begun to notice a change in him. Never an excessively voluble man in the first place, he'd grown even more quiet and withdrawn around 1964. He was troubled by a persistent, infectious sinus condition and, while just in his mid-fifties, was feeling the weight of his years perhaps more heavily than other men his age. He'd started out as a guy with a little radio shop. But now his business had grown exponentially and he shouldered a lot of responsibility.

One evening in December of '64, Fender VP Forrest White found Leo at his workbench long after most employees had gone home. He was huddled close to a space heater and clutching the collar of his jacket close to his neck against the unseasonably cold California winter that year. White recounted the scene in his memoir. "[Leo] said, 'Sit down, I have something to tell you. You know I haven't been able to shake this sinus condition, and I think it's time for me to get out. Don [Randall] and I have been talking to CBS Records about them buying the company.'"

The deal went through in January of '65. CBS acquired Fender for an unprecedented $13 million, the highest price ever paid for a musical instrument company at the time, and $2 million more than CBS had recently shelled out to acquire the New York Yankees baseball team.

"Monday evening, January 4, 1965, I went down to see Leo in his lab for the last time," White wrote.

We both found it difficult to act nonchalant. I helped him carry his personal belongings out to his car, pretended not to notice the tears in his eyes, and hoped he hadn't noticed mine. He got into the car and I walked to the side gate. He stopped briefly on his way out, paused and said, "I don't know what I would have done without you." I wish I could tell you what those words meant to me. He stepped on the gas and was out of the gate before I could answer. That was the last time I would let him out of the gate as I had done so many times before. I watched until his car was out of sight.

It was the end of an era. By the closing years of the sixties, guitarists were already speaking with awe of Fender's pre-CBS period. "Pre-CBS" became the watchword as musicians began searching for Fender guitars and amps from the golden years, before '65. Leo hung on as a consultant to CBS for a few years, but things weren't the same. Like all large corporations, CBS sought to maximize profits by cutting costs, and the quality of Fender gear suffered noticeably. New products didn't resonate quite as deeply with the market as the classic Fender designs had. How could they? They'd been dreamed up by a corporate committee rather than by an obsessive country music fan and gear geek going out to clubs night after night, talking to musicians, placing test instruments in their hands, and gleaning a profound understanding of their desires and dreams.

By the 1970s, Leo had recovered his health and gotten back in the game, launching the Music Man company with Forrest White and another partner, Tom Walker, at mid-decade, and G&L (for George and Leo) with George Fullerton in '79. Both companies produced well-designed and well-regarded guitars and amps. But they didn't change the world the way the iconic Fender guitars and amps had. The time for such mythic transformations had passed from the hands of guitar makers into those of visionary musicians.

Country legend and Gretsch guitar spokesman Chet Atkins

THE BLUES (AND COUNTRY) HAD A BABY

In the summer of 1943, the Number Nine Illinois Central train made its usual sixteen-hour climb from Memphis to Chicago. It was an uneventful trek for the railroad, but for one of its passengers—a handsome thirty-year-old black farmhand named McKinley Morganfield—it would always be remembered as the most monumental day of his life. Not that anyone could tell he was excited or nervous. His heavy-lidded eyes radiated an almost preternatural sense of cool as he watched the landscape slowly evolve outside the train window from emerald green pastures to gray industrial sprawl.

It was hard for him to believe that after thirty years of living and toiling in the cotton fields of Clarksdale, Mississippi, he was leaving his wood cabin for Chicago, a land so exotic he might as well be on a spaceship flying to Saturn. Wearing his only suit, and carrying a battered suitcase in one hand and a ten-dollar Stella acoustic guitar in the other, Morganfield knew he looked "country," but he was confident his ability to sing and play the blues would guarantee his survival in the city.

He was at least as good as his friend Robert Nighthawk, who'd left Clarksdale a couple of years earlier and was already making records for labels such as Victor and Bluebird. Truth was, he was *a lot* better. Since his early teens, Morganfield, known to his friends as Muddy Waters, had been honing his talent performing around the Stovall Plantation, where he spent long days plowing the fields followed by late nights entertaining tough customers in local juke joints. He was greatly influenced by other Delta bluesmen, such as Son House, Robert Johnson, and Charley Patton, but Waters had developed his own distinct sound, built around a deep, sensual voice punctuated by his stinging bottleneck slide guitar.

"I'd be hittin' my guitar, blowing a kazoo, and it was *gone*," Waters remembered. "People be dancin' like wild." He was a local legend, but at the age of thirty, he wasn't getting any younger and it was time to get a move on and make his mark in the city.

Besides, he never did like farming and all it entailed—picking and chopping cotton, taming the rough terrain in the hot sun. "I didn't like work, *period*," he told journalist Robert Palmer in 1978. "I loved the country—beautiful country, the Delta! But I would rather be in town playin' my guitar."

Muddy wasn't the only one determined to break the last chains of post-slavery plantation life. By the time he arrived in Chicago, tens of thousands of black Americans had already migrated there from the South. It might have been colder, dirtier, and more dangerous, but the factories and stockyard killing floors paid roughly four times more than work at the plantation—$2,000 a year on average, as opposed to $450.

Still, when Waters stepped off the train in Chicago, he was stunned. "It was the fastest place I'd ever seen in my life," he said. "Cabs dropping fares, horns blowing, the peoples walking so fast . . . and the big buildings."

He was as green as a Mississippi water snake, but over the next decade Mud would rise from the streets to become the undisputed king of Chicago blues, recording enduring classics for Chess Records like "Rollin' Stone," "I Got My Mojo Working," and "Mannish Boy." During that time he would also form the first significant electric band—that is, a group that used amplification for something more than sheer volume. Muddy and his self-proclaimed "Headhunters" would use electricity and distortion to create a sound that was as big, powerful, and modern as the locomotive he rode to town on. The band, featuring a singer, two electric guitars, an amplified harmonica, bass, and drums, would influence a vast array of blues and rock musicians who collectively shaped music in the twentieth century, including Chuck Berry, Elvis Presley, B.B. King, the Rolling Stones, and Led Zeppelin. If rock and roll were a virus, Muddy and his guitar were its patient zero.

WHEN WATERS HIT Chicago, it was primarily a jazz town. The sophisticated jump music of performers like Louis Jordan, Big Joe Turner, and guitarist (and Charlie Christian bandmate) T-Bone Walker were all the rage, while well-established blues performers such as Big Bill Broonzy and Memphis Slim were relegated to smaller clubs. Undeterred by the lack of musical opportunities, Muddy was ready to make his own luck. He hustled jobs, playing raucous house parties for $5 a night and all the whiskey he could drink, while working a succession of day jobs, doing everything from factory work to delivering venetian blinds.

Time and time again, Waters was told by local musicians that his raw form of country blues and bottleneck slide would never fly in the city, but he had enough evidence to the contrary. His performances at wild tenement get-togethers were incredibly popular with transplanted blacks, who enthusiastically consumed Muddy's emotive Delta-style blues like it was the sweetest home cooking, and he was confident in its power and broader commercial potential.

The only problem was, as mighty as his voice and guitar playing were, the city wasn't the country, and his acoustic guitar was

no match for the ambient blare and smokestack lightning of the
noisy Chicago streets. Muddy knew he needed something more if
he was going to wrestle the wild metropolis to the ground.

"The country sounds different than in the city—the sound is
empty out there," he recalled. "At night . . . just a guitar, man, you
play it at night out in the country, carries it a long way cross town."
This simply wasn't the case in the North. As fun as it was to play at
house parties, the close walls and bad acoustics of a rowdy apartment room filled with revelers threatened to swallow his music
whole before it could even reach the front door.

Fortunately for Waters, he'd found a solution to his problems
in the form of guitarist Jimmy Rogers, a fellow Mississippi trans-
plant who had heard about Waters from mutual friends. When
they first sat down to play, Rogers immediately recognized Mud's
potential and understood how to help him take it to another level.
An enormously empathetic musician, Rogers appreciated the raw-
ness of Waters's country approach, but, ten years his junior, he also
knew the sound needed to be brought into the modern era.

"Muddy had a Gretsch hollow-box [guitar]," Rogers told
writer Robert Gordon, "and I got him a DeArmond pickup put
on his guitar, got him a little amplifier, and then you could get a
sound out of it."

For the next several months, the duo jammed every chance
they could at Muddy's house on the West Side of Chicago, running through traditional songs and building new compositions
of their own while carefully constructing complementary sounds
and tones through their 15-watt Gibson amplifiers. Jimmy, with
his Silvertone archtop, concentrated on the more contemporary
single-note method, influenced by players like Charlie Christian,
while Muddy, on what was most likely a Gretsch Synchromatic
100, focused on the gritty rural slide technique created by Son
House and Robert Johnson. Together they forged a new sound, as
Rogers's slinky licks coiled and uncoiled around Waters's aggressively swampy grind. It sounded sexy and dangerous. Add Mud's

impassioned vocals to the mix and you had a sound that was big enough to knock plaster from ceilings, or peel paint from brick and steel. With two amplified guitars, they could do much more than fill an apartment with sound; they could dominate an entire club.

OF COURSE MUDDY and Jimmy weren't the first guitarists looking to expand their dynamic range. Charlie Christian was already turning heads with his playing on the Gibson ES-150. So why didn't they follow in his footsteps?

The simple answer is that, for a working-class musician, it wasn't that easy. Buying a $150 Gibson or Epiphone instrument was an expensive proposition in the forties, especially if you were struggling to make $5 a night. For men of their means, there was another option, one that was cheap and actually quite brilliant.

The DeArmond electromagnetic pickup was a stand-alone device that could turn any acoustic guitar into an electric instrument in seconds, and it cost a relatively manageable $25. Invented in 1935 by an enterprising ten-year-old guitarist named John Henry DeArmond, who fashioned a pickup from parts off an old Ford Model A, the unit clipped onto just about any guitar, giving Depression-era players a way to go electric without purchasing a new instrument. John's older brother, Harry, immediately saw the potential of the device and teamed up with a Toledo, Ohio, company named Rowe Industries. Together they oversaw the production of two models in 1939: the RH for round-hole guitars, and the FH for f-hole instruments.

The DeArmond pickups were a success, and enormously significant in democratizing the electric guitar for musicians like Waters and Rogers. And while they were inexpensive, they were by no means inferior products. Many aficionados consider the 1953 Model 1100, for example, to be among the best-sounding pickups ever made. Percussive, rich, and slightly twangy, the 1100 had a one-of-a-kind sound. It can fetch as much as $1,000 in today's market. The company went on to provide groundbreaking pickups for, most notably, Gretsch, Fender, and Martin, but those early pickups were some of the most important and unsung heroes in the popularization of the electric guitar.

MUDDY WATERS HAD always maintained that while his blues appeared to be simple, it was "the hardest in the world to play." He may have been right. For Waters, the blues was a fluid thing, and it had to flow, hesitate, or explode at any given moment, depending on what the singer was trying to express. Fellow musicians had to be vigilant to catch the dramatic pauses and the passionate out-bursts of joy or sorrow that were the hallmark of a great blues per-formance. The chord progressions might've been easy to master, but the art of maintaining the groove while capturing the shifting drama of the music was as subtle and complex as any performance by a classical string quartet.

It wasn't easy to teach, either, and was even more difficult to learn. Waters and Rogers spent long hours practicing and build-ing a sort of psychic connection that would allow them to shift dynamic gears at the drop of a bottle. For the next couple of years they played parties, networked the South Side blues clubs—such as the 708 Club, Smitty's Corner, and the Triangle Inn—and sup-ported other bluesmen, like harmonica legend Sonny Boy Wil-liamson and pianist Sunnyland Slim, while working on their soon-to-be revolutionary sound.

Occasionally they accepted outsiders into their ranks. For a while a flashy guitarist named Claude "Blue Smitty" Smith from Marianna, Arkansas, joined the duo. Smitty brought a new level of musical sophistication to the unit, and taught Waters and Rog-ers more than a few new tricks on the guitar, but he eventually left for a more stable job as an electrician. It was just as well, for it was his replacement that would help them make history.

Rogers lived only half a block from the center of Maxwell Street, a bustling Chicago marketplace that was a gathering place for street musicians looking to sharpen their chops and make a few bucks off passing crowds in the process. One morning he woke up to a "strange harp sound." The music was familiar, and yet so compelling that the guitarist put his clothes on and pushed through the busy streets until he found what he'd expected: the preposterously skinny, teenaged Marion "Little Walter" Jacobs, blowing some of the fiercest harmonica he had ever heard. The guitarist had only briefly crossed paths with Walter over the years, but he'd never forgotten his singular sound.

"He had a bass player and a guitar and a drum with him," recalled Rogers. "But the only thing that was really standing out to me was the harmonica. That's what I wanted to hear, and I knew how to back it up. And I sat in with them, and well, we had a wonderful time down there. That's the way we really met—*communicating*."

Still adjusting after Blue Smitty's departure, Rogers brought Walter to Muddy's home for a jam. Walter was young, high-strung, and arrogant, and his timing left much to be desired, but there was no arguing with his ear for melody and his lightning-fast chops. Profoundly influenced by swing jazz and bebop sax players like Charlie Parker, Walter was way ahead of the blues curve, and it was clear to Muddy and Jimmy that if they could rein in the eighteen-year-old, there would be very little that could stop the trio from being a force to be reckoned with in the blues world.

Little Walter knew he was brilliant, and was therefore reluctant to take orders from anyone, and even argued with veteran players such as Sonny Boy or Big Walter Horton when they tried to get him to slow down. You had to be careful when arguing with Walter. Rogers put it succinctly: "He was likely to kill you or anybody that crossed him." He was small and quick to anger, but there was something about the seriousness of Waters and Rogers and their ability to break down each song that appealed to the harp player, who deep down knew he needed to learn how to play within a groove if he was ever going to make it in a band.

Together they began forging the same kind of psychic bond with Walter that they had with each other. "Running patterns," they called it. By that time, Muddy and Jimmy were so in tune with each other that even the hurricane force that was Little Walter had to comply. And once the harmonica player found the groove, Waters and Rogers would start building and creating subtle variations until they would explode, sending waves of shrapnel-like bent notes and distortion toward audiences, who responded to the power and excitement by packing their performances.

The trio encompassed the past, present, and future of popular music in one compelling package. Even though Muddy's sound was rooted in the soil of the Mississippi Delta, playing through an amp modernized his style. The treble licks sliced deeper, his notes sustained longer and hung in the air like smoke. The sound he produced was industrial in strength—a primordial cry designed for modern ears.

It wasn't long before Waters, Rogers, and Walter, accompanied by a succession of drummers and bassists, came to own the Chicago blues scene. Their combined volume and absolute control over dynamics was unlike anything anyone had ever heard out of such a small group. Most significant was the notion that five men could generate that much noise and excitement; it pretty much sealed the doom of big bands, who were expensive to take on the road and difficult to maintain. The group would set the stage for rock bands to follow, who would use amplification to fill arenas, stadiums, and beyond.

But just as the unit was really starting to gel, Waters got his own break. In 1947 the legendary record company owner and producer Leonard Chess announced he was searching for a "rough blues singer," a musician who could authentically sing and play rural blues for his Aristocrat label (soon to be the eponymous

Chess Records). Recent successes by Lightnin' Hopkins for Aladdin Records and John Lee Hooker for Modern Records, who both played like they'd never left the Delta, convinced Chess that there was commercial potential for music that appealed to transplanted blacks nostalgic for simpler times.

Pianist Sunnyland Slim, who functioned as the record mogul's eyes and ears on the street, recommended Waters, who had remained true to his country roots even as he adjusted his sound and style for the city. But Chess wasn't remotely interested in Muddy's sensational band; he just wanted Waters.

Mud was disappointed to part with his bandmates, but he knew it was an opportunity too good to refuse. And so, in April of 1948, he became a solo act.

Chess got so much more than an authentic country sound out of Waters. Accompanied only by his amplified Gretsch acoustic and the ominous thump of upright bassist Big Crawford, Muddy recorded two milestones in blues history, "I Can't Be Satisfied" and "I Feel Like Going Home." While the production was sparse, Mud's bottleneck playing, channeled through an amplifier, gave his music an edge that was as funky and dirty as an Illinois factory. It wasn't the full-on assault of Muddy's band, but it was innovative still. Chess himself wasn't sure if he liked it, but when the first pressing of his single almost sold out in a day, he knew he would learn to.

After releasing smash after smash, Waters eventually convinced Chess to let him record with members of his band. Together, they would dominate the R&B charts during the mid-fifties with soon-to-be blues standards such as "I Just Want to Make Love to You" and "Hoochie Coochie Man." The Muddy Waters sound—sly, sexual innuendo issued over two stinging electric guitars, a wailing harmonica, and a throbbing rhythm section—would create a new paradigm for the blues.

•

FROM A MODERN perspective, it would be easy to imagine that the history of the electric guitar must largely have been a battle royale fought between Gibson and Fender, dominant as they are in today's market. But there were many other manufacturers equally important to the development of the instrument. As we have mentioned, some of Muddy Waters's earliest and most important electric sides were recorded using a hollow-body Gretsch with a DeArmond pickup. While it was not technically an electric guitar—it was an acoustic instrument retrofitted with an aftermarket device—both Gretsch and DeArmond would become major players in the solid-body guitar field.

Gretsch's origins are an archetypal New York story and, like Gibson's and Rickenbacker's, began with an immigrant from the Old World. Friedrich Gretsch arrived in Manhattan from Mannheim, Germany, in 1873. He worked briefly for the drum and banjo manufacturer Albert Houdlett & Sons. But by 1883, he'd Americanized his first name to Fred, started the Fred Gretsch Manufacturing Company in Brooklyn, and begun to build a product line that included drums, banjos, tambourines, and toy instruments.

The company grew steadily, but in 1895 misfortune struck. On a trip back to Germany, Friedrich died suddenly. He was only thirty-nine years old.

"He was traveling to Europe on a boat," explained great-grandson Fred Gretsch III, who still runs the company. "By the time he got to Hamburg, he was deathly ill, and he died a day or two later."

The leadership of the company passed on to Friedrich's eldest son, Fred—known as Fred Sr.—who was only fifteen at the time. "Even though my grandfather was only fifteen in 1895, my great-grandmother brought him into the business, rather than closing it down," said Fred III. "She must've been a heck of a business-woman: the mother of seven children and helping a fifteen-year-old son to run the company. Together they brought the business forward."

Mandolins were added to the line in 1900. And in 1916, the Fred Gretsch Manufacturing Company built a fine new headquarters for itself: a ten-story building at 60 Broadway in Brooklyn. Visible from the on-ramp to the Williamsburg Bridge connecting Brooklyn to Manhattan, the Gretsch building would be a landmark for successive generations of guitarists in the New York area.

Gretsch got increasingly involved in guitar making during the 1920s and 1930s, as guitars eclipsed banjos as the instrument of choice for dance band rhythm sections. During the twenties, these Gretsch-made guitars were marketed under the Rex and 20th Century brand names. None of these early guitars attracted much attention, but in 1939, Gretsch brought out the Synchromatic series—stylish archtops with flashy "cat's eye" sound holes that did much to put Gretsch on the map. That same year saw the release of the first Gretsch electric, the Electromatic Spanish guitar.

The Gretsch company underwent a series of managerial changes during the 1940s. Fred Gretsch Sr. left the company in 1942 and became a banker. Leadership of the company passed to his son William Walter "Bill" Gretsch, the father of the company's current head. But Bill Gretsch died in 1948, at age forty-one, and was succeeded by his brother, Fred Gretsch, known as Fred Jr. In the booming economy that took hold in the years after the end of World War II, Fred Jr. decided the time was right to stop messing around with the subcontract work they had been doing for Montgomery Ward and Sears, Roebuck, and to get serious about building and marketing high-quality guitars under the Gretsch name. As part of this impetus, Gretsch made a pact with Harry DeArmond; DeArmond pickups graced some of Gretsch's finest early-fifties guitars.

Solid-body electrics were still a new concept at the dawn of the fifties, but Fred Jr. had taken notice of Leo Fender, if only because

Leo had for a time encroached upon his Broadkaster brand name. But what really got Fred Jr.'s attention (and what would transform the way the electric guitar was conceived in America and abroad, as we'll see) was when his chief rival, Gibson, started producing the solid-body Les Paul model in 1952.

Ted McCarty, Gibson's president, recalled Gretsch's disbelief that Gibson was dabbling in such a tacky fad. In a 1992 interview McCarty said, "Fred Gretsch, who was a personal friend of mine, said how could you do this? I said, Fred, somebody's got to stop this guy Fender, he's just about trying to take over."

Fred may have been a skeptic, but it didn't take long for him to change his tune. After Fender and Gibson started selling solid-body guitars by the thousands, he responded quickly, and one year later the company introduced the 1953 Gretsch Duo Jet. It wasn't really a solid-body instrument. Hollow sound chambers within the body gave it a tone distinct from either the Les Paul or the Telecaster, a difference that found favor over the years with players ranging from Beatle George Harrison to punk rock icon Billy Zoom of the Los Angeles band X, to U2's the Edge.

The original Duo Jet was issued in black. But in 1954, Gretsch guitars started to become available in a kaleidoscopic range. Among them was the Gretsch Silver Jet, basically a Duo Jet done up in a silver sparkle finish, a look taken from Gretsch's drum department. As a major guitar manufacturer also very heavily invested in the drum business, Gretsch had a source of eye-catching materials that left its competitors in the dust.

The idea of applying drum surfaces to guitars was the brainchild of Jimmie Webster. Webster was an outgoing, backslapping ball of energy: a musician, inventor, pitchman, and marketing genius all rolled into one. As an artist/endorser he did tours and clinics to promote Gretsch instruments, dazzling potential customers with an unusual two-handed fretboard tapping technique (which rocker Edward Van Halen would stumble upon three decades later). He was also a marketing wiz, bombarding management and production people with wild ideas for finishes and gimmicks such as the T-Zone Tempered Treble, which was a very exciting name for a rather boring method of improving intonation using slanted frets.

But perhaps Webster's biggest contribution to Gretsch was corralling a particular young country guitar virtuoso into their fold. Gretsch was making great guitars, but they lacked a strong identity in the marketplace. The company was determined to find a marquee artist to attach their name to, someone who could bolster their image and their sales.

The notion of the signature model—attaching a noted player's name to a new guitar design—goes back at least as far as the 1830s, with collaborations between renowned luthiers such as René Lacote and Johann Stauffer and players such as Fernando Sor and Luigi Legnani. The idea was simple: if the best maker teamed up with the best player, they'd surely come up with something spectacular. Gibson had been achieving great success with their Les Paul signature models, as we'll see. And Gretsch had been courting the growing country market with models like the Round-Up, introduced in '53, so an alliance with a country star seemed an altogether wise course.

Fortunately for Gretsch, Webster knew exactly who to call.

BORN IN 1924 in the tiny, impoverished Appalachian town of Luttrell, Tennessee, the shy, asthmatic Chet Atkins found solace in his guitar. He'd started out on the ukulele, but when he was nine he traded his brother, Lowell, an old pistol and some chores for a guitar. Because of his illness, he was forced to sleep in a straight-back chair, in order to breathe comfortably. On those nights he would listen to the radio and play his guitar until he fell asleep, a habit that continued throughout his life.

Deeply influenced by the intricate fingerpicking of country guitarist Merle Travis and the jazz styles of Les Paul and Chicago guitarist George Barnes, Atkins eventually developed a remarkable, highly polished playing style that would earn him the nickname "Mr. Guitar." He was essentially a fingerpicker like Travis, but whereas Travis used his index finger for the melody and thumb for bass notes, Atkins expanded his style to include picking with the first three fingers. Chet's facility was so great, it often sounded like two people were playing at once (if not three), and he would amuse himself and astound audiences by playing two different songs simultaneously.

In 1942, the skinny, six-foot-tall eighteen-year-old became a staff guitarist at a radio station in Knoxville, Tennessee. He rapidly worked his way up the ladder, landing a recording contract five years later with RCA Victor in Nashville, where he became a triple threat—producing, recording, and arranging.

When Gretsch approached Atkins to endorse their instruments in 1954, the guitarist was intrigued. Both of his heroes, Travis and Paul, had signature models, and he aspired to be held in the same regard.

"At the time I was full of ambition," said Atkins. "I wanted to be known all over the world as a great guitarist, and that was one brick in the edifice that would help that happen." He agreed to work with Gretsch.

The first of many Chet Atkins models, the venerable 6120 debuted in 1955. Wanting to make a dramatic statement, Gretsch created an instrument that screamed "cowboy" perhaps a little too loudly. In addition to its campfire-orange finish, the archtop guitar featured a kitschy G-for-Gretsch logo branded into the front of the body and a 22-fret board engraved with a steer head, a cactus, and other western motifs.

Atkins himself was not crazy about the styling, and later modified most of it, but he was determined to support Gretsch's efforts to make him and his new guitar household names.

"I was very honest about it," said Atkins. "I played the Gretsch guitar, the orange one, even though I didn't like it."

Despite its garish design, or perhaps because of it, the 6120 was an overnight success, handily outselling Gibson's best-selling ES guitar, the ES-175, from 1955 to 1961. The guitar grew and evolved with the company itself, and it would go on to become perhaps their most revered model.

Much to Gretsch's delight, that same year the guitarist would also score two of the biggest hits of his career. His instrumental arrangement of "Mr. Sandman" reached #13 on the country charts and was followed almost immediately by another hit, "Silver Bell," a duet with country superstar Hank Snow. This meant that Atkins and his orange guitar would appear regularly on national television, cementing his image as one of America's premier guitarists and instrumentalists.

Additionally, over the next couple of years, the guitarist would oversee production and play rhythm guitar on some of rock and roll's most significant early records, including Elvis Presley's breakthrough RCA single, "Heartbreak Hotel" (which he arranged), and the Everly Brothers' smashes "Wake Up Little Susie" and "Bye Bye Love."

While much has been written about the influence of the blues on rock guitar, it is of equal importance to note the contribution of country music. Most of our best early guitar-playing rock musicians were from the South. Elvis Presley's guitarist Scotty Moore, who was highly influenced by Atkins, was from Tennessee. Buddy Holly was from Texas; Gene Vincent's guitarist, Cliff Gallup, was from Virginia; the Everly Brothers were from Kentucky; and they all had deep roots in folk music, western swing, bluegrass, and country. It was not an accident that most early rock music played by white musicians was called "rockabilly," which was essentially shorthand for hillbilly music infused with a large shot of African American–influenced rhythm and blues.

Presley, the King of Rock and Roll, summed it up this way: "The colored folk been singin' and playin' it just the way I'm doin it now, man, for more years than I know." But in other interviews he also described it as "hopped-up country." Both statements were true, and Atkins was a mover and a shaker at the center of all of it.

As a company that specialized in creating glitzy guitars that just happened to have a strong foothold in the country market, Gretsch was ideally positioned to become the axe of choice for the original rockabilly wild men with their outsized pompadour hairstyles and two-tone shoes. A circa '57 Gretsch 6120 was the vehicle that Eddie Cochran rode to fame on, with classic tracks such as "Summertime Blues" and "Something Else," songs that were reprised in later years by the Who and the Sex Pistols. Duane Eddy opted for a red 6120, purchased at Ziggy's Music in Duane's hometown of Phoenix, Arizona, and employed on instrumental hits like "Rebel Rouser" (which gave the word "twang" a permanent place of honor in the popular musicians' lexicon). And lead guitar man Cliff Gallup wielded a circa '55–'56 Duo Jet on such classic Gene Vincent hits as "Be-Bop-A-Lula"—a sound that made it to England and caused a young Jeff Beck and John Lennon to flip their wigs.

But Gretsch's impact on early rock and roll wasn't confined to rockabilly. Sometime in the mid-fifties, R&B great Bo Diddley took a Gretsch neck and pickups and attached them to a simple rectangular guitar body he'd made himself. A rock-and-roll archetype was born. Diddley went to Gretsch around 1958 and asked them to start making these distinctive guitars for him. With their five-alarm-red paint job and unique shape, they became an important element in Bo Diddley's distinctive visual and musical style. The great rock-and-roll originator also played a Jet Firebird in the studio and worked with Gretsch to create the rocket-shaped Jupiter Thunderbird, revived decades later by Gretsch's current management and ZZ Top's Billy Gibbons as the Billy-Bo Gretsch.

Meanwhile, Gretsch poster boy Chet Atkins had been made the head of RCA's Nashville recording studios in '57. There, he helped create the much-celebrated Nashville Sound, a more mainstream version of country music that emphasized vocals and smoothed out any rural edges with the use of strings and slick background harmonies. Beginning in the mid-fifties continuing through the early sixties, the Nashville Sound turned country from a regional, niche phenomenon into a multimillion-dollar pop-crossover industry, as Atkins produced massive hit singles by Don Gibson, Jim Reeves, Charley Pride, Porter Wagoner, and Dolly Parton.

"We took the twang out of it," said Atkins with pride. "In my case it went more uptown. I'd take out the steel guitar and the fiddle, which branded a song as strictly country."

While some criticized Atkins's productions as too slick, when later asked to define the Nashville Sound, the ever-shrewd guitarist responded simply by shaking some leftover change in his pocket and saying, "That's what it is. It's the sound of money."

As Atkins's prestige grew, so did Gretsch's line of Chet Atkins signature models. Introduced in 1957, the Chet Atkins Country Gentleman was a thinline hollow-body guitar—a slimmer version of the conventional hollow-body. It was built without sound holes, to attempt to contain feedback (though the company painted on fake f-holes just to make the instrument look kosher). The following year, Gretsch added the 6119 Tennessean model to the Chet Atkins line. It was essentially an affordable, single-pickup version of the 6120, although this model, like all Gretsches, would evolve in the years to come.

IN 1954, at the age of forty-one, Muddy Waters had finally made it to the top. Or so it seemed. "Hoochie Coochie Man" and "I Just Want to Make Love to You," released that year, became his biggest sellers and remained in the Top 10 R&B charts for more than three months. But the winds of change were blowing, and that summer, blues record sales suddenly plummeted, dropping by a dramatic 25 percent and sending shock waves through the Chicago music industry. Record execs blamed the poor economy, but as we've seen, a fresh and more youth-oriented brand of music was starting to sweep the airwaves, one that was built on the bones of the very R&B, blues, and country that they had so carefully nurtured. As Waters would later sing, "the blues had a baby and they named it rock and roll."

In '54, Elvis Presley paired the country tune "Blue Moon of Kentucky" with "That's All Right," a song originally performed by blues singer Arthur Crudup, and the single sold an impressive 20,000 copies. That same year, Bill Haley & His Comets sold millions with "Shake, Rattle and Roll" and "Rock Around the Clock." In response, Leonard Chess sniffed out and signed two young electric guitar–playing rockers of his own. Bo Diddley and his rectangular guitar would become an enormous commercial success; but it was Chuck Berry's crossover to the white teenage market that would make him a legend.

Charles Edward Anderson Berry, born to a middle-class family in St. Louis, Missouri, in 1926, was a brown-eyed charmer who loved the blues and poetry with almost equal fervor. After winning a high school talent contest with a guitar-and-vocal rendition of Jay McShann's "Confessin' the Blues," he became serious about making music and started working the clubs in East St. Louis, Illinois, located directly across the Mississippi River from his hometown, where he put all of his skills to good use. While Berry excelled at playing the blues of Muddy Waters and crooning in the suave manner of Nat King Cole, it was his ability to play "white music" that would eventually make him a star.

"The music played most around St. Louis was country-western and swing," Berry said in his autobiography. "Curiosity provoked me to lay a lot of the country stuff on our predominantly black audience. After they laughed at me a few times, they began requesting the hillbilly stuff."

The sight and sound of a black man playing white hillbilly music, combined with Berry's natural showmanship and his ability to improvise clever lyrics to fit any occasion, made him a top attraction with Missouri's black community. But Berry had bigger aspirations; he wanted to make records. While on a trip to Chicago he paid a fifty-cent admission fee to see his favorite blues singer, Muddy Waters, perform, and after the show he worked his way toward the bandstand and managed a few words with his idol.

"It was the feeling I suppose one would get from having a word with the president or the pope," Berry remembered. "I quickly told him of my admiration for his compositions and asked him who I could see about making a record."

Waters told the guitarist to see Leonard Chess. So, taking his hero at his word, Berry made a beeline for Chess Studios the next morning, introduced himself to the receptionist, and politely asked to see Chess. Remarkably, Chess waved him in, and Berry passionately delivered a well-rehearsed speech outlining his hopes as a musician. "He had a look of amazement that he later told me was because of the businesslike way I talked to him," Berry later said.

Hearing Chuck's homemade demo tape, the label president gravitated to a cover of "Ida Red," a 1938 song made popular by country swing band Bob Wills and His Texas Playboys. Chess recognized the crossover potential of a black artist playing country music, and he scheduled a session for May 21, 1955. After all, if a white man like Presley could make hit records by sounding black, why not try the reverse?

During the session, Chess demanded a bigger sound for the song and added bass and maracas to Berry's trio. He also told Berry to write new lyrics, insisting that "the kids want the big beat, cars, and young love." Chuck quickly responded with an outrageous story about a man driving a V8 Ford, chasing his unfaithful girlfriend in her Cadillac Coupe de Ville. The title was changed from "Ida Red" to "Maybellene," a name inspired by a brand of makeup teenage girls were wearing at the time.

And with it, rock and roll was born. Although the record made it only to the mid-20s on the Billboard pop chart, its influence was massive in scope. Here was a black rock-and-roll record with across-the-board appeal, embraced by white teenagers and southern hillbilly musicians alike (including Elvis Presley, who added it to his stage show).

And it was fortunate for the electric guitar that one of its earliest champions was not only an extraordinary musician and showman, but also one of pop music's greatest and most enduring singer-songwriters. With monster hits such as "Roll Over Beethoven" (1956), "Rock and Roll Music" (1957), and "Sweet Little Sixteen" (1958), Chuck Berry did much to forge the genre. His formula was ingenious: write lethally funny lyrics about the teenage experience, strap them into a high-octane groove, add a little country twang, shake it up with a showstopping guitar solo inspired by the likes of T-Bone Walker or Charlie Christian, and then watch the acclaim pour in. It was a recipe that would dominate popular music for decades to come. And if early listeners didn't understand how important his guitar was to the mix, Chuck soon made the connection explicit.

In his 1958 masterpiece, "Johnny B. Goode," Berry created the ultimate rock-and-roll folk hero in just a few snappy verses. As we all know, Goode wasn't pounding a piano, singing into a microphone, or blowing a sax. In his choice the electric guitar, something sleek and of the moment, the fictional character of Goode would forge an image of the archetypal rocker, doing as much to shape the history of the instrument as any real-life figure ever has.

The song's opening riff is a clarion call—perhaps the greatest intro in rock-and-roll history. It was played by Berry on an electric Gibson ES-350T, and it indeed sounded "just like a-ringin' a bell." The tale begins "deep down in Louisiana," where a country boy from a poor household is doing his best to get by. Johnny, we discover, "never ever learned to read or write so well," but he has something better than a formal education or a diploma—he has talent, street smarts, and a guitar. Johnny's Gibson is his instrument and also his ticket out of the backwoods.

After introducing our hero, the anthem turns to his guitar. It's portable—he could toss it into a "gunnysack" and practice anywhere, even beneath the trees by the railroad. It's astonishingly loud. More powerful than a passing locomotive, Johnny's soaring notes stop train passengers dead in their tracks.

By the last verse, the guitarist's reputation has spread far and wide. As his growing legion of fans and supporters cheers him on with shouts of "Go, Johnny, go," even his long-suffering mother is forced to concede that "maybe someday your name will be in lights."

"Johnny B. Goode" is a brilliant, uniquely American rags-to-riches story, but with a modern twist. Where Horatio Alger's nineteenth-century heroes rose from humble backgrounds to lives of middle-class security through hard work and virtue, Goode excelled on his own terms; he was uneducated, solitary. He was a bad boy, a story line all the more compelling to a generation of teenagers just beginning to identify with outsider icons such as James Dean and Elvis Presley.

It was a song that thrilled and exhilarated audiences both black and white. It became a massive crossover hit, peaking at #2 on *Billboard* magazine's Hot R&B Sides chart and #8 on the Billboard Hot 100. To teenage ears, Chuck's guitar signaled the dawn of a new era. The glorious peal of his 350T proclaimed that school was out.

John Lennon, Bob Dylan, Jimi Hendrix, Keith Richards, and Bruce Springsteen were just a few of the working-class kids who immediately grasped the sly moral of the song, and who recognized a good blueprint when they saw one.

"I could never overstress how important [Berry] was in my development," said Richards, perhaps the ultimate rock-and-roll outlaw.

Reflecting on the significance of "Johnny B. Goode" and his other hits, Berry later played down his originality. He was attempting to marry the diction of Nat King Cole, the lyrics of Louis

Jordan, and the swing of Charlie Christian, but with the soul of Muddy Waters. "Ain't nothin' new under the sun," he was fond of saying. But he was being modest. His synthesis of genres and his use of amplification were wholly original. If Christian introduced the electric guitar to a mass audience, Berry created its grandest mythology.

AS THE ELECTRIC guitar began to take on its signature shape—almost indistinguishable from the guitars of today—it bears noting how conspicuously sexy that design had become. With curves that cartoonishly mimicked the lines of a woman's hips, and an undeniably phallic neck, the guitar may have preceded the sexual revolution of the sixties, but it would become a perfect visual complement to it. Its provocative design was something Berry was one of the first to acknowledge, and that he rarely failed to exploit in his live shows.

While he had to be careful with how far he went—Chuck was one of the first black crossover rock-and-roll artists in a very racially charged time—he wasn't *that* careful. He often played to predominantly white audiences at rock-and-roll stage shows booked by DJ/promoter Alan Freed, or in Hollywood films such as *Rock, Rock, Rock!, Go, Johnny Go!,* and *Mister Rock and Roll.* During each appearance, Berry would kiss his Gibson or Gretsch on the neck, wrestling with it as he made it scream and swoon during his wild solos, jutting it lasciviously from his waist as he did splits.

The Gibson ES-350T was particularly well suited to Berry's gyrations. In the mid-fifties, electric guitar players had two choices: either a full hollow-body or a compact solid-body. Gibson had been receiving requests from players for something in-between the two styles, so in 1955 their first "thinline" electrics were developed. The guitar's medium build was a perfect fit for Chuck's high-energy stage presentation.

Chuck's guitar antics and wild gyrations were provocative

stuff for suburban kids, who were used to gently swaying crooners such as Frank Sinatra or Rosemary Clooney. And while they might not have understood all the implications of his act, one thing was clear: the electric guitar presented a seriously dangerous, sexy alternative to the comparatively staid piano or the sax.

BY THE END of the fifties, dozens of guitar-playing Johnny B. Goodes appeared, irrevocably changing the musical landscape, all playing in small electric combos resembling those pioneered by Chuck Berry and Muddy Waters.

As for Waters, he had a few more hits, including "Mannish Boy" in 1956 and "She's Nineteen Years Old" in 1958. But the music of a forty-something guitarist like Muddy was being overtaken by rock and roll, driving him back into the small blues joints from whence he came. As Waters ruefully noted, "[Blues] is not the music of today; it's the music of yesterday."

Little did he suspect that a few short years later, his music (along with that of younger acts such as Berry and Elvis) would find new life across the Atlantic, where it would be discovered by and inspire a generation of white British teens. They would go on to pick up electric guitars and start blues and rock bands of their own. The Rolling Stones (who borrowed their name from a Waters song), the Animals, the Yardbirds, Cream, and Led Zeppelin would pay homage—not to mention royalties—to those pioneers. Blues played on electric guitars, it turned out, was far from the music of yesterday. Indeed, it would be the music of today for decades to come.

Influential bluesman Freddie King
poses with his Gibson Les Paul
goldtop.

chapter 6

THE SOLID-BODY STRADIVARIUS

In the late winter of 1965, a young English guitarist wandered into a London music shop. He'd just made a bold and risky—some would say foolish—career move, quitting the band he'd been with since 1963 just as they'd scored their first hit record and were rapidly rising to fame. Success and recognition of that magnitude is the very thing most musicians dream of.

But then, Eric Clapton has always been a law unto himself. During his time with the Yardbirds—the band from which he had just resigned—he had been essential in carving out a greatly expanded, assertive, and adventurous role for the electric lead guitar in the mid-sixties music of the so-called British Invasion. But Clapton was displeased with the blatantly pop direction of the Yardbirds' breakthrough hit single, the harpsichord-driven "For Your Love." The guitarist had wanted the band to stick with the African American blues/R&B musical course they'd initially charted. Instead, in Clapton's eyes, they'd sold out. So he'd left in a huff.

Within two weeks of his departure, he'd accepted a gig with British bluesman John Mayall and his group, the Bluesbreakers. Mayall would come to be known as the father of the British blues scene. So if Clapton wanted to play blues and nothing but the blues, Mayall was his man. Of course, this meant a step down in terms of creature comforts and financial remuneration—sleeping rough in Mayall's incommodious van on small-time U.K. club tours while his former fellow Yardbirds and their new guitar player, Jeff Beck, jetted off to America and hordes of screaming teenage fans. But young Mr. Clapton was an idealist and man of principle, willing to suffer a little for the sake of his art.

He felt, however, that he needed a new guitar and amp for his new musical role. The Fender Telecaster and Vox amp he'd been playing had been fine for the Yardbirds. But now he required something with a bit more gravitas. A real grown-up instrument. And so he hit the music shops along London's Denmark Street and Charing Cross Road—a pilgrimage he'd been making regularly since he was a teenager.

"There were several stores that had electric guitars in their windows," the guitarist recalled in his 2007 autobiography, *Clapton*. "To me they were just like sweet shops. I would stand outside staring at these things for hours on end, especially at night when the windows would remain lit up, and after a trip to the Marquee [London's premier jazz/blues/R&B venue] I would walk around all night looking and dreaming."

Clapton knew exactly what he wanted—a Gibson Les Paul guitar like he'd seen his hero, bluesman Freddie King, playing on the cover of King's album *Let's Hide Away and Dance Away*. Clapton didn't manage to find a goldtop Les Paul model like the one on the album cover, but he came close enough, discovering a 1960 Les Paul Standard with a beautiful sunburst finish. Emerging from a dark-toned border, the guitar's natural maple-wood-grain top shone beneath glistening lacquer.

"It was almost brand new," Clapton would later recall, "in an original case with that lovely purple velvet lining. Just magnificent."

Clapton paired the guitar with a 50-watt Marshall amplifier and left the shop contented. He immediately put the new rig to work with Mayall, both live and in the recording studio, starting with a June '65 session for the single "I'm Your Witchdoctor"/"Telephone Blues," produced by none other than Jimmy Page, another guitarist who would become closely associated with the Gibson Les Paul. In April of 1966 this was followed by sessions for Mayall's second album, and first-ever studio LP, *Blues Breakers: John Mayall with Eric Clapton*. For this recording, as on the earlier single, Clapton insisted on recording his guitar and amp cranked up to live performance volume, a technique relatively unheard-of at the time. "The result," Clapton explained,

was the sound which came to be associated with me. It had really come about accidentally, when I was trying to emulate the sharp, thin sound that Freddie King got out of his Gibson Les Paul, and I ended up with something quite different, a sound that was a lot fatter than Freddie's. The Les Paul has two pickups: one at the end of the neck, giving the guitar a kind of round jazz sound; and the other next to the bridge giving you the treble, most often used for the thin, typically rock and roll sound. What I would do was use the bridge pickup with all the bass turned up, so the sound was also very thick and on the edge of distortion. I also always used amps that would overload. I would have the amp on full and I would have the volume on the guitar also turned up full, so everything was on full volume and overloading. I would hit a note, hold it, and give it some vibrato with my fingers, until it sustained and then the distortion would turn into feedback. It was all of these things, plus the distortion, that created "my sound."

Of course it wasn't only the guitar's sound that made the album so compelling. Clapton's handling of the instrument is masterful—

a riveting yin/yang of unbridled passion and uncanny control. His connection with the gritty truth of the blues cuts deeper here than on any of his work with the Yardbirds, or indeed any of the recordings that his fellow British blues interpreters, such as the Rolling Stones and the Animals, had done in the years immediately prior to '66. But at the same time, Clapton's performance on the album is markedly different from the playing of his African American blues mentors—exuding a cocky kind of rock-and-roll aggression that would set a benchmark for both rock and pure blues playing for decades to come.

For all these reasons, *Blues Breakers* is one of the most important guitar recordings of all time—kind of the *Sgt. Pepper's Lonely Hearts Club Band* for guitar players. The disc got to #6 on the U.K. charts when it was released in July of 1966. In the United States, it was more of a cult classic. Many only picked up on it retrospectively, after Clapton hit it big with his subsequent group, Cream, a year later. *Blues Breakers: John Mayall with Eric Clapton* remains one of the albums that guitar players are expected to know about. Many are intimately familiar with every note of the record's incendiary renderings of twelve-bar blues penned by Mayall and Clapton themselves, not to mention songs by blues giants including Ray Charles, Otis Rush, Freddie King, Little Walter Jacobs, and Robert Johnson.

As a cult album, everything about the package was fetishized, including the front cover photograph of the group seated on a curb in front of a paint-splattered, chalk-graffitied concrete wall. Clapton is seen reading a copy of the U.K. comic book *The Beano*. Apparently the guitarist was not in the best of moods the day of the photo shoot (he seemingly found album cover photos a bit too pop as well) and insisted on reading the comic, refusing to make eye contact with the photographer's lens, thus registering his boredom with the entire procedure. For this reason, the LP is often referred to as the "Beano" album.

It's interesting that, despite his vehement repudiation of the Yardbirds and all things pop, Clapton is by far the Mayall band member who most resembles a pop idol on the album cover, stylishly attired in Beatle boots, slim black trousers, and a black fur coat, sporting neatly trimmed muttonchop sideburns. In contrast, drummer Hughie Flint looks like an early-sixties beatnik, with a goatee and white poplin raincoat. Mayall and bassist John McVie more resemble campus folkies, in scruffy suede and denim, with hair somewhat less than immaculately groomed. Clapton was clearly another breed of musician—one soon to be known as a guitar hero.

The disc was released at a time when long-playing record albums and album cover graphics were gaining recognition as valid art forms. Music fans were beginning to value albums over the 45-rpm singles that had earlier driven the popular music market. At a time before the advent of guitar magazines or any kind of serious music journalism—let alone guitar instructional videos on YouTube—album cover art and liner notes were a prized source of all-too-rare information about musical artists.

So, even more than the "Beano" album's front cover photo, guitarists pored over the back cover's black-and-white shots of the band at work in the recording studio. In one of these, Clapton is seen playing his Les Paul Standard, a lit cigarette jammed between strings on the peghead. Off to his right, his Marshall amp is also seen. Even though the guitar is only partially visible in the photograph, and from a rear angle at that, the photograph was sufficient to send legions of guitar players scrambling to find Les Paul Standards of their own. The problem was that Gibson had discontinued the model in 1961, and there weren't that many available. It wasn't until Clapton and a few other mid-1960s guitar heroes picked up on the instrument that it came to possess the "holy grail" status that it still enjoys today.

Among the many guitar players impelled by the "Beano"

album to procure a Les Paul Standard of their own was a bearded Texan named Billy F. Gibbons, who'd just started a band called ZZ Top.

"As is well known by now, on the reverse side of that John Mayall and the Bluesbreakers LP, we see Clapton with a Les Paul and a Marshall amp in the background," Gibbons would later recall.

> And immediately those who could put two and two together began to suspect that this wonderful sound and its richness of tone might be a result of that combination. So go find a Les Paul sunburst and a Marshall amplifier—that became the goal. That Les Paul sunburst mystique fanned the flames of thinking, "This must be it. Get one of those and you're steps ahead." And by and large it's proven to be just that. Out of the 1,750 odd Les Pauls made in '58, '59, and '60, although each one has its stylized personality characteristics, I've yet to find one that is not rip-roaring groovy. They're all wicked.

Gibbons's own quest led him to a farmhouse in Texas, where he found and purchased the 1959 Les Paul Standard that he has played on every single ZZ Top album from the band's 1971 debut disc right up to the present day. Known by its nickname Pearly Gates—or sometimes Mistress Pearly Gates—the instrument is another one of the legendary Les Pauls from the '58–'60 golden period. Like Stradivarius violins, the most famous Les Paul guitars tend to acquire names and individualized, almost human personalities all their own. The '60 Standard that Clapton played on the Mayall album is often called the "Beano" guitar. Its mystique is enhanced by the fact that it was stolen from its owner in 1966, shortly after the *Blues Breakers* album was recorded, and has never been recovered.

The Stradivarius analogy is an apt one in other regards. The rich, sustained tone of these vintage Les Pauls is often described as violin-like. And as we'll see, the guitars' carved maple tops and opulent, book-matched maple-wood-grain patterns were directly borrowed from violin-making techniques. Also not unlike Stradivarius violins, the things are ultra-rare and incredibly expensive. In the early years of the twenty-first century, a sunburst 1959 Les Paul Standard that had belonged to guitarists Peter Green and Gary Moore sold for $2 million. Which, even allowing for inflation, is a pretty substantial appreciation for a guitar that retailed for about $280 brand-new in '59. If the Clapton "Beano" Les Paul ever turned up at auction, it would surely fetch a similarly astronomical sum. It is perhaps the most iconic iteration of one of the world's most iconic electric guitars.

Of the approximately 1,750 sunburst Les Pauls manufactured between 1958 and 1960, some 1,000 are still unaccounted for. Many may well have been destroyed, modified, cannibalized for spare parts, or converted into end tables. Of course, there are many other Gibson Les Paul models from years other than the '58–'60 Standards, and many of them are superb guitars, quite handsomely priced as well. But none of them quite measures up to the golden era "'bursts."

MANY OF THE guitarists who today venerate vintage Les Paul guitars have never heard the music of Les Paul. But they're most likely to have heard the music of Eric Clapton, Jimmy Page, Billy Gibbons, Duane Allman, Mick Ronson, Slash, and many other rock guitar gods who have ridden their Les Pauls to fame. Moreover, the sounds these players wrest from the instruments bear little resemblance to the tonalities the Gibson company and Les Paul himself were envisioning when the guitar was first designed.

The Les Paul guitar only came about because Gibson was desperately in need of a solid-body electric to rival Fender's Telecaster, which had made a substantial splash in the early 1950s. If Gibson was to maintain the leadership role it had established in the guitar market decades earlier, it knew it had to come up with a solid-body model that not only equaled the Telecaster, but exceeded it in every way. The task of doing this was spearheaded by Gibson's new president, Ted McCarty.

McCarty had been brought on board in 1948 to help Gibson out of its post–World War II slump. Wartime shortages, the necessity of retooling for the war effort, and the rise of competitors such as Gretsch and Epiphone had eroded Gibson's market share. It was a whole new world out there, and the company's owner, Maurice H. Berlin of Chicago Musical Instruments (CMI), wasn't about to let the company he'd acquired in 1944 get left in the dust. On the advice of his friendly rival Bill Gretsch, Berlin recruited McCarty to turn things around and get Gibson back on its feet.

McCarty was already a heavy hitter in the business. He'd played a key role at America's largest musical instrument company, Wurlitzer, where he'd gained expertise in manufacturing, retail, and even real estate over the course of his twelve years there. He was about to leave Wurlitzer to accept a post as assistant treasurer at the Brach's Confections candy company when Berlin asked him to visit Gibson's Kalamazoo, Michigan, facility, have a look around, and assess the situation there. McCarty's verdict was swift and characteristically blunt and to-the-point: the company's management was too top-heavy.

By all accounts, he was not a man to mince his words. Like many of the electric guitar's early innovators, Ted McCarty had come up during the hard years of the Great Depression. "He was a Golden Gloves boxer," says guitar designer and manufacturer Paul Reed Smith, who was mentored by McCarty in later years. "If he had a problem with another kid, he would nail him. The guy was tough."

Candy vs. guitars: Maurice Berlin didn't have an easy job luring McCarty away from the Brach's offer. Brach's was top dog in a huge market. Way more people buy candy than guitars. And, much like Leo Fender, McCarty wasn't a musician. Unlike Leo, however, McCarty doesn't appear to have had a musical passion anything like Leo's love of country music. So the opportunity to stay in the music business with Gibson wouldn't have been that much of an inducement. He was the kind of guy who looked at the bottom line first and foremost.

And he wasn't crazy about the idea of leaving Chicago's teeming metropolis, where Wurlitzer was headquartered, for the sleepy, small-town charm of Kalamazoo. The move would mean a major upheaval for both himself and his family. During his time with Wurlitzer, he'd had to relocate his wife, eleven-year-old son, and eight-year-old daughter to eight different cities. He wasn't particularly interested in going through all of that again. The Brach's job would have enabled Ted and his family to remain in their comfortable Colonial-style home in the Chicago suburb of Winnetka.

But the thing that was tempting about the Gibson offer was that it would give McCarty a chance to utilize the engineering degree he'd acquired from Purdue University but had never been able to use in a professional capacity. And not long after he'd accepted Berlin's offer and settled into his position at Gibson, McCarty realized that the job came with an intriguing engineering challenge right off the bat—to build a solid-body that would top the Telecaster and knock Fender off its perch.

He seemed almost to take the Telecaster's existence as a personal affront. This is an antipathy he shared with most of the guitar manufacturing establishment at the time. "Their attitude was, 'Forget it, because anyone with a band saw and a router can make a solidbody guitar,'" McCarty recalled. The difference was that McCarty didn't just "forget it." What was required was a solid-body electric guitar that *couldn't* be made by anybody with a band saw and a router. A guitar that was worthy of Gibson's long reputation for fine craftsmanship, but also something that was completely modern. To that end, around 1950, McCarty put together a team that included Gibson production chief John Huis, employees Julius Bellson and Wilbur Marker, as well as representatives of other Gibson departments ranging from the wood shop to the sales force. His approach was global—taking into account every-thing from the tree from which the guitar would be made to the way the finished product would look in a music store window.

McCarty's basic design strategy was to take all the proven virtues of Gibson archtop guitars—their distinctive hollow bod-ies, f-holes, and contoured tops—and adapt them to a solid-body instrument. From a marketing standpoint, he was playing the tra-dition card against Fender's innovation card. Perhaps the main challenge was to come up with a body shape that was functional, comfortable to play, fully and clearly a solid-body guitar, yet some-how reminiscent of Gibson's legendary archtops. But McCarty and his team couldn't just take a regular archtop shape and make it solid rather than hollow. The thing would weigh a ton. So, as Leo Fender and George Fullerton had done with the Telecaster, McCarty and his associates took the outline of a conventional hollow-body and shrank it down to manageable proportions. The body they designed was appreciably less thick than an archtop, but still a little thicker than a Tele.

To emulate the classic Gibson archtop look, the designers hit upon the idea of affixing a carved maple top onto a main body fashioned from mahogany. The arch is subtle, but it nonetheless imparts a sensuous contour to the instrument. Much thought went into positioning Gibson as the upmarket alternative to Fender, with all the gravitas of historical guitar craftsmanship on Gibson's side.

Significantly, McCarty and his team opted for a traditional glued-in dovetail joint to attach the neck to the solid body of the instrument—a key feature that would differentiate Gibson's new guitar from the bolt-on neck design of Fender solid-body electrics. This helps the guitar sustain notes longer and generally imparts a more traditional tonality to the instrument. Visually, the neck's fret inlays—the markings on a fretboard that help a player orient him- or herself, often simple dots or pairs of dots—have a distinc-tive trapezoidal shape. This, and also the shape of the headstock, were meant to emulate the look of Gibson archtops of the period.

Once McCarty's team had completed a prototype, they turned their attention to marketing their new instrument. The idea arose to make it an artist signature model, as they had done with their Nick Lucas model of 1928, a collaboration with the guitarist, film personality, and "Tip-toe Thru the Tulips" crooner, followed by a model with guitarist Roy Smeck, introduced in 1934. Smeck is arguably the "signature model king" of early electric guitar history, having also lent his name to instruments by Kay, Montgomery Ward, and others. The company's leaders felt they were taking a risk with the newfangled instrument, so they were keen to hedge their bets in any way they could.

It was Ted McCarty who proposed Les Paul as the man whose name should go on the guitar. Les Paul and Mary Ford were enormously popular at the time, with hits like 1950's "Tennessee Waltz" and '51's "Mockin' Bird Hill," "How High the Moon," and "The World Is Waiting for the Sunrise." The futuristic "New Sound" Les had forged on these recordings had made his name synonymous with electric guitar wizardry. So he was the ideal personality to be associated with Gibson's new solid-body guitar design.

"I said, 'What about Les Paul?'" McCarty later recounted. "Because at the time, he and Mary were at the top of the charts. I knew Les, and had been trying to get him to play Gibson guitars, because he was an Epiphone man."

Les Paul always told a different tale of the guitar's design origin. Perhaps not surprisingly, it featured himself in a much more central role. According to his account, he was approached by Maurice Berlin, who had laughed him out of the room when Les had showed him his Log guitar in the forties. But after Fender brought the Telecaster to market, Berlin purportedly said, "Go find that kid with the broomstick," and Les was duly summoned back to Gibson.

McCarty vehemently denied this account of the guitar's origin, saying, "We spent a year designing that guitar, and Les never saw it until I took it to Pennsylvania."

In any event, a resort in Pennsylvania's Delaware Water Gap was indeed where their contract was signed in 1952. The five-year deal gave Les 5 percent of the proceeds from every guitar sold.

Les claimed credit for originating the choice of the instrument's two initial colors, and perhaps he did. "The two I picked out originally were the gold and the black," he recalled.

> And they said, "Why in God's world do you want gold? That's the worst color. It's gonna turn green on you." They were against it. And I said, "Because it's rich. Because it represents the best, the greatest, the highest." Okay, so gold it is. And then they says, "Okay, now what about the other one?" What other one? Well they were gonna make two. "Okay let's see, what will the other one be? Well, black." Why black? Because then the audience can see your hands. That's all it was.

Gibson went with gold for the first production run of the Les Paul guitar. The goldtop model was introduced during the spring of 1952 at a price of $210, about twenty bucks more than a Telecaster. The newcomer did well, selling 1,716 units in 1952 and 2,245 in 1953, outselling all other Gibson electrics except for the archtop ES-125, and equaling or beating the Telecaster's production numbers during those two years. The Gibson Les Paul's special connection with the blues started right away. Prominent among the first guitarists of note to adopt the instrument were bluesmen John Lee Hooker, Guitar Slim (Eddie Jones), Hubert Sumlin, and Freddie King.

WHATEVER ROLE Les Paul may or may not have played in the actual design of the guitar, there could hardly have been a better person to promote the instrument. In 1952, he closed a deal to produce and costar in his own television program, *Les Paul and*

Mary Ford at Home, sponsored by Listerine mouthwash. The show was a variation on the popular sitcom, a genre that had taken root during broadcast television's early days with programs such as *The Life of Riley,* which debuted in 1948, *I Love Lucy, The George Burns and Gracie Allen Show,* and *Amos 'n' Andy,* all debuting in 1951.

But, as usual, Les had a few ideas of his own as to how the thing ought to be done. Rather than adhering to the usual half-hour, once-a-week sitcom format, he talked Listerine into doing several five-minute shows daily, squeezing in dialogue, music, and of course a plug for the sponsor's product. And rather than broadcasting from a television studio, the show was shot at Les and Mary's home in Mahwah, New Jersey, where they had eventually settled after leaving L.A. The concept was quintessentially Les Paul. Why go to a studio when you could do it at home? Also, the five-minute spots were historic forerunners of music videos—a pioneering form of short-attention-span entertainment.

In terms of content, *Les Paul and Mary Ford at Home* was very much in the mid-twentieth-century spirit of upward-middle-class mobility, security, and comfort. The cozy, suburban domestic settings around Les and Mary's home provided a unique backdrop for musical performances. Mary would be singing a tune while unpacking groceries or tending houseplants. Presumably, few viewers stopped to wonder where the heavily overdubbed three- and four-part vocal harmonies were coming from. Casually sitting at the kitchen table or on a chaise longue on a flagstone patio, Les would tear off lightning-fast licks on his Gibson Les Paul guitar. The show served to contextualize the electric guitar—still fairly novel at the time—alongside the electric toasters, vacuum cleaners, and other handy implements of middle-class suburban life. It was an early instance of what's now called product placement.

The Gibson guitar that Les was most often seen playing on the program was a model that the company had introduced in 1954, the Les Paul Custom. A handsome black guitar with white binding—Les often compared it to a tuxedo—it differed from its goldtop predecessor in a few ways. Apart from the obvious difference in color, the body was solid mahogany, rather than mahogany with a layer of maple on top. This gave it a slightly darker tone. Also, the metal frets on the fingerboard were smaller and set lower than Gibson's usual standard, making fretboard fingering easier and more comfortable. For this reason the guitar was nicknamed "the Fretless Wonder." Of all the many iterations of his namesake guitar, the Custom was the one that Les Paul personally preferred.

The Gibson Les Paul had begun to morph from a single instrument to a whole range of guitars. In 1954, the company also introduced an affordable student model, the Les Paul Junior. It lacked the fancy carved top of higher-priced Les Pauls—just a plain slab body with a single P-90 pickup rather than two. But it nonetheless offered Gibson quality and sound. Decades later, the Les Paul Junior would find favor with punk rock guitarists such as Johnny Thunders of the New York Dolls, Mick Jones of the Clash, and Billie Joe Armstrong of Green Day. The guitar's low-budget minimalism would appeal to many punk guitarists both aesthetically and economically.

These new models arrived at a time when the solid-body electric guitar market was starting to heat up considerably. As we've seen, 1954 was the year when the Fender Stratocaster was introduced, substantially upping the game. The curvaceous Strat was definitely not a plain "slab" guitar that could have been produced by anyone with a band saw and a router. And its sexy modernist contours tended to make Gibson's more traditional designs look staid. Beyond that, the Stratocaster possessed a few technical refinements that appealed to serious guitarists, such as a bridge allowing the height and intonation of each string to be adjusted individually and with an appreciable degree of precision.

Ted McCarty certainly wasn't about to take that lying down. He came up with his own highly adjustable "tune-o-matic" bridge and a new "stopbar" tailpiece, which transferred string vibrations to the guitar's body more effectively than the more old-school "trapeze style" tailpiece that had been used on earlier Les Paul models. Starting in 1955, these two pieces of innovative hardware would become standard equipment on all Les Pauls and many other Gibson models, and are still very much in use today. They're a key ingredient in the winning Les Paul formula.

Another vital innovation made its debut in 1957—the humbucking pickup. This one wasn't McCarty's idea, but rather the work of Gibson design engineer Seth Lover. It was the first really significant innovation in guitar pickup design since George Beauchamp's invention of the device in the 1930s. Lover's design addressed a problem that had been inherent in guitar pickups ever since the thirties—their susceptibility to electrical interference that generated a bothersome, nonmusical noise known as 60-cycle hum. This is created when the pickup's coil—a length of electrical wire wrapped around a magnet—interacts with electromagnetic fields generated by other sources, such as stage lighting equipment.

Lover's concept was to employ two coils rather than one, with electrical current flowing in a different direction through the wire in each individual coil. This pattern of current flow serves to cancel out, or buck, electrical interference, aka hum. Which is why the design is called a humbucking pickup, often referred to colloquially as a "humbucker." However, it also cancels out some of the pickup's treble response. As a result, humbucking pickups have more of a bassy tone, which isn't necessarily better or worse than the bright, trebly sound of a single-coil pickup. It's just different, and, like all tonal differences, more appealing to some guitarists than others. The warm, dark, bass-heavy sound of humbucking pickups would become a characteristic tonality of many Gibson electric guitars, and a key differentiating factor between the Gibson sound and the brighter, more sparkly Fender sound.

•

GIBSON BEGAN TO incorporate humbucking pickups into their high-end electric models in 1957, including the Les Paul model introduced in 1958—the iconic guitar that would come to be known as the Les Paul Standard.

The guitar's cherry sunburst finish evoked Gibson's long tradition of woodworking craftsmanship. The design was implemented on the Les Paul as a way of reviving flagging interest in the instrument. By 1957, the goldtops and black Customs weren't selling as well as they had earlier in the fifties. Something was needed to impart a new dose of visual excitement; and rather than going for a brighter or more garish solid color, Gibson went in a more traditional direction, implementing their now legendary sunburst finish, derived from violin making. The guitar top's natural, flame maple-wood grain glowed warmly beneath lustrous layers of artfully applied varnish. Redolent of fine furniture, this upscale look would captivate even casual fans. And as the wood grain on each individual guitar is as different and distinctive as a fingerprint, future guitar collectors would go into raptures over these instruments (while simultaneously reaching for their checkbooks).

The Les Paul is a heavy guitar—literally as well as sonically. Thanks to its thick mahogany and maple body, it weighs a good deal more than most other electric solid-bodies. Shoulder pain and injuries are one liability of wearing a Les Paul on a shoulder strap for long periods of time. But this weight and density also impart to the guitar one of its most highly valued tonal qualities—a great deal of sustain.

What is sustain? Think of a violinist bowing a string. For as long as the bow is kept in motion, which can be indefinitely in the case of a skilled violinist, the note will continue to hold out—or sustain—without fading, diminishing, or dying out. In contrast, think of plucking a string on a ukulele. The resulting note dies out fairly quickly; not a lot of sustain. This is why ukuleles are ideal for rhythmic, staccato strumming, whereas violins are ideal for playing legato melodies. So the Gibson Les Paul, with its capability to produce violin-like sustained notes, proved an ideal instrument to realize the quest that had begun with Charlie Christian—to bring the electric guitar forward as a melodic instrument rather than just a tool for rhythmic accompaniment.

In this regard, Les Paul's own quest with his Log guitar—to isolate string vibration from the guitar body completely—was a failure. Even solid-body guitars vibrate in response to string vibration. This is part of the inherent organic nature of wood. So it isn't actually possible to hear what a guitar string sounds like "all by its lonesome" just by creating a solid guitar body rather than a hollow one. Even solid wood colors the instrument's tone. But this turns out to be a good thing, as the Gibson Les Paul eloquently demonstrates. Listen, for instance, to the opening electric guitar notes to Santana's "Black Magic Woman/Gypsy Queen," played by Carlos Santana on his Gibson Les Paul. Consider how the notes seem to swell or blossom outward. This is the quintessential Gibson Les Paul tone.

Unlike with the Fender Stratocaster, then, which is still essentially the same instrument today that it was when it was first introduced in 1954, it took a period of some four years for the Gibson Les Paul to come fully into focus. And while there are guitarists who prefer goldtops, P-90s, trapeze tailpieces, and other elements of early Les Paul models, it is the Les Paul Standard that has proven to be true to its name, becoming the gold standard for the Les Paul model. Ted McCarty had hit a home run.

BUT HE WASN'T about to stop there. The Gibson chief was on a roll in '58. Along with the Les Paul Standard, Gibson introduced four more McCarty designs that year. Three of these were to become institutions in the realm of electric guitars. The fourth became a legendary phantom, often spoken of but rarely, if ever, actually seen.

Of the three, the most conventional in appearance was the

Gibson ES-335. On the surface it looks very much like a traditional archtop hollow-body electric, although the body is substantially slimmer—a thinline electric, as it was known. But underneath the 335's classic-looking arched top is a solid block of maple, not unlike a two-by-four, running down the center of the body. The 335 is a hybrid instrument, what's known as a semi-hollow-body guitar. It was McCarty's attempt to combine the best attributes of both hollow-body and solid-body electrics.

"I preferred the tone of the acoustic," he recalled, "and I thought the solidbody was a little harsh. I was trying to get some of the tone of an acoustic guitar in a solidbody—to mix the two. And the tone of the semi-solid did come out as a mixture of the two sounds. You could play it without having it plugged into an amplifier."

Much like the Les Paul, the ES-335 was an immediate success that would blossom into an entire range of similarly designed guitars. The ES-345 and ES-355 are both upscale variants on the 335 design, offering fancier appointments and stereo output jacks, allowing these guitars to be plugged into two separate amps at the same time. Like the Les Paul, the 335/345/355 range would become a staple of both blues and rock playing. Eric Clapton would play a 335 during the end of his tenure with Cream, around 1968. Jefferson Airplane guitarist Jorma Kaukonen prominently played a 345 in the same era. And B. B. King is most closely associated with the 355, one of many Gibson models that he played, and on which he bestowed the name "Lucille."

But if McCarty was looking back to Gibson's glory days as king of the archtop jazz box, he also had his eye squarely on the future. He knew that, in order to truly beat Fender at the solid-body game, Gibson would have to embrace the same mid-century-modernist vibe that Fender had with the Stratocaster and other instruments in their product line. His competitive spirit was getting revved up.

"Fender was talking about how Gibson was a bunch of old

fuddy-duddys, and when I heard that through the grapevine, I was a little peeved," he recalled. "So I said 'Let's shake 'em up.' I wanted to come up with some guitar shapes that were different from anything else."

So McCarty hired some outside designers to submit drawings of modernist guitar shapes. One of the most striking was an instrument with a body in the shape of the letter V. The neck was attached to what would be the bottom of the V, and the two outswept body wings bore an unmistakable resemblance to the space-age tail fins that Cadillacs, Fords, Chevrolets, and other Detroit cars were sporting at mid-century, which in turn were a visual trope of rocketry. The strings were anchored through the body itself (in the manner of Fender guitars), via a V-shaped metal plate that also evoked automotive hardware. To complement the radically angular V-shaped body, the guitar's headstock came to a rounded-off point, like the business end of a medieval battle weapon. Gibson introduced the guitar as the Flying V in 1958, manufacturing it from African limba wood, which the company branded under the name Korina. The wood grain was similar to the mahogany used on Les Pauls but much lighter in color—a hue not at all dissimilar to the blond wood furniture of Heywood-Wakefield.

But McCarty didn't stop there. The Flying V was only the first in a projected series of guitars he designated the Modernistic line. This also included a guitar released in 1958 as the Gibson Explorer. The Explorer's solid Korina-wood body is like a Cubist re-imagining of what a guitar looks like—wildly geometric, with upper- and lower-body bouts jutting boldly outward at sharp angles. The body shape echoes Fender's Jazzmaster, also released in '58, but is arguably even more radically modernist.

For all their flashy, futurist looks, however, the Flying V and Explorer were tonally and functionally not much different from the Les Paul—with dual humbucking pickups, a tune-o-matic bridge, and a glued-in dovetail neck/body joint. And if McCarty was counting on the V and Explorer's cutting-edge appearance to make them a hit, he was surely disappointed. The Flying V was the first Modernistic guitar to be released in '58, and Gibson shipped a mere eighty-one of them that year, not doing much better over the following few years.

Right from the start, the V was something of an outsider's instrument—although some of those outsiders were highly influential. The Flying V became the signature guitar for bluesman Albert King, a left-handed player who just flipped standard right-handed Vs upside down, playing them in a decidedly nonstandard D-minor open tuning. Then there was pioneering American-roots man Lonnie Mack, who retrofitted his V with a Bigsby tailpiece jammed into a lower-body wedge like some gender-bending appendage. The V was taken up by Dave Davies of the Kinks, noted for having the longest hair of all the mid-1960s British Invaders and for slashing his amp's speaker to get a raunchy, distorted sound, hailed as the harbinger of heavy metal. Even Jimi Hendrix adopted the Flying V as a second guitar to his beloved Stratocaster.

But apart from this handful of influential mavericks, the Flying V and Explorer didn't really come into their own until the advent of heavy metal rock in the seventies and eighties. It appealed to metal guitarists because it had that big, fat Gibson sound like a Les Paul but with a look much better suited to the spandex, leather, and big hair of metal's visual aesthetic. Indeed, the foundation of the entire eighties metal "pointy guitar" aesthetic can be found in the Gibson Flying V and Explorer. It's as if these designs languished in relative obscurity, like ancient seeds sealed in some Egyptian tomb, awaiting the dawn of the Metal Age to germinate.

In 1958, however, the Explorer sold even worse than the Flying V. Gibson shipping records show only eighteen Explorers—simply designated "Korina (Mod. Gtr)"—leaving the factory in 1958, followed by a mere three in '59. Given this dismal showing, Gibson decided not to put McCarty's third Modernistic design into production. It was to have been called the Moderne. The upper body was exactly like that of a Flying V, but with a curved, more abbreviated lower-body contour that actually sits better in the lap or on the knee than the straight-angle Flying V. The Moderne's flared headstock—oddly reminiscent of the cartoon character Gumby's head—was a silhouette never seen before or again in guitar design.

As far as anybody knows, no actual Modernes were produced in the late fifties. But there has been speculation that Gibson might have created one or more prototypes during the period. These putative late-fifties Modernes have been mythologized by collectors, sometimes called the Loch Ness Monsters of vintage guitars. If one were to appear on the vintage market, it would surely claim an even higher sum than even the priciest '58–'60 sunburst Les Paul Standards. Gibson would eventually revive the Moderne design and put it into production during—when else?—the "hair metal" eighties.

Seen from a long-term perspective, then, McCarty was ahead of his time. Even in the short run, his late-fifties output—the proliferation of Les Paul models, the 335/345/355 family, and the Modernistic/Korina guitars—effectively augmented Gibson's perennially popular jazz-box electrics. Which means that McCarty accomplished exactly what Maurice Berlin had hired him to do. He reestablished Gibson's leadership role after the lean World War II years. But, strangely, none of the Gibson solid-bodies that are so highly revered today—the Les Paul, the Flying V, and the Explorer—was much of a success initially. All three only remained in production for a few years. By 1961, even the Les Paul as we know it today had vanished from Gibson's product line.

In 1961, the company introduced a radically redesigned Les Paul. While the pickups and bridge remained the same, the body was roughly half as thick and the old single-cutaway design had been replaced by dual cutaways that terminated in pointed horns. Although Les Paul posed with the instrument in a photo for Gibson's 1961 product catalog, he was always quite vocal about hating the new look. Eventually his name was taken off the instrument and it was rebranded the Gibson SG (short for "Standard Guitar").

Disagreements over the redesign of "his" guitar were just one problem that confronted Les Paul in the early 1960s, and a relatively minor one at that. The advent of rock and roll had made Les Paul and Mary Ford records such as "Mockin' Bird Hill" and "Tennessee Waltz" seem hopelessly outdated and quaint. Their reign at the top of the charts was all over by 1961, and they divorced that same year. Les was dropped from Capitol Records in '62, the same year the Beatles began their rise to fame in the U.K. Exacerbating these career and personal crises, Les was stricken with Ménière's disease in 1962 as well, undergoing a bone graft operation on the little finger of his left hand in an effort to combat what was becoming an increasingly severe arthritic condition.

Amid all these difficulties, Les's relationship with Ted McCarty and Gibson continued to unravel. The cordial socializing that Les and Mary once enjoyed with McCarty and his wife had fallen by the wayside. And because Les no longer had the big hits and mass popularity, his name wasn't as valuable to the company as it had once been. In 1963, his contract with Gibson came to an end. It was not renewed.

But while Les battled myriad life crises, McCarty continued his battle with Fender for supremacy. In the early sixties, as we've seen, Fender had begun to use bold, bright automotive paint colors on their guitars. And in '62 the company had introduced the Fender Jaguar—a deliberate riff on the most popular European sports car of the day.

Never a man to be left gaping at the starting line, McCarty engaged automotive designer Ray Dietrich to design a new guitar for Gibson. In the first half of the twentieth century, Dietrich had created seminal designs for Packard, Chrysler, and Checker Cabs;

but in 1960 he'd retired to Gibson's home city of Kalamazoo, at age sixty-six. McCarty coaxed him out of retirement and set him to work on Gibson's newest challenge to Leo Fender.

The body shape that Dietrich came up with is similar to that of the Gibson Explorer, only with more rounded-off corners. Perhaps to de-emphasize that similarity, Dietrich reversed the outline of his guitar, making the lower-body bout significantly larger than the upper one—the opposite of the Fender designs.

When Dietrich's guitar appeared on the market in 1963, it was named the Gibson Firebird—a fairly obvious marketing ploy to echo the name of Ford's popular Thunderbird automobile. (The Pontiac Firebird didn't come along until four years later, in 1967.) The guitar's Firebird logo, which appeared on the instrument's surface, even bears a certain affinity to Ford's Thunderbird logos from the same period, sharing a common root in Native American iconography. When Gibson introduced a bass guitar version of the Firebird, they named it the Thunderbird.

Fender responded to the Firebird's release by claiming that the body shape infringed upon Fender's patent for the Jazzmaster. Gibson would eventually acquiesce, introducing a redesigned Firebird in 1965. The original models weren't selling that well anyway, so the company went with a more conventional design, flipping the upper-body bouts to create what are known as "non-reverse" Firebirds. While the model never became as ubiquitous as the Les Paul, the Firebird nevertheless ranks as one of the classic Gibson solid-bodies of the McCarty era, universally hailed as a golden age in Gibson's history.

AND JUST AS the Jaguar was Leo Fender's final great design for the company that bears his name, the Firebird was McCarty's last hurrah at Gibson. He left the guitar-making giant in 1966 to assume leadership of the Bigsby company. McCarty and Paul

Bigsby had been close friends for a long time, and the Gibson chief's adoption of Bigsby tailpieces on many Gibson electrics had helped to establish the Bigsby brand. So when Paul Bigsby felt like stepping down from his company in 1965, McCarty bought the company and moved it from California to Kalamazoo, bringing with him Gibson production chief John Huis, who had worked on the Les Paul and other great guitars of Gibson's McCarty years.

It is both strange and significant that four of the most towering figures in the early development of the electric guitar—Leo Fender, Paul Bigsby, Ted McCarty, and Les Paul—all got out of the game just as the rise of rock and roll was making the electric guitar one of the hottest commodities in the world. Leo, as we've seen, sold Fender in 1965 and went into retirement. That very same year, Les Paul retired from playing music, plagued by escalating health issues and a desire to focus on his inventions. And while McCarty's move from Gibson to Bigsby wasn't exactly a retirement, it was a substantial scaling back of his sphere of operations. Paul Bigsby died in 1968. But Fender, McCarty, and Paul would return as folk heroes of the guitar business during the classic rock era of the late sixties, the seventies, and beyond.

Leo Fender would bounce back to head up the Music Man and G&L companies. And when players like Eric Clapton and Mike Bloomfield repopularized the Les Paul toward the end of the sixties, Gibson put the model back into production, starting in 1968. Les Paul himself would eventually be reinstated into the Gibson fold, reveling in the legendary status conferred upon him by the instrument that bears his name. By 1976 he was back to performing and recording again, and never quit until shortly before his passing in 2009. And while Ted McCarty would never return to Gibson, he would become a design consultant to PRS (Paul Reed Smith) Guitars in the early nineties—feted and revered as one of the men who put the electric guitar on the map.

But nobody could have quite foreseen all this in '65 when a young Eric Clapton bought his first Gibson Les Paul, just as Leo

Fender, Paul Bigsby, and the guitarist Les Paul were deciding to call it quits. It was a very different world when the endgame rivalry between Fender's Jaguar and Gibson's Firebird was being played out. But that polarity remains an apt metaphor for the vital Fender/Gibson dynamic that would become central to the electric guitar as we know it today. The Fender aesthetic is still more akin to a European sports car—cool, curvy, and nimble. Whereas the Gibson vibe is closer to a mid-century Detroit luxury sedan—brash, massive, and heavy on horsepower and wood-paneled élan. Neither is better than the other. They're just different, often complementary. The bright, sparkly Fender tonality tends to sound beautiful alongside the fat-bottomed Gibson timbre. The Fender/Gibson dialectic, moreover, would inform solid-body guitar design for decades to come. To this day, electric guitar designers and builders will define and describe their work by referring to either Gibson or Fender construction principles. Many have sought to unite the best qualities of both in a single guitar.

But it would take a while for this dialectic to become the primary driver of electric guitar playing and design. The sounds and styles of other guitar brands would continue to make their voices heard as the rock-and-roll phenomenon found greater life in the 1960s.

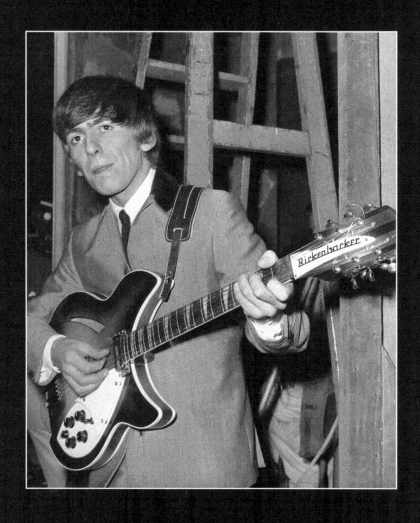

Rickenbacker's 360/12 electric twelve-string was an experimental new model in 1964; it took off once the Beatles' George Harrison adopted it.

THE FAB TWELVE

In New York City's cold, wet February of 1964, a series of interconnecting suites on the twelfth floor of the elegant Plaza Hotel was under a state of siege. Reporters, radio DJs, photographers, film crews, social climbers, hucksters, sharpies, and business opportunists of every description were working any angle they could manage in efforts to gain access. Right outside, on the southeast corner of Central Park, the icy pavements of Fifth Avenue and Fifty-eighth Street were mobbed with adolescent and preadolescent youths, mostly female, straining against police barricades that had been erected to prevent them from storming the entrances of the venerable neoclassical edifice. They too were willing to risk life and limb to get up to the twelfth floor.

In the half century since its opening in 1907, the Plaza had hosted royalty, movie stars, jet-setters, renowned authors, foreign dignitaries, and numerous other categories of VIP. But the hotel's seasoned staff had never witnessed anything quite like this. Even some of their own number, generally discreet to a fault, were silently hoping that a call for room or maid service might bring them to the twelfth floor. A special contingent from the Burns

Detective Agency was hired to stop interlopers who might attempt to get upstairs by presenting phony credentials or sneaking up a back stairway.

One person who found a welcome at the Plaza's besieged labyrinth of suites—sailing past the screaming throngs outside and tight security within—was an unassuming businessman in his mid-fifties named Francis C. Hall. He was the head of a modest-sized company in Southern California, and he had something that was very much of interest to the Plaza's twelfth-floor guests. Hall's company was the maker of Rickenbacker guitars.

Surrounded by assistants and one spouse, the preeminent occupants of the twelfth floor were four young rock-and-roll musicians from working-class Liverpool, England. They were a little nonplussed to find themselves the object of so much attention, but then it was much the same back home. Already a sensation of unprecedented proportions in the U.K., the Beatles were in New York to make their debut American performance on *The Ed Sullivan Show*, the popular TV variety program.

For that soon-to-be-historic telecast, which would draw a record 73 million viewers, the quartet's rhythm guitarist, John Lennon, would play a black Rickenbacker model 325 electric guitar that he'd purchased four years earlier in Hamburg, Germany. At the time of the purchase, the Beatles were just a bar band banging out rock-and-roll tunes in the seedy dives of the city's Reeperbahn red-light district. Lennon had subsequently played his Rickenbacker guitar on most of the early Beatles records that brought the group fame. The instrument had served him well, imparting a punchy, rhythmic sense of urgency to such tracks as the group's breakthrough American hits at the time, "She Loves You" and "I Want to Hold Your Hand."

And while the Beatles' lead guitarist, George Harrison, would be playing his Gretsch Chet Atkins Country Gentleman electric on the *Sullivan* show, he too was already a confirmed Rickenbacker fan. On a late-1963 visit to his sister in the United States, he'd purchased a solid-body Rick 425 at a music shop in Illinois. Harrison's 425 and Lennon's 325 had both done well for the band. The Beatles were keen to meet the man whose company made those fab guitars, and to check out a few new Rickenbacker models.

FRANCIS CARY HALL had already enjoyed a long and distinguished career in the electric guitar industry prior to his fateful encounter with the Beatles. The son of a Southern California shop owner, he'd inherited a keen business sense. By the late 1920s, when F.C. was still in his teen years, he'd found a way to monetize his youthful interest in electronics by manufacturing batteries at home and selling them through his father's store. This eventually grew into his own radio repair business, which by the late 1930s had evolved to become the Radio and Television Equipment Company (Radio-Tel), a major distributor of electronic parts and, eventually, Tele King television sets.

In 1946, Hall branched into another emergent technology, the electric guitar. Radio-Tel took on the distribution of the Hawaiian and lap steel guitars that Leo Fender had begun manufacturing. Also investing money in Fender's new enterprise, Hall played a vital role in the company's early success.

But in 1953, Fender decided to form its own in-house distribution company, effectively dispensing with Radio-Tel's services. So Hall purchased the Electro String company from Adolph Rickenbacker and turned his attention to developing and modernizing the Rickenbacker line of electric guitars.

The company had done well under Adolph's leadership, but it was still focused on the electric lap and pedal steel market that Electro String/Rickenbacker had launched in the thirties and had subsequently come to dominate. By 1953, however, it was clear that the times had changed. Hawaiian music and lap steels no longer enjoyed the widespread popularity they once did. And with the advent of the Fender Telecaster and Gibson Les Paul in the early fifties, it was clear that the electric Spanish guitar was the wave of the future.

The rock-and-roll explosion at mid-decade would escalate that wave to tsunami force. So, while maintaining Electro String's steel guitar market share, Hall set about developing a full line of Rickenbacker electric Spanish guitars, starting with the Combo 600 model in 1954. He also began courting alliances with the new breed of rock-and-roll guitarists and, for a while, had Ricky Nelson and his band playing Rickenbacker gear.

But the shift of focus from established American rock and rollers to a rising new British beat group was a quantum leap that would dramatically increase Rickenbacker's presence in the electric guitar market. It's important to bear in mind that the Beatles became huge in England a full year before they broke big in the States. At that time, Americans had much less awareness of what was happening in British life than they do today. Air travel was far less common; popular music, films, and television shows from the U.K. received little or no U.S. distribution. Post–World War II America just wasn't that interested in what happened overseas.

So how did Hall even know about the Beatles prior to their American breakthrough? The answer lies in the powerful sales and distribution network he had built up over the course of the preceding decades. A Rickenbacker regional sales rep named Harold Buckner had gotten wind of the Beatles' phenomenal rise to fame in the U.K. Also, the group's ascendancy had brought a wave of inquiries from several British companies hoping to land a contract to distribute Rickenbacker guitars—the Beatles' choice—in England. The contract ended up going to the Rose Morris company in England, who'd begun courting Hall quite aggressively, if cordially, even sending him newspaper clippings with photos of Lennon and Harrison playing their Rickenbacker guitars.

Lydia Catherine Hall—F.C.'s wife—began amassing a dossier on the Beatles, compiling a scrapbook that combined the clippings from Rose Morris with whatever other news items she could find on the group. (Mrs. Hall played an active role in her husband's business, perhaps most notably designing what would become the iconic Rickenbacker headstock logo.) Based on the data his wife had collected, Hall quickly saw the band's potential to become the biggest thing since Elvis Presley.

On January 2, 1964, Hall wrote to Buckner, saying,

> Buck, this is the hottest group in the world today, as they have the two top records by popular poll in Europe; and in addition, they have the top two LP albums for the same territory. If the boys are as popular in the United States as they are now in Britain, it will not be possible to make enough guitars to supply the demands. You may think I am boasting, but this is a fact.

Buckner's response was enthusiastic, but also cautionary. "Watch out for all those Fender promoters," he wrote, "or they'll have [the Beatles] playing [Fender] Jaguars and Piggybacks [that is, amps]. And don't say I didn't warn you."

So Hall got to work, contacting the Beatles' manager, Brian Epstein, in the U.K. Epstein was no stranger to working with musical instrument companies. He'd already negotiated a deal for the Beatles to use Vox amplifiers. By late '63/early '64, Epstein was being besieged by business offers, including licensing deals for Beatles wigs, dolls, lunch boxes, trading cards—a virtual avalanche of merchandise. He nonetheless found time to reply to Hall's query, which set up an exchange of transatlantic correspondence between the two men. In the end, an appointment was fixed for the afternoon of February 8, when the Beatles would be in New York to perform on *The Ed Sullivan Show.*

Hall enthusiastically wrote to Buckner: "I have a definite date to talk to the Beatles in New York; however *please* do not mention this to a soul, as I do not want our competition to know I will be in New York while they are there."

It was a major coup for Rickenbacker. Despite George Harrison's prominent use of Gretsch guitars, that company's own Jimmie Webster had failed to land an audience with the Beatles in '64. But somehow Hall had scored. Was it finesse? Timing? Sheer luck? Most likely a combination of the three.

F.C. and Catherine Hall traveled to New York in advance of the Beatles' landing there. They took a suite at the Savoy Hotel, near the Plaza, where the Beatles were staying. Joining forces there with Harold Buckner, they set up a display of Rickenbacker instruments and amps in their suite. It was similar to the kind of hotel-room marketing displays they were creating for trade shows at the time, only for a much more select audience in this instance. Cognizant of how much was riding on the occasion, Hall had even engaged Belgian jazz guitarist and harmonica player Toots Thielemans to entertain the lads from Liverpool. Thielemans's use of Rickenbacker guitars was what had influenced Lennon's purchase of one of the company's instruments back in Hamburg.

One can only imagine the level of anticipation in the room as the appointed time for the meeting drew near—let alone the consternation that must have arisen when the group failed to show up at the scheduled hour. But in due course the Savoy's telephone operator rang the suite with a message from Epstein: the boys were running a bit late, but they would be there shortly.

The Beatles had been at a rehearsal for *The Ed Sullivan Show* that afternoon. Or at least three of them—Lennon, bassist Paul McCartney, and drummer Ringo Starr—had been at the rehearsal. Harrison couldn't make it. He was confined to his bed at the Plaza with a case of the flu, hoping to recover sufficiently to perform well on the live telecast the following evening.

But once the three Beatles finished their rehearsal inside CBS-TV Studio 50 at Fifty-third Street and Broadway, they made their way over to the Savoy with Epstein and John Lennon's wife, Cynthia, in tow. On their arrival at the Rickenbacker suite, F. C. Hall presented them with a copy of their debut U.S. album, *Meet the*

Beatles, requesting that they autograph it. This was the first time Lennon, McCartney, or Starr had actually seen a physical copy of their first American record, and they were very pleased to do so. So Hall's gesture turned out to be an effective icebreaker.

Catherine Hall struck up a conversation with Cynthia Lennon, one that would result in a friendly exchange of letters and cards between the two women over the ensuing years. Meanwhile, the "boys" got busy with the guitars.

Among them was a new Rickenbacker model 325 for Lennon and a Rick 4001 bass for McCartney to check out. But of all the Rickenbacker guitars on display at the Savoy that afternoon in '64, the one that made the biggest impression was one of the company's brand-new instruments, a semi-hollow-body electric twelve-string guitar bearing the model designation 360/12 Deluxe. Lennon and McCartney both played it and were so impressed that they invited Hall and his party back to the Plaza to show the new twelve-string guitar to Harrison.

The problem, however, was that the horde of hysterical adolescents who had surrounded the Plaza had gotten wind of the fact that three of the Beatles were now at the Savoy. So they'd run the short distance to the second hotel and laid screaming siege to it, effectively blocking the Beatles' escape route. This kind of scenario had become an occupational hazard for the quartet and their management. Back in England, they'd evolved a whole set of strategies for evading frenzied fans, from sliding down laundry chutes to using decoy vehicles to distract overzealous well-wishers while the band escaped via another exit. But now they were in a strange city in a strange country, facing an unforeseen complication in a busy day filled with commitments and challenges.

And F. C. Hall found himself inside a scene that could have come right out of the Beatles' first feature film, *A Hard Day's Night.* Only this was real life, and there was a lot at stake for Rickenbacker's chief—an opportunity to increase his business exponentially. So Hall went down to the hotel lobby and had a word with the Savoy's bell captain. Hall was determined to find a way to get the Beatles, his own party, and the Rickenbacker twelve-string safely out of the Savoy and into the Plaza. He hadn't come this far to be thwarted by a mob of screaming kids.

The bell captain pondered the situation for a while, then remembered the existence of a tunnel leading from the hotel's basement to a discreet exit inside Central Park. He obligingly led the Lennons, McCartney, Starr, Epstein, the Halls, and Buckner down to a subterranean passageway. With F. C. Hall in possession of the 360/12 guitar, they traversed the tunnel's length, emerged in Central Park, and enjoyed a brief stroll over to the Plaza, which they entered unharassed, making their way up to the twelfth floor.

Sitting in bed in his room, Harrison was on the telephone doing a radio interview when Hall brought in the guitar. He played it for a while and even sang a little. The interviewer asked him if he liked the instrument, and he said, "Yes, it's a Rickenbacker."

It was one of those mystical meetings of player and instrument that would shape the course of popular music for decades to come. The plangent jangle of Harrison's Rickenbacker 360/12 on Beatles classics such as "I Should Have Known Better," "I Call Your Name," "You Can't Do That," and "Ticket to Ride" has become one of the great sonic signatures of mid-sixties pop music. In the process, the Rickenbacker 360/12 has been taken up by many hugely influential guitarists over the years, from Jim (Roger) McGuinn of the Byrds and Pete Townshend of the Who, to R.E.M.'s Peter Buck, U2's the Edge, and many others.

VOLUMES HAVE BEEN written attempting to explain the phenomenon known as Beatlemania. Certainly no prior British musical act had enjoyed anything approaching the Beatles' popularity in America, or indeed in the entire world. The Liverpudlian quartet were just four out of thousands of young Britons who had embraced skiffle music during the mid-1950s. Based on American folk music, skiffle favored amateur musicianship and a low-budget aesthetic that suited Britain's struggling post–World War II economy. All you needed for instruments was an inexpensive acoustic guitar, a serrated metal washboard for percussion, and a homemade bass fashioned from a broomstick anchored onto a metal washtub.

Like many of their generation, Lennon, McCartney, Harrison, and Starr had progressed from skiffle to the brand-new rock-and-roll sounds emerging from American artists such as Elvis Presley, Little Richard, Chuck Berry, Gene Vincent, Buddy Holly, and Carl Perkins, not to mention country music and Motown. Living in the port city of Liverpool, the incipient Beatles had access to more obscure records from the United States. American sailors would bring these discs with them when they landed in the city. This, for instance, is how Lennon got his fondness for the little-known R&B artists Larry Williams and Roy Lee Johnson, whose songs would be covered by the Beatles in their early career.

The Beatles had a few distinct advantages over other aspiring rock-and-roll groups of the day. Perhaps most important, they had a formidable songwriting team in Lennon and McCartney. At the time, it was still fairly unusual for recording artists in most genres to write their own material. Even major rock-and-roll artists, such as Elvis Presley, followed the time-honored music industry practice of recording material crafted by professional songwriters. Lennon and McCartney, however, had written the Beatles' first single, "Love Me Do," and it had become a hit. They next convinced EMI staff producer George Martin to go with another of their own compositions, "Please Please Me," as the Beatles' second single, rather than cutting the song Martin had selected, "How Do You Do It" by British tunesmith Mitch Murray. The latter song would indeed become a substantial hit for Gerry and the Pacemakers. But "Please Please Me" set the world on fire.

Second, of course, the Beatles were a damn good band. Their years in Hamburg had taught them to rock hard, play tight, and sing glorious three-part harmonies. Beyond just writing their own tunes, they represented a new kind of entity in rock and roll—a self-contained guitar and vocal band that had no distinct front person. The four of them came off as a collective phenomenon.

At the time, it was still very common for session musicians to play some or all of the instruments on recordings—even those by groups containing their own guitarists, drummers, and other instrumentalists. This was true of such groups as the Beach Boys and the Byrds, both of whom would score major hits that had instrumental tracks played by a group of L.A. session aces known as "the Wrecking Crew." The argument was that professional session musicians were more accomplished and disciplined. So they could nail a track more quickly than a young band that had just come up from the bars and clubs, thus saving hours of costly studio time. Session musicians could read music, and they belonged to musicians' unions, which was an important consideration in some territories.

But the Beatles were at the vanguard of new groups that shattered that whole system. It's true that George Martin had replaced Ringo with session drummer Andy White on "Love Me Do." But he soon came to realize that the collective energy the quartet generated on its own was far more valuable than a flawless or hassle-free performance.

And it was arguably the electric guitar itself that helped make this possible. Still a relatively new instrument at the time, it didn't carry the burden of tradition—the intimidating repertoire and legacy of virtuosity that belonged to instruments such as the violin, piano, or even saxophone. Rock guitarists were in the process of inventing their own tradition, forging their own vocabulary. As the players crafted their own guitar parts, an ability to read traditional music notation was of little or no value, and could even be a detriment to a player's authenticity. And authenticity would become a huge issue in the mid-sixties. The Beatles' recordings possessed a youthful exuberance that affected their young audience far more profoundly than the work of more accomplished session players "slumming" on a rock-and-roll date.

It was the start of an important paradigm shift in rock music. Rather than centering on the singing voice and visual image of one charismatic individual, a musical act's artistic identity began to be based on a distinctive *songwriting* voice that could be manifested by a group or an individual. Moreover, fans began to appreciate the unique playing style of each instrumentalist—how Ringo's approach differed from that of, say, the Rolling Stones' Charlie Watts, or the ways in which George Harrison sounded different from the Stones' Keith Richards. It was no longer enough just to sing well and look good. In the Beatles era and beyond, audiences began to favor artists who wrote their own material, played their own guitars, and had something to say for themselves, both in song and in interviews. It was the start of rock music's elevation from facile teenage entertainment to a valid art form—for many, the most important art form of the twentieth century.

As a result, the instruments played by this new breed of rock-and-roll artist would become a matter of supreme importance, even to the non-musicians among their fans. No longer a mere stage prop—which was essentially what it had been for Elvis—the guitar, particularly in its electric form, became charged with the mythic significance of Orpheus's lyre—an instrument imbued with a quasi-magical power to enthrall, entrance, and incite hysteria.

Of course, no one could have foreseen all this when the Beatles first hit America in '64—not even electric guitar manufacturers. Still, the Beatles' arrival and *Sullivan* debut conveyed a powerful sense that something completely new had landed on U.S. shores.

So the 73 million Americans who tuned into *The Ed Sullivan Show* on the evening of February 9 had a lot to digest—a kind of perceptual gestalt—when the Beatles took the stage. For some at the time, it seemed almost an overload of aural and visual stimuli. The quartet performed on a specially designed, modernist stage set, with geometric shapes veering inward in an exaggerated vanishing-point perspective, reframing the Beatles within the rectangular frame of viewers' television sets as if to say, "This is where it's at."

Along with wide-angle shots of the entire group, the camera came in for close-ups of each band member, giving more or less equal play to each Beatle. One round of individual shots offered subtitles with each band member's first name. Lennon's included the caveat, *Sorry girls, he's married*. For many viewers it was the first step toward discerning separate identities and personalities amid the collective phenomenon of four musicians in matching suits playing what seemed a radical new style of rock-and-roll music.

For nascent Beatlemaniacs, every detail seemed charged with significance. The group's hairstyles, devised by German artist Astrid Kirchherr, seemed shockingly in excess of standard male hair length at the time. In fact, much of the early American media coverage of the Beatles focused more on their hair than on their music. But while an older generation made bad-barber jokes, young viewers paid almost fetishistic attention to the Fab Four's hairstyles, their Cuban-heeled boots from London's Anello & Davide, and their stylish, slim-cut suits by London tailor Dougie Millings. Soon kids everywhere would be desperately scouring their hometown shops for anything remotely resembling these bold new fashions. Boys who could get away with it started growing their hair out and combing it down in the front, in emulation of Beatles hairstyles. Girls sought out clothes inspired by British couturieres such as Mary Quant—miniskirts and go-go boots. Fashion and music joined forces to create a dynamic new era in youth culture.

The Beatles' guitars commanded a huge amount of attention as well. They not only looked incredible, but were the source of this exciting new sound blasting from the minuscule speakers of several million home television sets. With its compact, violin-shaped body, Paul McCartney's left-handed, German-made Hofner 5000/1 bass guitar was the most traditional-looking stringed instrument on the stage that night (indeed, the Hofner company dates back to 1887). As such, it seemed to complement McCartney's persona as the nicest, homiest, most sensible Beatle—the one you'd least mind your daughter going out with. The Hofner 5000/1 became so closely associated with him that it would henceforth be known as "the Beatle bass," no matter who else played one. And the way McCartney wielded the instrument seemed to viewers an extension of his crowd-pleasing manner. He brought the headstock up close to his face and wiggled it each time the group went into one of its "Oooohhh" vocal harmonies, eliciting a collective, cathartic, and deafening wave of screams from the audience. On these cues, the television camera would cut to audience reaction shots. It was almost as if the bass's headstock were wired to the theater seats, transmitting a kind of electric current to fans each time McCartney wiggled it.

George Harrison's dark brown Gretsch Country Gentleman guitar seemed a trifle too large for him, enhancing his boyish charm as he picked and fretted the instrument with a look of stern concentration. With its bewildering array of gleaming knobs and switches, it seemed a very grown-up guitar. Harrison had chosen the Gretsch in emulation of the big archtop guitars played by his rock-and-roll elders and heroes—Carl Perkins, Eddie Cochran, and Duane Eddy, not to mention the seminal country picker Chet Atkins. He'd purchased it four months earlier at the Sound City music shop in London—his third Gretsch guitar, with several more to follow during his tenure with the Beatles.

But John Lennon's Rickenbacker 325, with its angular contours, was by far the most unconventional and modern-looking guitar played in the *Sullivan* telecast. Its slender black body blended with Lennon's black jacket in such a way that it seemed to disappear from view at certain camera angles—the instrument merging with the performer's body—leaving the impression that the instrument's body consisted solely of its semicircular pickguard. The guitar seemed to form part of Lennon's defiant, bowlegged stance. And while few viewers would have been able to pick out individual guitar lines, the joyous, clangorous wall of sound generated by these instruments telegraphed an incredible sense of exuberance and liberation for a generation of American baby boomers coming of age. Their peers all around the world felt very much the same.

F.C. AND CATHERINE HALL were present as the Beatles' guests at the historic *Sullivan* telecast. A portion of F.C.'s head is even visible in some of the footage from the performance. It is not known what the couple, then in their mid-fifties, made of the event, though their son John—the current head of Rickenbacker—got the impression that they weren't unduly impressed with the music. This culture-defining moment did, however, represent the realization of the dream F.C. had set in motion eleven years earlier, in 1953, upon purchasing the company from Adolph, when he'd embarked on the task of modernizing Rickenbacker.

One of Hall's first moves at that time had been to hire the German-born guitar designer Roger Rossmeisl. It was Rossmeisl who would go on to design the sharp-looking guitars that helped rocket Lennon and Harrison to fame.

A stylish, handsome man of twenty-seven when he joined the Rickenbacker staff, Roger Raimond Rossmeisl was the son of German jazz guitarist turned luthier Wenzel Rossmeisl and Elizabeth Rossmeisl (née Przbylla), a singer who performed under the stage name "Lollo." Wenzel gave his son some instruction in guitar building, but Roger also attended the prestigious Mittenwald school of instrument making in Germany. He eventually went to work for his father, who had launched a company producing

archtop jazz guitars. Wenzel had named the brand after his son—
Roger Guitars.

The company managed to survive the extremely difficult
World War II years in Germany. In 1946, Roger spearheaded a
move into electric archtops. But the company suffered a major setback in 1951, when Wenzel was jailed for a currency violation of
Germany's foreign exchange laws. Roger took over the business,
but he apparently lacked his father's management skills. Also, the
younger Rossmeisl's fondness for luxury and high living helped
bring the company to financial ruin.

To escape his creditors, Roger decided to immigrate to the
United States. He wrote to Gibson's Ted McCarty, who paid Rossmeisl's fare from Germany and gave him a job at the Gibson factory in Kalamazoo, Michigan. This, however, did not last very
long. Rossmeisl clashed with McCarty, who did not care for the
young man's ideas for improving on their classic designs. And at
this point, not long after World War II, Rossmeisl had apparently
fallen afoul of anti-German sentiment at the factory, particularly
among workers of Dutch descent.

So Rossmeisl used the pretext of vacation leave from Gibson
to travel out west and land a gig playing guitar on a ship bound for
Hawaii. Following the vessel's return voyage to L.A., he took a job
at Rickenbacker.

Rossmeisl's design work for Rickenbacker combined the Old
World classicism of Mittenwald violin-making; the jazzy flair of his
namesake, Roger Guitars archtops; and a sleek, industrial, modernist aesthetic that seemed attuned to the sensibility of Germany's Bauhaus school of design. He tended to simplify and sharpen
the angles of more traditional guitar designs. Some of the rounded
contours became more pointed. The traditional violin-style f-holes
became elongated slashes. Every surface and detail of the electric
guitar, as reimagined by Roger Rossmeisl, became streamlined in
a new, harmonious whole.

"Roger certainly had a sense of style and design," said John Hall, son of F. C. Hall and Rickenbacker's current owner, who knew Rossmeisl personally. "The guy was a real sharp dresser. He always had impeccable clothing—the latest styles. You can see that in photos of him. He also had a Sunbeam Alpine sports car. He had a real sporty kind of outlook on things."

While Rossmeisl's life would spiral tragically downward into alcoholism and an early death, his years at Rickenbacker represented a high point for him both professionally and personally. He and his wife would visit the Hall family at Christmas bearing lavish gifts. The presents were "very creative and unusual," the younger Hall recalled. In the late fifties, Rossmeisl designed the Rickenbacker Capri series of guitars, which would morph into the 300 series, which included both John Lennon's 325 and George Harrison's 360/12.

"He became the father of our modern Rickenbacker design," Hall said.

The twelve-string guitar had been around for ages in its acoustic form, finding a home in folk music and blues through the work of performers such as Leadbelly, Blind Willie McTell, and Pete Seeger. Where a standard guitar has six strings, a twelve-string has six *pairs* of strings, known as "courses." The two strings in each course are spaced closely together, so that the player's fretting finger can press both down simultaneously. The twelve-string guitar produces a bigger, more sonorous tonality than its six-string counterpart, a sound that Pete Seeger once described as "the clanging of bells."

Prior to Rickenbacker's introduction of the 360/12 in 1964, both Gibson and a tiny company called Stratosphere had attempted to market twelve-string electrics. But neither had met with any real success. Had it not been for the Beatles, the Rickenbacker twelve-string electric design might have fallen by the wayside, too—which would have been a shame, given both the visual and tonal beauty of the instrument.

In electrifying the twelve-string guitar, Rickenbacker introduced a few innovations. The way the courses were strung was slightly different, resulting in a new kind of tonality. Second, an ingenious new headstock arrangement had tuning keys for the principal strings facing outward, in the conventional manner, while keys for the doubled strings faced backward. It's a subtle difference to the non-player, but as Harrison is alleged to have said of the Rickenbacker's revised design, "Even when you're drunk you can still know what string you're tuning."

The Rickenbacker 360/12 that Hall brought to Harrison at the Plaza was the second ever manufactured. (The first went to Las Vegas entertainer Suzi Arden, a personal friend of Hall's.) Harrison ended up keeping the guitar for his own, and would later acquire a second 360/12, putting both to excellent use. Lennon would commission Rickenbacker to make him an electric twelve-string version of the small-bodied model 325 that he favored. Hall's hunch that the electric twelve-string's innovative design and distinctive sound would appeal to the guitarists in a groundbreaking musical group paid off in a big way. Design work on the 360/12 had begun in 1963, the same year that Beatlemania took hold in England, and in that regard the instrument and the group that made it famous were completely contemporaneous.

The Beatles' prominent use of both Rickenbacker and Gretsch guitars in the early years of their career brought about a tremendous increase in sales for both companies. In the pre–Fab Four 1961–63 period, Gretsch produced an average of 5,000 guitars per year. By 1965, at the height of Beatlemania, that number had jumped to 13,000 units per year. Harrison's preferred Country Gentleman 6122 was one of Gretsch's biggest sellers, with production jumping from an annual average of 200 in 1962 to 1,400 by 1965. At Rickenbacker, the story was much the same. The company had to move into a larger building to step up production, upgrading manufacturing equipment and employee compensation.

While Harrison generally deployed the Rickenbacker electric twelve-string for chiming, melodic guitar parts, he tended to use his Gretsches for grittier leads, and also passages that showed off the strong country influence in his playing, such as the concise, eloquently terse solo in "Can't Buy Me Love." Like many of their British Invasion contemporaries—perhaps most notably Keith Richards and Brian Jones of the Rolling Stones—Harrison and Lennon weren't locked into strict lead guitar/rhythm guitar roles. There was a greater freedom of interplay between guitarists in early- to mid-sixties rock music, before lead guitar became the rarefied domain of virtuoso players such as Jimi Hendrix and Eric Clapton.

ALONG WITH HAVING SPORTS CARS, mansions, and posh girl-friends, rock guitarists who land on top of the charts will most certainly spend their newly acquired cash on some new axes. The Beatles were no exception, amassing an array of Gibsons and Epiphones early on. But it's not so much the guitars themselves as what the Beatles did with them. They were brilliant innovators in the nascent field of rock guitar aesthetics, crafting both highly original chord progressions and a fascinating array of new guitar textures never heard before. Where jazz guitarists tend to innovate through harmonically clever and virtuosically dexterous note choices, remaining relatively indifferent to tone, rock guitarists tend to innovate sonically, often going to great lengths to coax arresting, startling, or mesmerizing sounds from their guitars, amps, and other equipment. It's a holistic approach that embraces the entire signal path, from strings to speakers. And, in a rock context, the Beatles are the towering figures at the dawn of this tradition—the gateway, if you will, to Hendrix, Townshend, Beck, and other rock titans.

The Beatles' 1964 single "I Feel Fine" opens with the first-ever deliberate and imaginative deployment of guitar feedback on a rock record. John Lennon and his bandmates had come upon the sound accidentally and decided to put it to creative use. They were fortunate in having a producer, George Martin, who was not only willing to adopt their unconventional creative ideas, but also able to provide the technical know-how necessary to implement them.

The Beatles also pioneered the use of "backwards" guitar for the solo in their 1966 song "I'm Only Sleeping"—achieved by recording a guitar part and then flipping the tape reels around on playback to create a surreal, dreamlike sound. This would become a hallmark of the psychedelic period, just getting under way at the time. No stranger to innovation himself, Paul McCartney was arguably the first musician to run a bass guitar signal through a fuzz pedal, which he did on the Beatles' 1965 recording "Think for Yourself." The same device was responsible for the guitar lead in the Stones' "Satisfaction," released that same year.

THE SUCCESS OF the Beatles in 1964 touched off a full-scale British Invasion of what were then called "beat groups" from the U.K. The Dave Clark Five, the Animals, the Rolling Stones, the Kinks, the Yardbirds, Herman's Hermits, the Hollies, the Zombies, the Searchers, the Moody Blues, Gerry & the Pacemakers, Manfred Mann, Freddie & the Dreamers, Billy J. Kramer & the Dakotas, and numerous other electric guitar–driven English rock-and-roll groups enjoyed massive worldwide hits in the mid-sixties. In the United States, the network television shows *Shindig!* and *Hullabaloo,* along with variety programs such as Ed Sullivan's and a handful of local rock-and-roll shows in major U.S. markets, afforded fans precious opportunities to see the new British groups in action.

In Great Britain, too, the Beatles and their contemporaries represented the first major new movement in rock-and-roll music and culture since the music's original breakthrough in the mid-fifties. And this time, it was a homegrown phenomenon. Young Britons eagerly tuned into ITV's program *Ready Steady Go!* each week to watch England's newest hit-makers perform their latest songs. But the new sounds created a great, and often hostile, divide in British youth culture. The fashion-forward Mods embraced the new British-made rock—particularly that of the Who, the Kinks, and Small Faces—along with the contemporary sounds of American Motown and Jamaican ska, known as "blue beat" at the time. On the other hand, there were the Rockers, who clung to the old sounds of artists such as Elvis and Gene Vincent and the 1950s "greaser" style, with slicked-back hair and leather motorcycle jackets. Asked by an interviewer in a scene from *A Hard Day's Night* if he was a Mod or a Rocker, Ringo Starr replied, "I'm a mocker."

The music of these new bands from Britain was all heavily influenced by American rock and roll, blues, and R&B. And they were playing it, for the most part, on Gretsches, Rickenbackers, Gibsons, Epiphones, and other American guitars. So why, then, did it sound so distinctly English? There are several factors, among them the cultural differences between the young British musicians and the predominantly African American artists they were emulating. But it would be difficult, in assessing the beat-group sounds coming out of the U.K. in the mid-sixties, to overestimate the role played by British-made Vox guitar amps. The sound of the British Invasion is very much the sound of Vox.

The amplifiers grew out of a partnership between businessman and accordion player Tom Jennings and guitarist Dick Denney, who first met during World War II while working at a munitions factory in Britain. The two men formed Jennings Musical Instruments (JMI) in 1957, and began producing amplifiers, and later other products, under the Vox brand name. JMI brought the first Vox amplifier, the AC15, to market in early 1958. Designed by Denney, the 15-watt guitar amp was markedly different from the amplifiers that Leo Fender and other American innovators had been designing and marketing. Vox amps employed different tubes and a different configuration of components to create a bright, highly dynamic tonality that would become closely identified with the "jangle" of the British Invasion sound. In the vivid language of noted amp expert, guitarist, Marshall amp design consultant, and former vice president of marketing for Fender Ritchie Fliegler, a Vox amp from this period is "on 10 and wailing the whole time it's on."

The 30-watt Vox AC30 was introduced in 1959, and remains one of the standards in rock guitar, still very much in use today. But the thing that really crystallized Vox's wow factor was the advent of the company's Top Boost circuit—essentially an extra treble control—for the AC15 and AC30. Top Boost is what's largely responsible for the brilliant timbre of something like the guitar intro to the Beatles' "Eight Days a Week."

Shortly after launching JMI and Vox amps, Jennings and Denney opened a retail shop at 100 Charing Cross Road in London, with a nearby manufacturing facility in Dartford, Kent. Their goal from the start was to get into the burgeoning market for electric guitar gear that had been initiated by the advent of rock and roll in the mid-fifties. They scored a major triumph in late 1959 when the Vox AC30 became the amp of choice for the Shadows, Britain's top rock-and-roll band at the time, led by bespectacled guitarist Hank Marvin. The Shadows had a dual-pronged career. On the one hand, they were the backing band for the popular U.K. rock-and-roll singer Cliff Richard, sometimes described as "the English Elvis Presley." But the Shadows also released a very successful string of guitar instrumental tracks on their own. When they deployed their Vox AC30s on their 1960 instrumental hit "Apache," it did not go unnoticed.

Most of the young, soon-to-be British Invaders were huge Shadows fans. "Before Cliff and the Shadows, there had been nothing worth listening to in British music," John Lennon once said. Lennon and Harrison had named an early instrumental of theirs "Cry for a Shadow" in honor of the group, emulating the Shadows' sound and style.

So it was no mere whim that brought Brian Epstein into

JMI's Charing Cross Road shop in July of 1962. He offered store manager Reg Clarke a deal: If Clarke would supply the Beatles with free Vox amps, the group would agree to use Vox amplification exclusively and also lend their image, likeness, and words of endorsement to Vox ads and other promotional endeavors—a true PR and marketing bonanza. Of course, the Beatles were still a virtually unknown commodity in the summer of '62. They'd just barely managed to secure their recording contract with EMI, having been turned down previously by Decca. They had yet to score any hits. But Epstein nonetheless assured Clarke that his boys were going to be "very big indeed."

Clarke phoned his boss, Tom Jennings, to ask what he should do. The store manager later said he would never forget Jennings's response to Epstein and his offer: "What does he think we are, a fucking philanthropic society?"

Clarke nonetheless made a pact with Epstein, thereby saving himself and Jennings the ignominy of going down in history— along with Decca Records' Dick Rowe—as men who had been foolish enough to turn down the Beatles. And so John Lennon and George Harrison each got a tan Top Boost AC30. These were promptly put to use onstage and, on September 4, 1962, at Abbey Road Studios in London, where the Beatles recorded "Love Me Do." Paul McCartney got his first Vox bass amp in early 1963. JMI would continue to supply the Beatles with Vox gear throughout their career, crafting louder and louder amps to compete with the decibel levels generated by audiences filled with screaming young Beatlemaniacs.

Like everything else surrounding the Beatles, Vox amps looked as fabulous as they sounded. While Dick Denney brought engineering talent to the equation, it was Tom Jennings who had a flair for stylish visual design. The amps' diamond-pattern grille cloths, bold VOX logos, and space-age chrome stands all became vital British Invasion signifiers.

Tom Jennings had obviously changed his tune about philanthropy. By the mid-sixties, Vox product catalogs were proudly displaying a photographic who's who of British Invaders, including the Rolling Stones, the Kinks, the Animals, the Dave Clark Five, Manfred Mann, the Hollies, the Searchers, and many others. Also seen with their stacks of groovy Vox gear were several of the British Invaders' key American counterparts, such as the Standells, the Sir Douglas Quintet, and, fittingly enough, Paul Revere & the Raiders.

OF ALL THESE new rock-and-roll groups, it was of course the Rolling Stones who had claimed a place right alongside the Beatles at the top of the heap. The Stones' manager, Andrew Loog Oldham, shrewdly saw the efficacy of marketing the Stones as a kind of anti-Beatles. To young rock-and-roll audiences at the time, the Rolling Stones offered a kind of primal, dark, Dionysiac alternative to the Beatles' more sunny, well-groomed Apollonian appeal.

While a lot of this was just media hype, there was nonetheless an essential difference between the Beatles and Stones. It was—and remains—immediately discernible in their music. Unlike the Beatles, the Stones started out as blues and R&B purists. While they'd been profoundly affected by the birth of rock and roll in the mid-fifties, they'd focused their attention on the music's African American antecedents in a way that the Beatles hadn't. A big part of it was being from London, where a small but enthusiastic blues/R&B scene had grown up.

It had originated in an enthusiasm for "trad," or traditional African American jazz—what we might now call Dixieland or New Orleans jazz—that had taken hold of England in the fifties. Trad was part of a larger appreciation in Britain at the time for the many genres that make up what is now called Americana, or American roots music. A key figure on the trad scene was trombone player and bandleader Chris Barber. He'd touched off the skiffle craze by fostering the career of guitarist, banjo player, and vocalist Lonnie Donegan.

And—perhaps more significant, given the direction guitar-based rock music would take over the next three decades—Barber also brought African American blues into the U.K. by promoting concert appearances and tours by seminal bluesmen such as Big Bill Broonzy, Muddy Waters, and the harmonica/guitar duet of Sonny Terry and Brownie McGhee. In the audience for many of these early blues dates, assiduously taking in every detail, were future British rock stars such as Eric Clapton, Jeff Beck, and, of course, the Rolling Stones.

One of the bluesiest elements in many of the early Stones recordings is electric slide guitar, often played by one of the group's founding members, Brian Jones. A heavy hitter on the London R&B scene—arguably heavier, at that time, than the Stones' cofounders, Mick Jagger and Keith Richards—Jones is often credited as the first musician in England to play slide guitar. Performing at early London venues such as the Marquee and the Ealing Jazz Club, he had even billed himself as Elmo Lewis—a tribute to American bluesman and slide guitar pioneer Elmore James, combined with the first part of the young guitarist's given name, Lewis Brian Hopkin Jones.

It was also Jones who gave the Rolling Stones their name, appropriating the song title "Rollin' Stone" from pioneering bluesman Muddy Waters. Even more so than the music of Elmore James, Waters's music would have a tremendous influence on the Stones. Sharing a squalid London flat with Jagger and another friend, Jones and Richards would spend hours listening to records.

"When we started playing together," Richards said, "we were listening to Jimmy Reed and Muddy Waters—the two-guitar thing, the weaving. We did it so much, which is the way you have to do it. So we both knew both guitar parts. So then you get to the point where you get it really flash and you suddenly switch—

the other one picks up the rhythm and the other one picks up the lead part."

"I hope they don't think we're a rock and roll outfit," Mick Jagger told London music rag *Jazz News* in '62. This quote was often cited ironically in later years, when the Stones became known as "The World's Greatest Rock and Roll Band." But it was an important distinction to make in London of 1962.

"British R&B bands, we called them at the time," recollected Giorgio Gomelsky, who managed both the Stones and the Yardbirds early on, and ran London's "most blueswailing" nightclub, the Crawdaddy. "Because rock and roll was not that. It was considered white, surfing, teenybopper music—the corporate rock of that time. All these people like Fabian, these sort of pseudo Elvis Presleys."

Even in '62, though, there was a note of hypocrisy—or perhaps just plain hype—in Jagger's claim that his band was not "a rock and roll outfit." The early Rolling Stones would cover Chuck Berry and Buddy Holly songs, just as the Beatles would do. But aligning oneself with more traditional African American styles was a badge of authenticity on the tiny London scene that fostered the early Stones. Two early Stones members, Geoff Bradford and Brian Knight, had actually quit the band because they took exception to Richards's fondness for Chuck Berry.

"The very little budding blues scene in England—all four hundred of us—were split into two camps," according to Gomelsky. "'That version of Chuck Berry is not blues.' 'Yeah, but that version of so-and-so is not rhythm and blues.' *Blues Unlimited,* one of the big fanzines at the time, were distributing pamphlets. All these disputes were going on and at the same time bands were playing and the scene came about. And [the disputes] didn't make any difference afterward."

In this context, it's significant that the Rolling Stones' first single was a Chuck Berry cover, "Come On," released in June of 1963. It was rock and roll enough to launch the Stones out of the insular London R&B scene and into the same wide world of hysterical teenage fan adulation that the Beatles had both generated and attracted.

"We were a blues band," Richards commented years later, "[but] we made just one little pop record and it became a hit. Or semi-pop. And suddenly chicks screamed at you and you're not playing for anybody anymore. You're just wondering how the hell you're going to get off this stage and safely get out of this town before you get ripped to shreds . . . Weird, manic. And you're thinking, 'But I'm a blues player!'"

"The Stones weren't really a girls' band, man," Gomelsky reflected. "None of the R&B bands were. Ninety percent males used to come to the shows, among them the Pete Townshends, Eric Claptons, and Jimmy Pages . . . all those people. The Beatles were more a girls' band. But, in the end, you can't resist the sexual economics."

Which is to say that the Stones were a gateway to the blues for many young musicians and listeners, both American and English. By covering so many blues classics by artists such as Muddy Waters and Howlin' Wolf, the Rolling Stones aroused a powerful curiosity about the originals in the minds of adventurous young guitarists seeking new sounds and inspirations. With a dearth of written information about these artists available at the time, Stones fans traced down the names in the songwriting credits on the group's albums and singles. (*Who is McKinley Morganfield? Ah, it's this guy they call Muddy Waters. Who the hell is Chester Arthur Burnett? Oh, that's Howlin' Wolf.*)

It was an act of cultural appropriation, certainly. But the Rolling Stones in particular were eager to share the limelight with their blues heroes, exposing them to an enthusiastic new audience that, in years to come, would provide African American bluesmen with a significant new source of income in record sales and song royalties. One of the Stones' greatest coups was to arrange for Howlin' Wolf to perform on America's premier pop-music television program, *Shindig!*, in 1965. The sight of a large, black man in his mid-fifties shakin' his thang before an audience of somewhat bemused white American teenagers and a spellbound Brian Jones remains one of the strangest and most evocative video artifacts of the mid-sixties.

Much like the bluesmen of old, Keith Richards and Brian Jones started out playing fairly modest electric guitars made by Harmony, the American company that specialized in affordable instruments, selling many through retail outlets such as Sears in the States. Jones played a Stratotone and Richards a Meteor. But they gradually worked their way up to better guitars as the Stones' popularity grew, Jones gravitating toward a Gretsch Anniversary model and Richards an Epiphone Casino, both hollow-body instruments. High-quality electric guitars were still hard to come by in the U.K., as indicated by the fact that Lennon and Harrison had bought their Rickenbacker electrics in Germany (where distribution was a bit more reliable) and the United States, respectively.

Fame brought the Stones their own endorsement deal with Vox. An early Vox promo shot captures the brief period when the Rolling Stones wore matching band outfits, featuring leather vests. Many of the early Stones recordings, not to mention live shows, were done on Vox amps, principally AC30s. Jones also became closely associated with the teardrop-shaped Vox Mark III electric guitar. The idea for the instrument came from Vox chief Tom Jennings, as part of his ongoing quest to position Vox as makers of not just amps but the absolutely coolest-looking instruments on the scene. To that end, Jennings instructed Vox chief design engineer Mick Bennett to craft an electric guitar with a body shape resembling that of a lute. The prototype was given to Brian Jones.

It was an obvious choice. The visual reference to the Renaissance lute suited Jones's romantic public image. His fluffy mane of "Prince Valiant" blond hair had always set him apart, giving him an air of almost feminine vulnerability that appealed to young girls in a powerful way. Jones was always the most flamboyant dresser among the Stones, and the uniquely shaped white guitar seemed an extension of his image and persona, much in the same way that Lennon's Rickenbacker 325 was part and parcel of his identity as a performer. Vox also made a twelve-string version of the Mark III for Jones. They created a teardrop-shaped bass guitar for the Stones' bassist as well, marketed as the Vox Bill Wyman model. Production models of all these teardrop instruments, as well as the more angular Vox Phantom models, became highly sought-after items among up-and-coming guitarists and aspiring future rock stars during the mid-sixties.

Instrumentally, Brian Jones was the Stones' most "outside the box" thinker. It was he, for instance, who took a metal slide to a Rickenbacker electric twelve-string to create the signature riff on the band's 1966 hit "Mother's Little Helper." This was far from standard procedure. The guitar, moreover, was just one of many instrument choices for Jones. He played harmonica predominantly on a lot of the early Rolling Stones recordings. And as the group developed stylistically, he branched out into a kaleidoscopic array of instrumental colors—Indian sitar, Appalachian dulcimer, recorder (the wooden flute heard on "Ruby Tuesday"), marimba, organ, piano, saxophone, and pretty much anything else that came to hand in the recording studio. This became a key role for him as Jagger and Richards's ascendancy as the Stones' songwriters thrust them into a leadership position that Jones once saw as his own.

"Brian was always searching for another sound," Richards recalled. "As a musician he was very versatile. He'd be just as happy playing marimba or bells as he would guitar. Sometimes it was, 'Oh make up your mind what sound you're going to have, Brian!' 'Cause he'd keep changing guitars. He wasn't one of those guys who said, 'Right, here's my axe.'"

Jones's multi-instrumental tendencies, combined with his drug-fueled personal decline, would lead Richards to assume a more prominent guitar role as the sixties progressed. In August of 1964, Richards acquired what would become an iconic instrument for him—a 1959 Gibson Les Paul Standard equipped with a Bigsby tailpiece that had been installed by the instrument's previous, and original, owner, British guitarist John Bowen. It became Richards's main guitar between '64 and '67, seen by many Americans for the first time when he played it on the Rolling Stones' debut *Ed Sullivan Show* performance, on October 25, 1964.

"It was my first touch with a real great, classic rock and roll electric guitar," Richards said in 1997. "And so I fell in love with [Les Pauls] for a while."

Richards's 1959 Gibson Les Paul Standard has become the stuff of rock-and-roll legend. Stories circulated that it is the same guitar later owned by Eric Clapton and Jimmy Page. (It's not.) In 1967, Richards sold the guitar to Mick Taylor, who within two years would become Brian Jones's replacement in the Rolling Stones. But as the existence of the myths themselves attest, Richards's 1959 Gibson Les Paul Standard has come to be regarded with awe. It's seen as a gateway instrument—a harbinger of the late-sixties age of the guitar hero. Shortly after Richards took up the Les Paul Standard, guitar icons such as Eric Clapton, Jimmy Page, and Mike Bloomfield all did the same, playing that instrument on some of their most significant recordings. So, just as the Stones turned a generation of guitarists onto the blues through their covers of songs by Muddy Waters, Howlin' Wolf, and other American bluesmen, "Keef" is seen as forging the path that made the Les Paul Standard one of the most important instruments in rock history.

AMONG ITS MANY other contributions to popular culture, the British Invasion era gave the world some of the greatest electric guitar hooks ever recorded. In this area as well, the Beatles and the Stones were at the head of the pack. The mid-sixties rock-and-roll market was very much based around hit singles rather than album sales. In order to stay in the game, groups had to come up with a new chart-topping track every month or so. An attention-grabbing introductory guitar riff was an essential part of the format. Guitar intros had been around since the dawn of rock and roll in the fifties in the exemplary work of guitarists such as Chuck Berry and Carl Perkins. But these intros were often just that, a perfunctory two or four bars of electric frenzy that would then give way to a vocal and never be heard again, except perhaps at the end of the song.

The art of the almighty riff hit a new height in the mid-sixties. Designed to grab and hold the listener rapt, the riff would not only introduce the tune; it also become an integral part of the song's spine, underpinning a verse vocal melody, as in the Beatles' "Day Tripper," or driving home a money-shot chorus vocal, as in the Rolling Stones' "Satisfaction." Chordal arpeggios and patterns, such as those in the Animals' "The House of the Rising Sun" or the Searchers' "Needles and Pins," could be equally effective. The tone of the electric guitar was in itself a signifier of excitement. Perhaps the greatest example of this is the single guitar chord that opens the Beatles' "A Hard Day's Night." The timbre of Harrison's Rickenbacker 360/12 through a Vox amp, shadowed by Lennon's Gibson J-160E, also played through a Vox, is a musical statement in itself.

One key difference between the Stones and the Beatles is that the latter were working in the studio with a formally trained musician and record producer, George Martin, whereas the Rolling Stones' earliest recordings were produced by their manager, Andrew Loog Oldham. Both were excellent producers in their own right, but they were very different in style and approach. Martin was somewhat older than the members of the Beatles, an avuncular figure who was very open to the group's creative ideas but also made sure that everything went down to tape in accordance with proper EMI technical standards. Oldham was somewhat closer in age to the Stones, and had had no prior experience as a record producer when he began working with them. As a result, the artist/producer relationship was more one of lads running amok together in the studio. Also, while the Beatles almost always recorded in the familiar and controlled environment of EMI's Abbey Road Studios in London, the Stones ventured further afield into less familiar studios on less familiar turf. They worked at the RCA facility in Hollywood, and Chess Studios in Chicago, where their heroes Muddy Waters, Howlin' Wolf, Little Walter, and others had made historic blues recordings.

All of which contributed to a perception of the Rolling Stones as having a more raw sound than the Beatles. This in turn fueled the Stones' image as a dangerous, outsider alternative to the Beatles. However cordial relations between the two groups may have been, "Stones vs. Beatles" became the dialectic that defined much of pop music in the mid-sixties. Bands tended either to be rough and ready, Stonesy, bluesy, R&B-inflected outfits—like the Kinks, the Who, the Animals, and the Yardbirds—or more Beatlesque groups with pristine vocal harmonies, in the manner of the Hollies and the Zombies. Needless to say, their guitar choices were also often based on those of the band(s) they emulated.

THE PROFOUND CULTURAL impact of the British Invasion did much to encourage teenagers on both sides of the Atlantic to get hold of some electric guitars and form rock-and-roll bands in the basements and garages of their parents' homes. If anything was more exciting than growing your hair out and suiting up in groovy Mod gear, it was kitting yourself out with an electric guitar and amp, recruiting some friends, and actually trying to make music like the Beatles, the Stones, and other British Invaders.

As a result, the demand for electric guitars went through the roof. At the top of the food chain, premier American makers such as Gibson, Fender, Gretsch, and Rickenbacker all went into manufacturing overdrive. But a flood of inexpensive foreign imports from Japan, Germany, Sweden, Italy, and other countries began to flow into both the U.S. and the U.K. Teisco Del Reys, Kents, Silvertones, Ekos, and Hagstroms were among the overseas brands often sold through department stores rather than specialist music shops. American brands such as Harmony, National, Valco, Kay, and Airline also came in at bargain prices. Many were starter instruments, some better than others. Players who showed some ability and genuine interest might move on to a higher-quality guitar.

So the British Invasion was to guitar music roughly what the Gutenberg Bible and advent of printing had been to literacy. It touched off a cultural explosion. Playing music—and specifically electric guitar music—became a vernacular pursuit, the musical voice of the masses. And garage bands became the primary arena for this new musical conversation.

The garage rock groundswell that had begun with the rise of amateur surf instrumental bands a few years earlier gained dramatic momentum in the months and years after the Beatles' early-1964 U.S. debut on *The Ed Sullivan Show*. By the mid-sixties, garage rock had emerged as a distinctive rock-and-roll subgenre in its own right, with regional, national, and sometimes international hits by garage outfits such as the Standells, the Shadows of Knight, Question Mark & the Mysterians, the Music Machine, Music Explosion, the Sonics, and the Knickerbockers. The sound tended to be a few shades raunchier than the Stones or the Kinks at their rawest, and the overall garage band aesthetic was a bit more low-budget than what the bigger English and American groups were doing at the time. But that was all part of the appeal. The "anyone can do it" accessibility of mid-sixties garage rock would become a major inspiration for punk rock a decade later, not to mention several garage rock revivals.

With young guitarists on both sides of the Atlantic seizing Rickenbackers, Gretsches, and other electric guitar models, the British "Invasion" had given way to an impassioned, creative, two-way dialog between British and American rock musicians. By 1965, musical ideas and influences were traveling both ways, back and forth across the Atlantic at the speed of sound. This dynamic cultural exchange would shape the course of rock music in the decades that followed. The shared basic language of this inspired détente was the broad lexicon of American roots music. But in embracing it as their own, the Beatles, the Stones, and other British groups transformed it into something new and exciting. And in bringing it all back home, the Americans took British innovations and traditions on board. The strategic alliance that made all this possible, the marriage of American guitars and British amps, proved to be one made in rock-and-roll heaven.

The 1968 Fender Stratocaster that
Hendrix played at Woodstock sold
for $2 million in 1998.

chapter 8

THE REVOLUTION
WILL BE AMPLIFIED

Facing the largest audience he'd ever played to in his life, Jimi Hendrix flashed the peace sign with his left hand as his right began fingering a melody on the maple fretboard of his white 1968 Stratocaster. The tune was a familiar one, although not one of Hendrix's many hits. Recognition rippled like an electric current through the rain-soaked, mud-sodden, drug-hungover but still largely jubilant crowd that had made it through to the final performance at the Woodstock Music and Art Fair on the morning of August 18, 1969.

Hendrix was playing "The Star-Spangled Banner."

It was an unusual song choice for a rock show. But even more striking was what the guitarist did with it. His interpretation of the well-known composition's first few phrases was faithful to the original, if decidedly nonchalant. While playing, he reached across to adjust the tuning on his guitar, something that had been giving him trouble throughout his set at Woodstock. But at the conclusion of the melodic phrase that accompanies the line "through the perilous fight," Hendrix began to embellish the melody with improvised trills and melismas, claiming the age-old patriotic tune as his own—and on behalf of the newly fledged Woodstock Nation.

But mayhem didn't truly break out until the part about "the rockets' red glare." That's when Hendrix stepped on one of the effects pedals at his feet, unleashing an explosion of wild, atonal, freeform guitar feedback. This in itself was nothing new. Hendrix and other guitarists had been exploring the disruptive musical potential of guitar feedback for several years prior to this. But here he was putting the sound to thematic use—taking a well-known hymn to an American battle victory as an occasion to plunge his listeners into the chaotic and disquieting sonic reality of battle itself. And he was doing so at a time when resistance to America's involvement in the Vietnam War had reached a fever pitch among youth culture. The message was not lost on his audience. Although the performance was strictly instrumental—everyone knew the words anyway—Hendrix was employing his electric guitar to make an eloquent and impassioned political statement.

The ominous duotone wail of a European police siren blasted from Hendrix's Marshall amps to accompany—and offer mutely ironic comment on—the line "the bombs bursting in air." Hendrix was yanking vigorously on the Stratocaster's vibrato arm, eliciting descending shrieks in a playing technique that would come to be known as "divebombing." But perhaps the most poignant moment followed the melodic passage for the line "that our flag was still there." Here Hendrix played taps, the mournful bugle melody performed at military funerals. At that point, some 30,000 American lives had been lost in President Lyndon Johnson's escalation of the Vietnam War.

By the time the piece's concluding chords rang out, it was clear that Jimi Hendrix had done something truly radical with the electric guitar. Something that outshone even his prior stellar accomplishments on the instrument. In the years immediately preceding Woodstock, the electric guitar had accompanied many songs of protest and conscience. But in Hendrix's masterful hands the instrument itself did the talking. He had transformed the electric guitar into an instrument of political commentary and social change.

Looking on from backstage, Michael Lang—the Woodstock festival's idealistic, youthful, curly-haired promoter—was deeply moved by Hendrix's performance.

" 'The Star-Spangled Banner' really spoke volumes to everything we were doing," Lang later commented. "Everything we'd been through."

If a poll were taken to determine the single most influential electric guitar performance in the instrument's entire history, the majority of votes would most likely go to this tour-de-force musical moment. For many, the very words "electric guitar" will immediately evoke visual images of Hendrix at Woodstock, attired in a Native American–style white leather tunic, fringed and turquoise-beaded, with a red headband wrapped around his Afro, his white Stratocaster hanging upside down from a shoulder strap (which is how the left-handed guitar titan played it). The instrument he played that day has itself taken on the aura of a holy relic. Purchased for a reported $2 million in 1998 by Microsoft billionaire Paul Allen, the Hendrix Woodstock Strat now resides in the collection at Allen's Experience Music Project Museum in Seattle, where thousands annually make a pilgrimage to see it.

Apparently, though, Hendrix's performance of "The Star-Spangled Banner" at Woodstock was an impromptu one. If he'd been planning to do it, he hadn't shared that information with his bandmates. They were as surprised as the audience when he whipped it out.

"On that song, Jimi started and I played the first five or six notes with him," recalled Billy Cox, Hendrix's bassist at Woodstock. "Then I said, 'Wait a minute, we never rehearsed this before. This is quite different.' And it was 'The Star-Spangled Banner,' one of the greatest solo songs of the festival."

Legendary as it is, however, the Woodstock set was hardly one

of Hendrix's greatest live shows. Incessant rain and poor organization combined to create a performance space that posed a
formidable challenge for all the artists who played at the festival.
Backstage amenities were few and mud-sodden. The stage itself
was still being built as the musicians played. Giant cranes and
other construction equipment can be seen in the background in
photos and film footage of Hendrix and other acts.

"The rain really put a wrinkle in the electrical connections,
power . . . all of that stuff," recalled bassist Jack Casady of Jefferson Airplane, who also performed at Woodstock. "They tried to
put up a couple of tarps to keep the rain off the stage. But the tarps
just became water collectors. They'd start to sag and the water
would come gushing down onto speakers, amplifiers, and everything. So there was a serious danger of getting a nasty shock, if not
electrocuted outright."

The moist conditions also wrought havoc with the tuning of
Hendrix's Stratocaster. But even more significant, he was backed
that morning by the under-rehearsed and ill-prepared Gypsy Sun
and Rainbows, an ad hoc aggregation of musical colleagues and
jam buddies that Hendrix had recently put together following
the mid-1969 dissolution of the group that had brought him to
fame, the Jimi Hendrix Experience. Drummer Mitch Mitchell,
a veteran of the Experience, was the only player besides Hendrix
who'd had prior experience performing for a really large audience,
although the Woodstock crowd outnumbered any audience they'd
previously faced.

"Jimi looked out [at the audience] and said, 'Oh my God,'"
Cox recalled, "because he had never played for that many people.
Mitch just said, 'Oh,' and I said, 'Why did you guys get me in the
middle of this?' But Jimi looked at it with his infinite wisdom and
he says, 'They're sending a lot of energy to the bandstand. So what
we're going to do, we're going to take that energy, absorb it, and
send it back to them.' We got onstage and we played for two hours."

Not that it was two hours of unrelenting brilliance. The uneven set was largely held together by Hendrix's own coruscating virtuosity. And if this meant stepping forward for a solo rendition of "The Star-Spangled Banner," so be it.

Of course the performance subsequently drew the outrage and ire of conservatives, who denounced it as disrespectful and unpatriotic. Hendrix backpedaled at the time, saying, "We're all Americans . . . it was like 'Go America!' We play it the way the air is in America today. The air is slightly static, see." But the guitarist knew full well what he'd been doing. Hendrix had spent a brief period in the army. He'd been forced to enlist as an alternative to being jailed at age nineteen for riding in stolen cars. He'd hated every second of military life and had been discharged as being unfit for duty, just barely missing deployment to Vietnam himself. But in the late sixties, an African American performer still had to be cautious about making public political statements. Radicals such as the Black Panthers were starting to speak out, but entertainers had to tread carefully. Besides, he'd already made his statement onstage at Woodstock. Hendrix was a master of the mutely articulate gesture.

"He would never raise his voice above a whisper," recalled Hendrix's fellow guitar hero Jeff Beck. "It was all in his expressions, in the hands. Unbelievable comedy and profound statements just by the raising of an eyebrow."

Among Hendrix's many achievements, he played a key role in reviving interest in the Stratocaster in the late sixties, a time when it had fallen out of favor. As we've seen, the British Invasion had brought Rickenbackers and Gretsches to the forefront. And by mid-decade, serious guitarists were starting to gravitate toward Gibson Les Pauls. The Stratocaster had come to seem a bit passé . . . First introduced in 1954, it was associated early on with the boy-next-door charm of Buddy Holly and, a little later, the clean-cut, fun-in-the-sun surf music sounds of the Beach Boys. Neither of these would be regarded as the epitome of cool at the decade's end.

But Hendrix turned all of that around by embracing the Stratocaster as his main instrument. The spoken line "You'll never hear surf music again," in his 1967 recording "Third Stone from the Sun," can be read as a nod to his willful and inspired transformation of the Stratocaster's sound and image. No longer a musical surfboard, the Strat had been transformed into a multidimensional space hopper. Fifteen years after its inception, the Stratocaster experienced a rebirth, a glorious Second Coming, in the gifted hands of Jimi Hendrix.

The last great hurrah of the counterculture sixties, Woodstock was the third in a triumvirate of music festivals that defined the era. In so doing, they served to delineate and dramatize the expanding role of the electric guitar within the counterculture zeitgeist.

I. A TOOL OF CAPITALISM?
DYLAN GOES ELECTRIC

It's fairly common knowledge that Bob Dylan caused a furor by appearing onstage with an electric guitar at the Newport Folk Festival. Many people even know that this momentous event occurred in 1965. But from a distance of half a century, it's difficult to grasp the full significance of this brief, three-song electric performance. It really is the "big bang" that created not only rock music as we know it today but also much of what we remember today as the counterculture sixties.

The festival itself had been taking place annually at Newport, Rhode Island, ever since its 1959 inception as a spinoff of the Newport Jazz Festival. By that point, a widespread and enthusiastic folk music revival was well under way in America. It had begun during the 1930s and '40s with the work of archivists and musicologists such as John and Alan Lomax, who traveled to rural areas recording and collecting the traditional songs sung by farmers, laborers, and other largely nonprofessional performers. This in turn had led to the emergence of prominent professional folksingers such as Woody Guthrie and Pete Seeger in the late forties. These and many other folksingers strongly allied themselves with liberal political causes, including civil rights and the labor movement.

The core audience.for folk music was largely collegiate—young, well informed, and progressive-minded—although the fifties gave rise to a wider, less politicized audience for more mainstream folk ensembles such as the Kingston Trio, the New Christy Minstrels, and Peter, Paul & Mary. From edgy radicals to more accessible acts, the common denominator that united all of these performers under the "folk" rubric was the use of traditional acoustic instrumentation—guitars, banjos, mandolins, dulcimers, zithers, autoharps, harmonicas, accordions, and other homespun implements. There was a strong sense that these were instruments "of the people." The folksinger's commitment to these instruments was ideological—moral, even. They were the honest tools of those in service of a righteous cause. Woody Guthrie famously emblazoned his acoustic guitar with the slogan THIS MACHINE KILLS FASCISTS, thus beginning a long tradition of using a guitar as a political statement—a tradition that would come to include both Jimi Hendrix and Guthrie's fervent admirer Bob Dylan.

Dylan had emerged within the folk scene of the early sixties. He quickly became noted as a supremely gifted writer of anthemic political songs such as "Masters of War," "Blowing in the Wind," "With God on Our Side," "A Hard Rain's Gonna Fall," "The Lonesome Death of Hattie Carroll," and "The Times They Are A-Changin'," compositions that spoke out eloquently against war, racism, and other social ills. Like many folksingers, he played acoustic guitars—a variety of Martins and Gibsons—and harmonicas held in playing position by a metal rack around his neck.

But Dylan was also a baby boomer. He had grown up on the first great wave of rock and roll, and had played in rock bands during his high school years. And, like many his age, he'd become deeply enamored of the music that the Beatles and the Rolling Stones brought to the fore in the mid-sixties. So it was natural for him to want to incorporate some of the electric guitar sounds he was hearing from those groups into his own music. Electrified timbres also seemed to suit a new direction his lyrics were taking at the time, veering away from political themes and more toward personal concerns and free-associative, surrealist imagery.

In March of 1965, Dylan released his first recordings with electric guitar, bass, and drum kit accompaniment as part of his fifth album, *Bringing It All Back Home.* It was followed three months later by his first hit record, the fully electrified six-minute opus "Like a Rolling Stone." These recordings were generally reviled by folk purists, who felt that Dylan had betrayed their cause. Feelings of this nature were very much in the air when, just a week after the release of "Like a Rolling Stone," Dylan appeared at Newport, backed by a full electric blues/rock-and-roll band.

It was his third Newport performance. Over the course of the previous two, he'd confirmed his stature as king of the festival and the new young champion of folk music. But the reception he received was somewhat more ambivalent when he stepped onto the stage dressed in a slim-cut leather jacket, with a sunburst 1964 Fender Stratocaster hanging from his shoulder and flanked by five musicians with even more electric instruments. It must have seemed like a hostile takeover to some of the folkies in attendance—a suspicion apparently confirmed when Dylan and his group launched into a frenetic, up-tempo performance of "Maggie's Farm" from *Bringing It All Back Home.* Lyrically, the song has been interpreted as a middle finger raised at folk music. But even those who didn't catch the words certainly got the message anyway. For many in attendance, those electric guitars were a far bigger insult than being flipped the bird. As the song crashed to a raucous halt, Dylan and his band were greeted with a mixture of cheering and booing.

It has retrospectively been claimed that reports of the audience's negative response were greatly exaggerated. Yet boos are clearly audible in recordings of the set. One report has claimed that an audience member jeered, "Go back to *The Ed Sullivan*

Show!"—an unfavorable reference to performances by the Beatles, the Rolling Stones, and other pop groups on the popular television program.

"The electric guitar represented capitalism . . . the people who were selling out," the folksinger Oscar Brand later commented, in explanation of the crowd's response.

Dylan and his band followed "Maggie's Farm" with two more songs: "Like a Rolling Stone" and an early draft of a song Dylan would record soon thereafter, "It Takes a Lot to Laugh, It Takes a Train to Cry." Neither did much more than "Maggie's Farm" to win over skeptics in the audience. One of them, Pete Seeger, the evening's host, wasn't thrilled. At the concert's outset, Seeger had announced from the stage that the night was going to address serious issues such as civil rights and the Vietnam War. Now here was young Dylan screeching inscrutably about jugglers, clowns, and chrome horses to strident, electrified accompaniment. Not that Seeger could hear much of the lyrics, which was a big part of his beef.

"I was absolutely screaming mad," he recalled. "You couldn't understand a goddamn word of what they were singing." On being forcibly kept from the sound mixing board, where he'd hoped to adjust the balance more in favor of the vocals, Seeger remarked, "If I had an axe, I'd cut the cable." (It was later reported—erroneously, Seeger claimed to his dying day—that he had actually made such an attempt.)

AS MUCH AS people took note of the new, leather-clad Bob Dylan, many were equally shocked or entranced—depending on their perspective—by the intense, wild-eyed young man to Dylan's right, playing frenzied lead guitar through an Epiphone Futura amp. This was Michael Bloomfield of the Paul Butterfield Blues Band. Hunched over his white 1963 Fender Telecaster, Bloomfield was particularly manic on "Maggie's Farm," answering Dylan's vocal lines with snarling bursts of wicked-fast blues riffing. He acquitted himself equally well on the remaining two tunes, his grainy licks and manic meter straining at the boundaries of the song arrangements like a wild horse bolting a racecourse fence.

Bloomfield had played lead guitar on the studio recording of "Like a Rolling Stone." The hot-wired frenzy of his Telecaster stylings are essential to the track's giddy forward momentum, building climactically to set up each "How does it feel" refrain. His playing would become integral to the album Dylan would soon release, the groundbreaking *Highway 61 Revisited*.

The two men were kindred spirits. Dylan and Bloomfield had both grown up Jewish in the American Midwest. Both had become passionately involved in the folk music scene, Bloomfield studying acoustic guitar at the Old Town School of Folk Music in his native Chicago. They'd first met at a club Dylan had played on the Chicago folk circuit, an encounter Dylan would later remember more vividly than Bloomfield.

"He played all kinds of things," Dylan recalled. "Big Bill Broonzy, Sonny Boy Williamson—that type of thing. He just played circles around anything I could play, and I always remembered that."

But folk and acoustic blues represented just one area of Bloomfield's expertise. From his teen years onward, he had also been venturing into the sweatbox blues clubs of Chicago's African American South Side, where pioneering electric bluesmen like Muddy Waters, Howlin' Wolf, and Magic Sam were dishing out dirty amped-up blues to boozy, boisterous crowds on a nightly basis. Turning his attention to the electric guitar, Bloomfield was soon good enough for Waters and other leading Chicago bluesmen to invite him to join them onstage. He became close friends with Waters, Big Joe Turner, and other seminal blues musicians, drinking and getting high with them, traveling with them, and generally absorbing their wisdom and way of life.

In the late 1950s and early '60s, a young white guitarist rarely gained that kind of intimate access to the source of the electric blues.

"I remember going to some of those blues clubs much later, in 1965," recalled Bloomfield's friend, Jefferson Airplane lead guitarist Jorma Kaukonen, "and you needed somebody to go with, otherwise you'd get your ass whipped. Michael came up through the real, no-bullshit blues scene."

There was a definite buzz on Bloomfield when Dylan tapped him to perform on "Like a Rolling Stone" and the other tracks that would go to make up *Highway 61 Revisited.*

"I saw him at a few parties," Bloomfield recalled of Dylan, "and then out of the clear-blue sky he called me on the phone to cut a record. So I bought a Fender, a really good guitar for the first time in my life, without a case, a Telecaster . . . I had never been on a professional, big-time session with studio musicians. I didn't know anything. I liked the songs. If you had been there, you would have seen it was a very disorganized, weird scene. Since then I've played on millions of sessions and I realize how really weird that Dylan session was."

Dylan was attempting something unprecedented; the intuitive, largely unspoken understanding between Bloomfield and Dylan was vital to making *Highway 61* the brilliant, revolutionary album that is so revered today. And as Dylan's role on electric guitar was not that much different from what he played on acoustic guitar—a strummed chordal accompaniment to his vocals—it was Bloomfield's job to find the right embellishments and tonal colors on lead guitar.

"It was never like, 'Here's one of the tunes and we're gonna learn it and work out the arrangement,'" Bloomfield said of the sessions. "That just wasn't done. The thing just sort of fell together in this haphazard, half-assed way. It was like a jam session . . . [Dylan] had a sound in mind, because he had heard records from the Byrds that knocked him out. He wanted me to play like [Byrds guitarist Roger] McGuinn. That's what he was shooting for. It was even discussed. He said, 'I don't want any of that B.B. King shit, man.' Dylan would play me Cher's versions of his songs. And different English versions, Animals versions, but the Byrds sound is what he wanted to get in his sessions."

At the time he went into the studio with Bob Dylan, Bloomfield had already joined the Paul Butterfield Blues Band. The group had been signed to Elektra Records, but had yet to release a recording. Formed by Chicago-based blues harmonica ace Paul Butterfield, the group was the first racially integrated electric blues band that had come to prominence, with Howlin' Wolf's rhythm section of bassist Jerome Arnold and drummer Sam Lay playing alongside Butterfield, Bloomfield, second guitarist Elvin Bishop, vocalist Nick Gravenites, and keyboard player Mark Naftalin.

Along with John Mayall, the Butterfield Band is at the generative heart of the sixties counterculture's subsequent passionate embrace not just of the blues, but also the language and other aspects of African American culture. For years to come, a blues jam would be taken as a measure of a band's authenticity and essential truth.

And inadvertently, the Butterfield Band inspired Dylan's decision to go electric at Newport. They had also played at the festival, at a Saturday afternoon blues workshop, but had been given a condescending spoken introduction by Alan Lomax, who evidently shared the folk-purist disdain for electric instrumentation, and also apparently had a problem with white people playing the blues. This incensed both Dylan and his manager, Albert Grossman. The latter actually came to blows with Lomax over the incident.

But while those two titans of the folk business rolled in the dust trading punches, Dylan came up with a far better plan of retribution; he'd have members of the Butterfield Band back him up on a selection of his new electric songs during his festival performance on the evening of Sunday, July 25, 1965. Albert Grossman employee and roadie Jonathan Taplin was present when the momentous decision was made. "Dylan just got a hair up his ass:

'Well fuck them if they think they can keep electricity out of here. I'll do it.' On a whim, he said he wanted to play electric."

Mike Bloomfield was delegated to assemble the backing band. Assuming lead guitar duties, he put the Butterfield rhythm section of Arnold and Lay together with organist Al Kooper, who'd also played on "Like a Rolling Stone," and electric pianist Barry Goldberg. A hasty rehearsal took place the evening before the performance at the home of festival organizer George Wein. (This is why Dylan and his group only performed three songs together the following evening. That's all they'd had time to prepare.)

Peter Yarrow, of Peter, Paul & Mary, was the sound engineer for the evening, and in film footage of the afternoon soundcheck with Dylan and his band, Yarrow is seen pleading with the musicians to remember their soundcheck volume levels and not to deviate from them during the show. Yarrow had taken on an immensely challenging job. Electric guitars have a much wider dynamic range—the sonic distance between a whisper and full blast—than their acoustic counterparts. During the concert, Yarrow quickly learned what all rock soundmen now know: bands play louder when they're all vibed up in front of an audience than they do at soundcheck. But live sound reinforcement for rock bands wouldn't reach anything like maturity until way into the seventies. It's a very different craft from miking up some folkie grandma with a dulcimer in her lap.

That night, Dylan and his electric band followed traditional banjo picker Cousin Emmy onto the Newport stage. By the time they'd left it, both folk music and rock music had been changed deeply and permanently. As an indicator of the performance's cultural importance, the Stratocaster Dylan played at Newport sold for a record $965,000 in 2015.

Bloomfield's Newport Tele didn't do too badly either when it sold for $45,000 in a 2015 auction, a pretty good price for an instrument that had been heavily hacked up and butchered after leaving Bloomfield's hands. Heritage, the auction house that handled the sale, billed the instrument as "the guitar that killed folk."

WITH THE NEWPORT set and *Highway 61*, Bob Dylan officially joined a movement he had helped inspire when rock and pop acts like the Byrds, the Turtles, and Cher had begun recording electrified versions of his songs, and making hits of them. The first salvo had been fired by the Byrds' 1965 recording of Dylan's "Mr. Tambourine Man," which prominently featured the same Rickenbacker 360 electric twelve-string model that George Harrison had popularized. "Folk-rock" was the name given to this new musical hybrid. It was the first of many hyphenated rock subgenres that would arise in the years to come. And in many ways it was the most important. Folk-rock represented an unprecedented merging of the collegiate folk audience with the fanatically devoted teen audience that had sprung up around the Beatles, Stones, and similar artists. With this convergence of two different but closely aligned tribes, rock music came of age as a credible and vibrant art form.

Clocking in at six minutes and thirteen seconds, "Like a Rolling Stone" broke the age-old three-minute song limit of Top 40 radio. Columbia, Dylan's record label, was reluctant to release it for that reason, but it was a smash hit nonetheless—and despite the fact that its multi-verse format owes more to folk balladry than anything that had hitherto happened in rock and roll or any other pop genre. Dylan's wildly imagistic lyrics had liberated rock and pop tunesmiths from having to write exclusively about romance, cars, or surfing. This would have a powerful effect on songwriters such as John Lennon, who almost immediately began crafting more introspective material.

Dozens of folk-rock groups—including Buffalo Springfield, the Byrds, the Lovin' Spoonful, Simon & Garfunkel, the Mamas & the Papas, and many lesser-known, one-hit wonders—began to emerge in '65 and '66. Protest music—from Springfield's "For What It's Worth," to Barry McGuire's "Eve of Destruction," to Simon & Garfunkel's "The Sounds of Silence"—became popular as the collegiate folk community's political engagement and social activism spilled over into the rock-and-roll arena. The youthful sound of the electric guitar was integral to all these recordings.

What Dylan had done at Newport was to make manifest a fundamental but hitherto unarticulated truth—rock-and-roll music, as it existed at that time, essentially *was* electrified folk music. As with true folk music, there was no system of formalized instruction for rock, nor were there any reliable written transcriptions of rock-and-roll songs, let alone rock guitar solos. Rock electric guitarists learned their craft by copying what they heard on records or getting together informally with like-minded players to trade information and licks. That is, they made it up as they went along. In this regard, rock at this juncture was more *folk* than folk. You could go to a place like the Old Town School of Folk Music to learn the intricacies of acoustic fingerpicking. There was no equivalent for rock guitar.

As liberating as Dylan and folk-rock were for songwriters, their rise to prominence was an equal boon for electric guitarists. Along with political sensibilities, the collegiate folk audience brought new listening habits to the rock forum. People began to listen to rock music seriously and analytically, rather than just as a backdrop for dancing or beach parties. This meant that they began paying more attention to instrumentalists. The prospect of being taken seriously as a musician began to attract folk players into the rock idiom. Many of the rock era's most influential electric guitarists—including Stephen Stills, Neil Young, Jerry Garcia, Jorma Kaukonen, and Roger McGuinn—had all started out as folkies, subsequently making the switch to electric.

But it was Michael Bloomfield who opened the door. While the term "guitar hero" has become overused, Bloomfield was nonetheless the archetype for this cultural phenomenon—the first guitarist to captivate the newly emergent rock audience with his virtuosity and imaginative approach to the instrument. His work on *Highway 61* gave him a high degree of visibility at a time just before the ascendancy of Clapton, Hendrix, and all the other iconic players whose names are perhaps more widely known today. Together with the poet Allen Ginsberg, Dylan, Bloomfield, and Kooper also exemplified a new breed of Jewish American cool—urban, literate, laconically hip. Dylan printed his poetry and stream-of-consciousness prose on his album back covers and inner sleeves. Bloomfield was a voracious reader. When he came upon a book he particularly loved, he was known to have eaten the pages, as if hungry to absorb the wisdom and beauty contained therein. This hunger and obsessive, almost psychotic, sense of urgency came across dynamically in his playing.

Following the *Highway 61* sessions, Dylan offered Bloomfield a spot in his touring band, but Bloomfield declined the offer, preferring to stick with Butterfield and the blues, even though that option promised less financial reward than being Dylan's guitar man. The position ended up going to Robbie Robertson, along with the group we know today as the Band. Booing and jeering the electric guitar became a semi-regular ritual as that ensemble toured England with Dylan in 1965–'66. Cries of "Judas!" from disgruntled audience members were not uncommon. At one infamous concert, Dylan responded to the accusation by saying, "I don't believe you; you're a liar," before introducing "Like a Rolling Stone" and instructing his band to "Play it fucking loud."

Given Mike Bloomfield's ambivalent attitude toward fame, and the kind of mass hysteria it can induce, it was probably for the best that he stepped off the Dylan roller coaster when he did. His position with Butterfield certainly afforded more opportunity for instrumental improvisation than there would have been backing a poet/lyricist like Dylan. Bloomfield's work on the Butterfield Band's eponymous debut album in '65 and their '66 follow-up, *East-West,* was assiduously studied by guitarists. Along with spirited interpretations of the twelve-bar Chicago blues format, *East-West*'s hugely influential title track was an epic thirteen-minute instrumental piece that incorporated elements of jazz and Indian classical raga improvisation on electric guitar.

This was music to sit and listen to with focused, meditative attention, very much the way one listens to jazz, for instance. But where the saxophone was perhaps the ultimate instrument for jazz improvisation, the electric guitar took on that role in the burgeoning new rock medium, which was expanding to embrace elements of jazz, blues, folk, and raga, among other stylistic mediums. At this time, young rock fans had also started to embrace something that had long been a favorite among jazz musicians and some of their listeners—marijuana. This too would color the new attitude toward the appreciation and consumption of rock music then fomenting.

Dylan had somewhat famously introduced the Beatles to pot in 1964, and young fans of both acts were soon following suit. Beyond that, hallucinogenic drugs such as LSD, psilocybin, and peyote were also coming into vogue, popularized by counterculture figures like Harvard psychologist Timothy Leary and novelist Ken Kesey with his bacchanalian acidhead entourage, the Merry Pranksters. The kind of music that Bloomfield and the Butterfield Band were creating on "East-West" made ideal listening for people in the states of expanded consciousness and heightened sensory awareness fostered by marijuana and hallucinogens. Bloomfield is said to have composed "East-West" in the aftermath of an LSD trip.

BLOOMFIELD USED HIS popularity to act as a tireless advocate for the blues. It was he who convinced entrepreneur Bill Graham to book B. B. King into Graham's influential San Francisco rock concert venue, the Fillmore. Graham had never heard of King.

"Bill hired B.B. just on Michael's word that this guy was the best," recalled Butterfield vocalist Nick Gravenites. "And it was from that point that Bill started to hire blues bands along with the hippie bands. It was essentially Michael clueing him in that there were all these great bands out there that he could hire."

But of course Bloomfield's influence was most strongly felt among other guitarists. It was during his time with Butterfield that Bloomfield switched from his Telecaster to a 1956 Gibson Les Paul goldtop. His purchase of the instrument did not go unremarked in the electric guitar community. With the Les Paul out of production at the time, a market for vintage ones quickly took shape. This was the start of the vintage electric guitar boom that would become a multimillion-dollar business in subsequent decades.

"Prior to Bloomfield, I saw very little evidence of interest in paying much for a used electric rather than a new one, and recognizing one as being special," the noted vintage guitar dealer and authority George Gruhn recalled. "But when Bloomfield did it, it happened almost overnight."

By 1967, Bloomfield had moved on to a new band, the Electric Flag, and a new guitar, a 1959 sunburst Les Paul Standard. His switch was motivated in part by Eric Clapton's use of a '60 Standard on the Mayall/Clapton "Beano" album. But Bloomfield had also spent a lot of time playing a Standard owned by a friend, Lovin' Spoonful guitarist John Sebastian. Once again, his change of instruments had a dramatic and immediate effect on the vintage guitar market, doing much to cement the Standard's reputation as the ultimate Les Paul and, indeed, the ultimate electric guitar.

"When Bloomfield was playing a goldtop, people didn't want the sunburst [Standard]," Gruhn recalled.

> People told me, "The Standard's not the right guitar. Those tune-o-matic bridges kill sustain. And those metal-covered humbucking pickups, they just sound sickly sweet and syrupy. They don't have bite like those good P-90s." They'd pay me six or seven hundred dollars for a goldtop. But for a sunburst, they didn't want to pay more than two-fifty. But within two weeks after Bloomfield switched to a 'burst that

all changed. There was one guy who'd told me how the tune-o-matic and humbuckers were no good—he denied ever having said anything of the sort.

Bloomfield's '59 Les Paul Standard also figured prominently on the cover of the guitarist's post–Electric Flag recording project, the monumentally influential *Super Session* album with keyboardist and fellow *Highway 61* sessioneer Al Kooper. In his newly assumed role as an A&R man for Columbia Records, Kooper had the idea of assembling a rock album the same way jazz albums are created—by bringing together a group of handpicked instrumentalists and allowing them to stretch out and improvise in the studio. Released in May of 1968, *Super Session* was so successful that it engendered a follow-up concert recording later that year, *The Live Adventures of Mike Bloomfield and Al Kooper.*

Unfortunately, Bloomfield's career started to go downhill after that. Chronic insomnia, drug use, and a deep-seated antipathy toward commercial success all combined to make him an unreliable performer. He'd miss concert and recording dates, something he repeatedly did with Kooper. His indifference to fame or fortune made him generally unwilling to jump through all the hoops that go with a career in music. He remained sporadically active throughout the seventies, but died a sad, premature, and drug-related death in 1981. The influence he exerted in the latter half of the sixties, however, cannot be overstated. Bob Dylan himself called Bloomfield "the best guitar player I ever heard, on any level."

II. MACHINE-GUN LOUD:
FROM TOWNSHEND TO HENDRIX

The vogue for extended rock guitar improvisation manifested itself just as strongly, if somewhat differently, in England as it had in the United States in 1965. One of the groups at the vanguard of this phenomenon was the Yardbirds. They were the first big rock band that had people focusing on the guitar playing more than the vocals. During the Yardbirds' early career (1963–65), with Eric Clapton on lead guitar, they'd established a format for inserting passages of freeform electric guitar and amped-up blues harmonica soloing into their songs. This became known as a "rave-up," an abrupt shift in tempo from the main body of the song, building to a climax fueled by an ascending bass line. It was at this time that CLAPTON IS GOD graffiti started appearing on the walls of London.

As a guitarist, how do you follow that? Impossible—unless you're Jeff Beck. When Beck replaced Clapton in the Yardbirds in mid-1965, the band was able to forge even more adventurous new paths for the electric guitar. And Beck was able to pursue experimental sonic directions he'd started with earlier groups such as the Night Shift and the Tridents, exploring musical applications for electric guitar feedback, distortion, and other sounds hitherto considered undesirable.

"I had a terrible amp back then that fed back anyway," Beck later explained. "When we started playing big ballrooms, you'd turn up the volume and . . . wheeeeee. And everybody would start looking at me thinking I wanted to be dead because I'd made this mistake. So I had to turn a horrible sound into a tune, to make them think I meant it. That's where it all came from—the inability of sound systems to cope with the needed volume."

Unlike Clapton or Bloomfield, Beck was no blues purist, although he could certainly whip out a wicked twelve-bar when the occasion demanded. His early influences were more along the lines of country and rockabilly players such as Chet Atkins and Cliff Gallup, the lead guitarist in Gene Vincent's band, and Les Paul's "New Sound" recordings of the fifties.

Beck's tenure with the Yardbirds, starting in 1965, gave him an opportunity to bring his own new sounds to the top of the pop charts, beginning with the hit single "Heart Full of Soul." Released in June of that year—a month before Dylan went electric at Newport—it was the follow-up to "For Your Love" (the hit debut single that had caused Clapton to quit the band because it wasn't a blues number).

Yardbirds producer/manager Giorgio Gomelsky hired a sitarist and accompanist on tabla (a pair of Indian hand drums) to play on "Heart Full of Soul." They were accomplished Indian classical musicians—which turned out to be a problem. The rhythmic organization of Indian classical music is very different from that of Western music. So the sitarist and tabla player couldn't nail the song's very basic four-beat time signature.

"It was totally magical, what he was doing," Beck said of the sitar player, "but it just didn't have any groove to it. I showed him on guitar what I thought would be a good idea [for the song's main riff]. And everybody said, 'That sounds great. Let's just leave that.'"

Two things enabled Beck to emulate the sound of the sitar. One was the fact that, unlike most rock guitarists, he picks with his fingers rather than a guitar pick. The technique enabled him to sound a sitar-like drone on his guitar's open D string, while employing other fingers to play the song's main riff on the higher strings, bending notes microtonally in an intuitive approximation of Indian classical scale intervals.

The other thing that enabled Beck to emulate the buzzy string sound of the sitar on his Esquire was an electrical device connected between the guitar and the amp—a fuzzbox, or fuzz pedal. Foot-pedal effects devices for guitarists would soon become commonplace, but they were still fairly novel in 1965, Gibson having introduced what's generally acknowledged to be the first fuzzbox, the Maestro FZ-1, back in 1962. The device had been invented to emulate the way a tube amplifier sounds when turned up sufficiently to produce distortion—a raw, grainy sound that occurs when the overdriven amp starts to produce harmonic overtones not present in the original signal.

The fuzzbox that Beck used for the main riff on "Heart Full

of Soul" was a device lent to him by his close friend Jimmy Page, a custom box designed and built by Roger Mayer, who would go on to create guitar effects devices for Jimi Hendrix, Bob Marley, and others. Beck's use of fuzz on "Heart Full of Soul" predated Keith Richards's prominent use of a Gibson FZ-1 fuzzbox on the Rolling Stones' "Satisfaction" by a little over a month. It is truly a landmark recording. For the song's guitar solo, Beck opted to use another early fuzz pedal, a Sola Sound Tone Bender. Soon, an ever-growing array of effects pedals would provide guitarists with a relatively easy and affordable way to customize their tone.

Mid-sixties Yardbirds tracks such as "Happenings Ten Years Time Ago," "Heart Full of Soul," "Shapes of Things," and "Over Under Sideways Down" played a vanguard role in establishing the late-sixties vogue for psychedelic rock music. The sound was very much based around fuzzy sitar emulations and extended electric guitar improvisations loosely emulating Indian classical scales. Psychedelic rock would form the context for Jimi Hendrix's emergence in 1967. The electric guitar simulations of bomb blasts and ambulance sirens in Hendrix's Woodstock performance were first heard three years earlier on the aforementioned "Happenings Ten Years Time Ago," one of the few Yardbirds tracks to feature both Jeff Beck and Jimmy Page.

IN TERMS OF exploiting feedback and other noisy artifacts of electric guitar pickups and amps, there was one guitarist in London at the time pushing the envelope even further than Beck or anyone else. That was Pete Townshend of the Who. The son of a professional big band sax player, Townshend had absorbed a variety of guitar influences growing up—from jazzmen like Wes Montgomery and Johnny Smith, to country and early rock players such as Chet Atkins and James Burton, to bluesmen including John Lee Hooker.

But Townshend brought another, entirely different set of influences from his training in contemporary visual arts at Ealing Art College during the Who's formative years. While there, he studied with Gustav Metzger, one of the chief founders of the "auto-destructive" movement in art. Metzger's work included things like acid action painting, which involved flinging hydrochloric acid onto sheets of nylon, causing the nylon to corrode in an array of colors. His *Construction with Glass* consisted of glass sheets suspended from a gallery ceiling by adhesive tape. As the tape gave way, the glass sheets crashed and shattered onto the concrete floor below.

"Auto-destructive art is an attack on capitalist values and the drive toward nuclear annihilation," Metzger wrote in a 1961 manifesto. And in an earlier manifesto, from 1959, he'd stated, "The amplified sound of the auto-destructive process can be an element of the total conception."

Young Townshend took this very much to heart, applying it to his guitar playing. Where the youthful Jeff Beck had attempted to make "a tune," in his own words, from accidental bursts of feedback, Townshend deliberately sought ways to maximize the atonal and disruptive qualities of feedback. Onstage, he would slam his guitar into the amplifier's speaker cabinet, making it howl with feedback, and rub the rough metal clutch of a mic stand up and down the guitar strings to create a screeching cacophony. Another strategy was to flick the pickup-selector toggle switch up and down violently.

"The toggle switch thing was to make the guitar sound like a machine gun when it was feeding back," Townshend explained.

> To me the guitar was a symbol. It was a metaphor for a machine gun. And the only thing you could do with a machine gun in the sixties was break it across your legs. That's what I did. Because I was in this mode where the guitar was a weapon, most of the techniques I used were very violent, virulent, and aggressively expressive. They were all part of the art school tradition that I'd got of breaking the

rules. I was at an art school where the course was dedicated to breaking the rules, and I just drafted that into my work as a guitar player.

Some of these subversive sonic strategies made their way on to early Who singles such as "Anyway, Anyhow, Anywhere" and the Mod anthem "My Generation." Back in 1964, as we've seen, the Beatles had incorporated the first-ever use of guitar feedback on a pop record, in the intro to their single "I Feel Fine." One year later, Townshend took that a step further by integrating feedback into the guitar solo in "Anyway, Anyhow, Anywhere"—a tactic that would soon be employed by countless rock guitarists. As for "My Generation," it is particularly notable for its outro barrage of chaotic wailing feedback and frenzied drumming—a suitably apocalyptic conclusion for a record that contained the famous line "Hope I die before I get old."

Sonic phenomena such as these were even more dramatically felt in the Who's live performances. Along with his exceptional abilities as a songwriter and guitarist, Townshend was much more of a showman than contemporaries such as Clapton, Beck, or Page. He developed a series of dramatic gestures to reinforce his aggressive guitar techniques. The most famous of these is the "windmill," a move Townshend originally appropriated from Keith Richards but took to much more dramatic extremes. The Townshendesque windmill is a frenetic circular flailing of the right arm, like a clock run amok, to drive home his power chords.

But of course the ultimate in aggressive electric guitar performance technique pioneered by Townshend was smashing his guitar to splinters—slamming it down hard on the stage, the amplifiers, drums, and anything else that came within range until the instrument was destroyed. For many years, this was the cathartic climax to live performances by the Who, almost the inevitable outcome of their intensely furious approach to playing rock music. But like many innovations, it was born of a freak accident. This one took place in the autumn of 1964 during a gig at London's Railway Hotel, a cramped performance space with a low ceiling.

"I started to knock the guitar about a lot, hitting it on the amps to get banging noises and things like that, and it had started to crack," Townshend recalled.

> It banged against the ceiling and smashed a hole in the plaster, and the guitar head actually poked through the ceiling plaster. When I brought it out, the top of the neck was left behind. I couldn't believe what happened. There were a couple of people I knew from art school at the front of the stage and they were laughing their heads off. One of them was literally rolling about on the floor laughing and his girlfriend was kind of looking at me smirking, you know, going, "flash cunt" and all that. So I just got really angry and got what was left of the guitar and smashed it to smithereens. About a month earlier I'd managed to scrape together enough [money] for a 12-string Rickenbacker, which I only used on two or three numbers. It was lying at the side of the stage, so I just picked it up, plugged it in and gave them a sort of look and carried on playing as if I'd meant to do it. The next week I went back there [to the Railway], and there was a whole crowd waiting to see this lunatic break his guitar.

Townshend had done his art school mentor proud. If, as Gustav Metzger had written, auto-destructive art was an attack on capitalism, and the electric guitar, as folksinger Oscar Brand had said, was a symbol of capitalism, what could be more revolutionary than smashing a guitar? Shocking, confrontational, or provocative gestures have always been a key ingredient in rock music, from Presley's pelvic gyrations onward. But Townshend's guitar smashing took this to a new extreme, one that defied the centuries-old tradition that musicians are supposed to love and cherish their instrument. In this context Townshend and the Who are often, and rightly, regarded as forerunners of punk rock, also notable for its defiant non-musicianly stance.

All theory aside, the Who's gear bashing was just incredibly exciting—an acting-out of the audience members' youthful frustrations and anger at authority. The ultimate "fuck you" gesture. But on a pragmatic level, it was also a damnably expensive enterprise for a band just struggling to establish itself. Townshend had played Rickenbacker guitars early on with the Who. But these are relatively fragile instruments that smash a little too easily, as the incident at the Railway Hotel had proven. So Townshend switched to Fenders for a while. They're more rugged—built to withstand punishment. And they were designed for ease of repair, so guitar necks, bodies, pickups, and other spare parts could be salvaged from each evening's wreckage and recombined to build new guitars.

During the Who's early career, Townshend played through Fender amps as well. But he was soon to play a key role in the development of what would become the ultimate rock guitar amp, the 100-watt Marshall stack.

LONDON-BORN BIG BAND drummer, vocalist, and tap dancer Jim Marshall had opened a drum shop on Uxbridge Road in London in 1960. He soon expanded into the sale of other musical instruments, including electric guitars and amps. This was at the urging of local rock musicians who began to frequent his shop, among them Pete Townshend. Marshall had long been a friend, and even former bandmate, of Townshend's sax-playing dad, Cliff. This might well have predisposed the London shop owner to favor young Peter and his typically astute observations.

"Pete was one of the ones who came to me and said, 'In the music shops of West London they treat us like idiots because we play rock and roll. So why don't you sell amplifiers and guitars in your shop?'" Marshall recalled. "I said, 'Well, I know a lot about drums but not guitars and amps. But I'll have a go at this.' I did and it was successful right from the word go."

Along with Townshend, the notable or soon-to-be-notable guitarists who frequented Marshall's shop included Ron Wood of the Faces and Rolling Stones, Ritchie Blackmore of Deep Purple, and session guitar ace Big Jim Sullivan. Having persuaded Marshall to sell guitar gear, these players next suggested that Marshall turn his hand to building guitar amps and selling them at his shop. "They came to me and said that the guitar amplifiers then available weren't built for their type of music," Marshall recalled.

While Marshall had done electronic work on fighter aircraft during World War II, he'd had no prior experience with audio electronics. He had, however, hired a young musician named Ken Bran to do amp repairs at the shop. To this he added a third team member, a promising apprentice technician from EMI named Dudley Craven. By 1962 the three of them had come up with a prototype 35-watt guitar amp. It was based on a Fender Bassman amplifier, Fender amps being a big seller at Marshall's shop. But the design employed some different electronic components—ones that were more readily available in the U.K. at the time.

Also, rather than housing the electronics and speakers all in the same enclosures, Marshall decided to have separate enclosures for each—a "head" containing the electronics and front-panel volume and tone controls, and a larger cabinet containing just the speakers. This design had been used by other amp manufacturers, including Fender, but it would become more of a necessity as guitar amplifiers grew louder and more powerful. The separate enclosures did a better job of isolating the electronics, which do the delicate work of amplifying a signal, from the speaker cabinet and its violent sonic vibration. Within a few years, rock guitarists would be stacking one cabinet atop another to achieve even greater volume levels.

Jim Marshall himself devised the cabinet design, which contained within it four 12-inch speakers wired up to deliver maximum power, and a panel sealing off the back of the enclosure. The Marshall speaker cabinet's closed back also gave it a different sound from Fenders and other amps with open-back cabinets. This, combined with the different components in the circuitry, made for a completely new and distinctive tonality—one that would become known as the legendary "Marshall sound." Prior amplifiers had been designed to avoid distortion. The Marshall amp was designed from the ground up *specifically* to distort, and to sound great doing so. Originally christened the Mark II, this early Marshall amp was eventually named the JTM45. The initials stood for Jim and Terry Marshall. (Terry was Jim's son, a sax player in a local London group called the Flintstones.)

By late 1962, the JTM45 was in production and selling briskly. As a domestic U.K. product, it offered better value for money than U.S. imports such as Fender amps, which were costly to ship across the Atlantic. And the Marshall amp was specifically voiced for the way young London was making rock music at the time. As Jim Marshall ramped up the manufacturing side of his business, he, Bran, and Craven were continually fine-tuning and upgrading the JTM45 in the eternal quest for more volume and better tone.

This was one of Jim Marshall's many gifts: his willingness to listen to young rock musicians. Most of his generation despised the belligerent primitivism of rock and roll. Marshall took a broader view. He once attended an early Who show with Pete's dad. As a guy who built and sold music gear for a living, Marshall was quite pleased to see the up-and-coming pop star bashing the hell out of his equipment. The need to purchase replacements was inevitable.

"When Pete started to knock his equipment about, Cliff and I thought, 'The kid's gone stark-raving mad,'" Marshall recalled. "But we quickly realized it was a new form of showmanship that we wouldn't have thought of in our day."

A war of acquisition broke out between Townshend and the Who's bass player—and compulsive shopper—John Entwistle.

"I bought some of the first Marshall cabinets ever made,"

Entwistle later recollected. "I bought one and Pete bought one. I bought another one and Pete bought another one. And I said, 'Well, is it loud enough? Fuck, I'll buy two more.'"

But if you have more speaker cabinets, you need a more powerful amplifier to drive them. Which is why Townshend walked into Marshall's shop in 1965 and demanded a 100-watt amplifier—twice as loud as the one Clapton used on the "Beano" album. Townshend's request would result in what may well be the ultimate rock guitar amp, the Marshall Super Lead model 1959, which first hit the market in 1965. This model and other iterations produced between 1965 and '69 are known as "plexi" Marshalls, nicknamed for the Plexiglas Marshall logo on the front of the amp. They are considered the most desirable and collectible Marshall amps.

Prior to this, the guitar amp had been a fairly anonymous piece of technical equipment—functional, utilitarian, not much different than a microphone stand or drum throne. It was something to be positioned as unobtrusively as possible onstage, low and to the rear, out of the sight line of audience members. But with the advent of the Marshall stack, amps became towering phallic monuments—tall as a human being and integral to the visual aesthetic of rock music in concert. The amp became part of the show—not to mention a more active partner in the creation of electric guitar tonalities. Townshend's new 100-watt behemoth enabled him to generate frenzied feedback and doomsday distortion tones that mirrored the crazy, rebellious, sexual energy of sixties youth gone wild.

By 1967, however, Townshend had moved on from Marshall to Hiwatt amps, which were initially distributed by the U.K. music retailer Sound City. The amps were similar in design to Marshall's, although built to stringent military specifications and thus more durable on the road. By some accounts, Townshend had moved away from Marshall because the Who had rung up a huge debt at Jim Marshall's shop by replacing equipment destroyed onstage, and they couldn't pay. But Townshend was also relentless in his quest for the ultimate guitar tone, and worked as closely with Hiwatt on amp design as he'd done with Marshall. In this way, he's a key figure in the Les Paul tradition of guitarists who get deeply involved in the "under the hood" technicalities of equipment design as a way of realizing their musical vision.

ONE OF THE things Jimi Hendrix most wanted to do when he first hit London in late 1966 was meet Pete Townshend. This was a fairly easy thing for his manager, Chas Chandler, to arrange, as he had recently negotiated a deal for Hendrix to record for the Who's label, Track Records. The former bass player for the Animals, Chandler had moved in the same British Invasion world as Townshend and the Who. But now he'd switched his focus to artist management and had discovered a phenomenally promising young guitar player in New York, a veteran of the African American chitlin' circuit named Jimi Hendrix. In his mid-twenties at the time, Hendrix had made a splash on the Greenwich Village club scene, but had a much larger vision in mind. And a substantial part of that vision was the kind of larger-than-life sound that Townshend was coaxing from his amps.

The Who was in the recording studio when the two great architects of rock guitar met for the first time.

"Hendrix came to see me at IBC Studios and asked me what kind of amplifiers I should buy," Townshend recalled. "Well, he didn't actually say anything. Chas Chandler asked me what sort of amplifiers he should buy. And I said, 'I like Hiwatts'—or Sound City, as they were called then—'but he might prefer Marshall.' And Jimi said, 'Well, I'll have one of each.' For the first few dates that I saw, he was using both."

Like most people who met Hendrix, Townshend noticed the guitarist's soft-spoken, almost painfully shy demeanor, which contrasted starkly with his out-of-control stage performances. "Jimi was covered from head to foot in dust," Townshend recalled of that first meeting. "He looked like he'd just come out of a skip, where you put builder's rubbish. He was very scruffy and his military jacket had obviously seen better days. His skin was pale, and he was immediately nervous and shy and couldn't speak—didn't speak. I just put out my hand and said, 'I've heard a lot about you.'"

At the time of the meeting, Townshend was playing Fender Stratocasters, and so was Hendrix. The latter guitarist had been given his first Strat during his time in Greenwich Village. The donor was friend and early benefactor Linda Keith, who at the time was Keith Richards's girlfriend and is said to have been the inspiration for the Stones' song "Ruby Tuesday." The white Stratocaster she gave to Hendrix had been purloined from Richards himself. Hendrix had wanted one because it was the type of guitar played by two of his biggest idols, Buddy Guy and Otis Rush. And Linda Keith knew where to get one, appropriating the Strat without Richards's knowledge.

It had been Linda who had spotted Hendrix in a Greenwich Village club and told Chandler to go check him out. Hendrix was then performing at the Cafe au Go Go in the Village with bluesman John Hammond—son of pioneering record executive John Hammond Jr., the man who had been instrumental to the success of Charlie Christian, among many others. But Hendrix also had his own group, Jimmy James and the Blue Flames, who were playing at a variety of Village clubs, including Cafe Wha?, which is where Chandler first heard him.

The former Animals bassist was hardly the only musician in town eager to check out the Village's new guitar sensation. Mike Bloomfield had also been tipped off about Hendrix. There was a kind of connection there already. Hendrix was a rabid fan of Bob Dylan—another artist who'd launched his career from the Village—and Bloomfield had of course served as Dylan's guitarist. At this early point in Hendrix's career, he'd already begun covering Dylan's "Like a Rolling Stone." This was of particular interest to Bloomfield, who'd played lead guitar on the original recording and now found himself gigging in the Village with the Butterfield Band right across the street from where Hendrix was performing.

"I was the hotshot guitarist on the block," Bloomfield later told *Guitar Player* magazine.

> I thought I was it. I'd never heard of Hendrix. Then some-one said, "You got to see the guitar player with John Ham-mond." I went right across the street and saw him. Hendrix knew who I was and that day, in front of my eyes, he burned me to death! I didn't even get my guitar out. H-bombs were going off, guided missiles were flying, the surf, waves . . . I can't tell you the sounds he was getting out of his instru-ment. He was getting every sound I was ever to hear him get, right there in that room with a Stratocaster, a [Fender] Twin [amp] and a Maestro Fuzz-Tone [pedal], and that was all.

Bloomfield introduced himself, saying, "Man, where you been?" To which Hendrix replied, "I been playing the chitlin' cir-cuit and I got bored shitless. I didn't hear any guitar players doing anything new and I was bored out of my mind."

Had Hendrix remained in the Village, performing as Jimmy James, he might not have won the adulation of anyone outside of a handful of guitar fanatics and Manhattan hipsters. It was Chan-dler's inspiration to bring the guitarist over to England, team him with a British rhythm section—bassist Noel Redding and drum-mer Mitch Mitchell—and dress them up in the Swinging London "psychedelic dandy" fashions then being pioneered by cutting-edge new boutiques like Granny Takes a Trip—billowing, ruffled shirts and wildly multicolored frock coats. Chandler also coached Hendrix's nascent songwriting gift, providing input and lending him science fiction books to help fire his imagination.

The result was an utterly unique fusion of chitlin' circuit soul and the amped-up excitement of Swinging London. No performer of African heritage had gone headlong into psychedelic rock in quite the same way before. In his dynamic stage performances Hendrix channeled all the great bluesmen and showmen who had gone before, copping moves from T-Bone Walker, Guitar Slim, Chuck Berry, and Buddy Guy—playing the guitar behind his head and between his legs, and picking the strings with his teeth. To this he added Townshendesque aggression and feedback-frenzied guitar mangling.

But it was Hendrix's formidable playing technique that saved the whole thing from being mere pastiche. He exploited the full sonic potential of the Stratocaster to a degree that seemed to transcend the laws of physics. Leo Fender and his design team had built the Strat for both comfort and speed, with all controls and the vibrato arm within intimately easy reach of the player's hand. Hendrix, however, obviated all that by flipping his Strats upside down and playing them left-handed. By restringing his right-handed guitars for left-handed playing, he put the strings in a different relationship to the pickups than they would be on a conventionally setup Strat. Right away, this changed things around sonically. Turning the body upside down positioned the controls in awkward places, but Hendrix's hands were so big that this didn't present him with as much of a problem as it would a player less digitally endowed. As a musician who later worked with Hendrix marveled, "His fingers were like rulers."

No wonder all the top British guitar gods suddenly felt a few shades less divine.

"I shared with Eric [Clapton] that, fucking hell, when I first saw Jimi play I wanted to go and kill myself," Townshend confided.

And he said, "Well I did too. But I didn't think that would've affected you. I mean, he wasn't in your arena." But he *was*. He was someone working with showmanship, which is one of the directions where rock and roll was inevitably going to go. Jimi was one of the people who showed that there was something you could do in the curve of an arm or the movement of the tongue, the stance of the body and hairdo . . . where you combined showmanship and stagecraft. It was the beginnings of the great genius.

One thing that Hendrix brought to the stage—and which became a key factor in his massive popularity—was a frankly and blatantly sexual style of performance, flicking his tongue in a none-too-subtle simulation of cunnilingus, stroking his guitar like a lover, or shoving the neck between his legs and yanking it onanistically. Townshend's performance style was more about anger than sex. Hendrix was the most overtly erotic rock-and-roll performer since Chuck Berry and Elvis Presley. But where Elvis had wiggled his hips at an uptight, straitlaced post–World War II America, Hendrix was strutting his stuff before a newly sexually liberated audience.

One can easily see how blues-oriented British guitarists such as Eric Clapton felt especially intimidated by Hendrix. These were guys who had come up pretty much worshiping the image of the African American bluesman. They'd devoted themselves to emulating this musical style, only now to be confronted with the real deal—an authentic new-generation bluesman who was also embracing the Brits' own musical contributions to create some new strain of cosmic mojo.

Authenticity was everything to Clapton, so the guitarist was impressed when Hendrix suggested that they jam on Howlin' Wolf's "Killing Floor" the first time they met and played together, at a late-1966 gig at Central London Polytechnic with Clapton's new band at the time, Cream. Clapton, like Townshend, was an old British Invasion cohort of Chas Chandler's, so it was relatively easy for Chandler to facilitate a first meeting between Hendrix and Clapton at the London venue.

"I thought it was incredible that he would know how to play this," Clapton said of Hendrix's choice of "Killing Floor,"

as it's a tough one to get right. Of course Jimi played it exactly like it ought to be played and he totally blew me away. I mean you're jamming with someone for the first time, most musicians will try to hold back, but Jimi just went for it. He played the guitar with his teeth, behind his head, lying on the floor, doing the splits . . . the whole business. It was amazing and it was musically great too, not just pyrotechnics. Even though I had already seen Buddy Guy and I knew that a lot of players could do this kind of stuff, it's still pretty amazing when you're standing right next to it. The audience were completely gob-smacked by what they saw and heard too. They loved it and I loved it too, but I remember thinking here was a force to be reckoned with. It scared me, because he was clearly going to be a huge star, and just as [Cream] were finding our own speed, here was the real thing.

Jeff Beck witnessed a similar phenomenon when Hendrix jammed with Clapton at the London School of Economics. "Eric was up front doing his stuff in front of all the girlies and along comes Jimi who sits in and upturns the apple cart." Beck, too, initially felt like packing it in after witnessing Hendrix's uncanny merger of showmanship and musicianship.

"Even if it had been crap, and it wasn't, it got to the press," he said. "People wanted that. They were just starved for theater and outrage. Any of us could be fantastic and stand there like a bunch of librarians. Regardless of great music, that's still pretty boring to look at. Then Hendrix comes along, plays fabulously well and also does tricks, almost circus tricks, with the guitar."

As it turned out, there was enough room in the burgeoning

late-sixties rock scene for Hendrix, Townshend, Clapton, Beck, Page, and many other adventurous electric guitarists. All of these musicians found creative ways to employ the new range of tonalities opened up by the big 100-watt amplifiers. And by the decade's second half, all would be working in the power trio format, with electric guitar, bass guitar, and drums forming the entire instrumental lineup of bands such as Cream, the Who, the Jeff Beck Group, and Led Zeppelin.

Marshalls and Hiwatts going into distortion created such a big, harmonically dense sound that there was no longer a need for a second guitarist or keyboard player to fill up the tonal canvas. Having a mere three instrumentalists in the band also created more space for each to improvise wildly and create elaborate parts. Bassists and drummers were no longer confined to a support role. And indeed, bass players such as Jack Bruce of Cream and John Entwistle of the Who became instrumental idols in their own right, as did Cream's drummer, Ginger Baker, and the Who's inimitable Keith Moon. But most of all, the era belonged to the guitar hero—larger-than-life shamans of the six-string.

NOT THAT IT happened overnight. Hendrix really struggled to get by when he first hit London. Chas Chandler had had to sell the bass guitar he'd played in the Animals at one point, in order to finance early Hendrix recording sessions. At the very end of 1966—December 20, to be precise—they'd been able to release a debut single on the Who's Track Records label. It was a recording of "Hey Joe," a tune that had been covered by many rock bands of the mid-sixties, with notable recordings by the Surfaris, the Leaves, the Standells, the Seeds, Love, the Music Machine, and the Byrds all predating the Hendrix disc. Hendrix's own version is based quite heavily on a recording of "Hey Joe" by a folk-rock artist named Tim Rose, who took the song at a much slower, more somber tempo than earlier interpreters—an approach perhaps better suited to the song's tale of a man who kills his unfaithful lover and must flee to escape the hangman's noose.

Although the Jimi Hendrix Experience's recording of "Hey Joe" failed to chart in the States, it was a major U.K. hit of early 1967. This gave Chandler and the group sufficient traction to record a debut album, although they were still scrambling to book sessions during late-evening downtime hours when studio rates were cheaper. By this time, Hendrix had found another key collaborator, the aforementioned guitar effects wizard Roger Mayer. A university-trained mechanical and electrical engineer, Mayer was working by day for the British Admiralty and teaming up with Hendrix at night to create a kaleidoscopic array of hitherto-unheard guitar tones generated by means of custom-built fuzz pedals, treble boosters, phasers, flangers, octave dividers, and wah-wah pedals.

The result of all this creative experimentation was released to the public on May 12, 1967, bearing the title *Are You Experienced*, the debut album from the Jimi Hendrix Experience. It was one of several epoch-defining albums released that year, a list which also includes the Beatles' *Sgt. Pepper's Lonely Hearts Club Band* (June 1), Pink Floyd's *The Piper at the Gates of Dawn* (August 5), Jefferson Airplane's *Surrealistic Pillow* (February), Cream's *Disraeli Gears* (November 10), and the Doors eponymous debut LP (January 4). All these records formed the soundtrack for the emergent hippie counterculture and psychedelic scenes that had blossomed in San Francisco, London, and elsewhere. Hippiedom was a smorgasbord of ideas and lifestyles, some inherited from the Beat generation of the fifties—Eastern spirituality, free love, pacifism, political activism, vegetarianism, and of course experimentation with psychedelic drugs.

But rock music was the glue that bound all this together, something that all the counterculture subcultures could—and did— rally around. In 1967's Summer of Love, rock became a blazing sun, giving life and light to a number of satellite art forms—poster art, album graphics, light shows, fashion, film, experimental theater, new literary forms, and a new strain of music criticism that, for the first time, endeavored to write seriously and creatively about rock. In this cultural stew, the rock guitarist became the new Da Vinci, the new Shakespeare, the new Paganini—the romantic artist-hero par excellence. And Jimi Hendrix was the indisputable king of them all. His otherworldly guitar tonalities and adventurous playing seemed a direct evocation of the psychedelic experience. The sound was recognizable as an electric guitar, but, like one who embarks on an LSD trip, the instrument had clearly entered another dimension.

At a time before keyboard synthesizers became widespread, the electric guitar—fully rigged with a panoply of effects pedals and powerful new amps—became the musical instrument with the most wildly varied and expressive range of tonal possibilities. There was no instrument better equipped to express and reflect not only the hallucinogenic experience but also all the profound changes taking place in society during the latter half of the sixties.

III. THE BIRTH OF CLASSIC ROCK

Big Marshall amps, feedback, and aggressive onstage theatricality had all come into Jimi Hendrix's stage act directly from Pete Townshend and the Who, as we've seen. This indebtedness became a major issue for both guitarists at the Monterey International Pop Music Festival, which took place in California in June of 1967. The Who and the Jimi Hendrix Experience both had a lot riding on Monterey. The festival would serve as the major American debut for both acts. Hendrix had never played the States with the Experience, and while the Who had been going strong for two years in England, their management hadn't been able to get them over to America before '67.

So here were two groups brand new to the American audience, both presenting a bold new approach to the electric guitar. Apart from a few die-hard rock fanatics, no one knew the genealogy of this approach. So whichever one went on second was in danger of seeming derivative of the other.

Monterey was a big deal in general—the first rock festival and, as such, the mother of all rock fests to come. Without Monterey, Woodstock might never have happened.

The idea of putting on a rock music festival had originated in a conversation between L.A.-based record producer Lou Adler, guitarist/singer/songwriter John Phillips of the Mamas & the Papas, and Paul McCartney. "We were talking about how rock and roll, although it was expanding as far as talent and the writing, was not considered an art form in the same way that jazz and folk were," Adler recounted.

Adler and Phillips had also discussed how high-visibility festivals and concert series had played a key role in legitimizing both folk music and jazz as major art forms in years gone by. They wanted to do the same thing for rock music. Together with a few other organizers, including Beatles publicist Derek Taylor, they found the Monterey County Fairgrounds, located in an idyllic Northern California beach town. The fairground had long been home to the Monterey Folk Festival and the Monterey Jazz Festival. So it was the perfect venue. Two years after the electric guitar and rock music had muscled their way into Newport, the music was about to receive its very own festival.

It didn't hurt that Monterey is just two hours south of San Francisco's Haight-Ashbury district, ground zero for the emergent psychedelic rock scene. The festival was as much a coming-out party for hippiedom and psychedelia as it was a showcase for exciting new rock talent. Brian Jones from the Rolling Stones flew over from England to check out the scene and introduce some of the acts—including the Jimi Hendrix Experience. He was accompanied by Nico, the beautiful blond German actress, Warhol scenester, and Velvet Underground vocalist. The San Francisco

Bay area had already been the site for love-ins, be-ins, acid tests, and other counterculture gatherings, but Monterey was the first time they were scored by three days' worth of top musical talent playing a daring and vibrant new form of rock.

The idea was to bring together the best and brightest of current rock and pop acts of the day. This included emerging stars like Janis Joplin with her band Big Brother and the Holding Company, and kindred spirits from related genres such as soul music megastar Otis Redding and Indian classical maestro Ravi Shankar. The bill also included the Byrds, Jefferson Airplane, Canned Heat, Moby Grape, the Butterfield Blues Band, the Electric Flag, Buffalo Springfield, the Grateful Dead, Country Joe and the Fish, and Quicksilver Messenger Service. All were major "buzz bands" of the day. Many featured highly regarded electric guitarists such as Quicksilver's John Cipollina, the Airplane's Jorma Kaukonen, the Dead's Jerry Garcia, Canned Heat's Henry Vestine, and Barry Melton from Country Joe and the Fish. Counterculture guitar hero Mike Bloomfield was there as well, performing with both the Butterfield Band and the Electric Flag.

The majority of the acts were American. But the promoters asked both McCartney and Rolling Stones manager Andrew Loog Oldham what the hottest thing in England was at the moment. The reply was immediate and unanimous: the Who and the Jimi Hendrix Experience. Both acts were booked and scheduled to perform on the festival's final evening, Sunday, June 18.

And that was the problem. The two bands were slated to play back-to-back. Neither one wanted to follow the other onto the stage. Which led to one of the festival's legendary nonpublic performances—a backstage confrontation between Pete Townshend and Jimi Hendrix. The two men were friends and colleagues as much as they were rivals. So the scene was hardly hostile or angry—just intense and a little strange.

"Jimi was on acid, and he stood on a chair playing the guitar," Townshend later recalled.

I was trying to get him to talk to me about the fact that I didn't want the Who to follow him onto the stage. I said, "For fuck's sake, Jimi, listen to me. I don't want to go on after you. It's bad enough that you're here. It's bad enough that you're gonna fuck up my life. I'm not gonna have you steal my act. That's the only thing we've got. You're a great genius. They'll appreciate that. But what do I do? I wear a Union Jack jacket and smash my guitar. Give me a break; let me go on first." And he was, I thought, teasing me; you know, standing on a chair playing the guitar and ignoring me. But Brian Jones told me later on that he was just fucking *completely* whacked on acid.

Townshend was in a bit of a weak position. The Who's management had been unable to meet the cost of shipping the group's backline of Sound City amps over to the States. So for the Monterey concert and other U.S. tour dates in '67, Townshend and bassist John Entwistle would be playing through American-made Vox Super Beatle amps, the result of an endorsement deal put together by their management. With the Super Beatle, Vox had forgone the tubes that had given earlier amps their distinctive color, in favor of the recently adopted transistor. Super Beatles were notorious for the amount of hiss they produced, and the transistor tone seemed tinny and "pinched" in comparison with the warmth and wallop of tubes. Consequently, the Super Beatle was a model that nobody very much liked, not even the Beatles.

Hendrix, on the other hand, would have his usual tube-driven powerhouse backline of British Marshall stacks. So the conflict over which group would play first wasn't only about seeming like a copycat. Townshend also knew that if the Who followed Hendrix, his guitar sound wouldn't have the same impact.

Hendrix was nervous about the gig as well. His chair-standing routine with Townshend may have been more a display of stage fright than arrogance.

"Monterey was predominantly a music festival, done up the way it's supposed to be done up," Hendrix later said. "Everything was perfect. I said, 'Wow! Everything's together! What am I gonna do?' In other words, I was scared at that, almost. I was scared to go up there and play in front of all those people. You really want to turn those people on. It's just like a feeling of really deep concern."

Finally the decision was made that the Who would go on first. Some accounts say this was the result of a coin toss by John Phillips. According to other stories, Townshend forced the issue and Hendrix said, "That's fine, you go on first. But I'm pulling out all the stops."

Both sets were huge triumphs and festival high points, making a profound impression on the audience and launching major U.S. careers for both bands. But it's interesting to compare the concluding moments of each band's performance. Townshend smashed his Stratocaster in much the same way as he'd been doing since 1964—violently, angrily, but with a kind of youthful exuberance glinting through the anger. As always, Townshend was mirroring the rebellious, anarchistic side of youth culture. This was all new to America at the time, and many in the audience were truly shocked.

"That was something that I couldn't fathom," Mamas & the Papas singer and Monterey headliner Michelle Phillips later commented. "We took such care of our instruments. My God, if we saw a crack in a guitar we went crazy. They were like religious symbols to us. It seemed ungodly to smash your instruments."

But when Hendrix set his Stratocaster alight at the conclusion of his set, it seemed more religious ritual than sacrilege or act of subversion. It wasn't the first time he'd ended a performance in this manner. He'd done it at least once before in England, at the Finsbury Park Astoria Theatre, at Chas Chandler's prompting. But, like the Who's act, it was all new to America.

Fire is, of course, an ancient symbol of spiritual purification and transformation, and Monterey would prove an important rite of passage for Hendrix—a return to his homeland as a conquering hero. His guitar burning at Monterey seemed almost an eroticized sacrifice to propitiate whatever domestic deities might have been presiding over Monterey. Looking at film footage of the event, it's clear that it *was* a sacrifice for Hendrix to torch the instrument. He was more of a traditional musician's musician in that regard—in love with his axe. He kisses the guitar before setting it down on the stage, dropping to his knees, and straddling the instrument. After squirting cigarette lighter fluid from a small can onto the guitar, he drops a match onto it, waving his long slender fingers in the air above the instrument as if conjuring a spirit. Only once the thing was flaming did he pick it up and start smashing it, Townshend style, almost as an afterthought.

The two performances aptly reflect the dual faces of the rock guitarist in popular culture at the time—the anarchist warrior striking out against the oppressive old order, and the tantric shaman ushering in the new Age of Aquarius.

MONTEREY WAS ONE of the main catalysts in bringing psychedelic rock music and the hippie counterculture into the mainstream. It was part of a cultural shift that author Charles A. Reich would call "the greening of America" in a best-selling 1970 book of that title. Soft drink ads for Coca-Cola, 7UP, and Fanta began to sport psychedelic graphics, rock music, and counterculture slogans such as "Do Your Own Thing." Counterculture themes formed the premise for television shows ranging from *The Mod Squad* to *Rowan & Martin's Laugh-In* and *The Smothers Brothers Comedy Hour.* Only the latter program had any kind of actual underground cred, in part owning to appearances by musical guests including Cream, the Who, the Doors, Jefferson Airplane, and other rock luminaries.

All of those bands enjoyed stellar record sales in the period between 1967 and the decade's end, as did the Jimi Hendrix Experience. The prominent vogue for electric blues and blues-rock guitar playing also gave rise to new heroes such as Johnny Winter, and Alvin Lee from the British group Ten Years After. Composer, satirist, and counterculture antagonist Frank Zappa began to move in more of a heavy guitar direction as the decade wore on, a direction cemented by his landmark 1969 solo album, *Hot Rats.*

The emergence of freeform FM rock radio in the latter half of the sixties provided an outlet for all this music to be heard. A higher-fidelity medium than AM radio, FM had long featured classical and "easy listening" programs. But a 1964 FCC ruling that AM stations could no longer just simulcast their AM signals on FM sent stations scrambling for new content. This provided an opening for progressive-minded DJs, such as San Francisco's Tom Donahue and New York's Scott Muni, to start broadcasting an eclectic blend of cutting-edge music based on their own personal tastes rather than a predetermined format. These DJs and those that followed their lead tended to favor long-form rock tracks with plenty of electric guitar soloing.

Often this rock music would be contextualized alongside traditional folk, blues, Indian raga, classical, and even poetry readings. But increasingly, rock music became the main draw, helping to foster album sales for the artists featured. In the U.K. a similar phenomenon took place with the rise of "pirate radio"—actual illegal radio stations broadcasting from ships just off the British coast, to circumvent BBC regulations and restrictions.

FM rock radio became the beacon, beaming into the suburbs and hinterlands the new underground rock sounds that had been brewing in the clubs, concert halls, and recording studios of London, New York, L.A., San Francisco, and other major cities. Broadcast in stereo—as opposed to AM radio's monaural signal—FM became an ideal medium for the dynamic, ambitious new style of electric guitar–driven rock music that had sprung up in the wake of Hendrix's *Are You Experienced* and like-minded discs.

Seeking a new, post-Yardbirds musical direction, Jeff Beck saw where all this was heading, although he had to talk his manager/

producer at the time into taking it seriously. More of an old-school pop radio guy, Mickie Most had been trying to push the guitarist in a pop vocal direction.

"He couldn't see a market in America for underground, hooliganistic kind of rock and roll," Beck said of Most. "In fact, he was explicit in '67–'68 when I was in big trouble with my musical career and direction. He said, 'Oh, that Jimi Hendrix; all that twang twanging and feedback nonsense, it's all finished.' I said, 'Excuse me, it's just starting.'"

Beck was right, of course, which is perhaps why he named his debut solo album *Truth*. A landmark recording, often cited as a precursor to heavy metal, *Truth* featured future Rolling Stone Ron Wood on bass and Rod Stewart on vocals. Among other things, it is the album that launched Stewart's career in a big way. But *Truth*'s main delight was, and remains, the sound of Jeff Beck, armed with a 1959 Gibson Les Paul, embracing the heavier new guitar sound just coming into vogue at the time, and that he had pioneered.

Beck's old friend Jimmy Page also saw the direction in which rock music was heading—and the electric guitar's enormous potential as a tool for crafting epic, episodic, bombastic tracks tailor-made for FM rock radio's stereophonic signal. To that end, he assembled Led Zeppelin in '68. The quartet's self-titled debut album hit like a ton of bricks in January of '69.

"I also knew that stereo FM [rock] radio was emerging in America for albums," Page later said of Led Zeppelin's genesis, "and I wanted to develop our songs emotionally, beyond just lengthy solos."

Not that there was any shortage of those. Both *Truth* and *Led Zeppelin* rely heavily on twelve-bar blues numbers, launching pads for epic electric guitar soloing. But both discs, each in its own way, take in a much broader range of musical moods, referencing folk and, in Page's case, a hint of raga—all styles that had been intermingling since '65 and were now swimming together in the free-form FM stew.

Needless to say, these developments served to boost sales in electric guitar equipment, as well as in record albums. "From 1966 onwards Marshall enjoyed explosive growth and consolidated their position as the world's premier rock guitar amplifier," wrote amp historian Michael Doyle in 1993. Marshall-style brands such as Hiwatt and Orange also did well. New effects pedals began to flood the market, and, as we've seen, the Gibson Les Paul was back in production by late 1968. And thanks largely to Jimi Hendrix, the Fender Stratocaster was also enjoying a resurgence in sales.

THE HUGE POPULARITY of heavy, electric guitar–driven rock was certainly one of the main paving stones along the road to Woodstock. Significantly, the original design for the festival poster featured a dove perched atop a flute. But the flute was quickly changed to a guitar neck.

The rock festival concept had become popular in the aftermath of Monterey, but Woodstock was by far the largest, and the one with the most far-reaching cultural consequences. The August 1969 Woodstock Music and Art Fair was billed as "An Aquarian Exposition: Three Days of Peace and Music." But it might just as accurately have been billed as "Monterey for the Masses." Whereas the audience at Monterey was estimated at being somewhere between 25,000 and 90,000, the Woodstock crowd has been reckoned to have numbered between 400,000 and 1,000,000.

That was the difference that two years made. Few Americans, or people anywhere for that matter, had heard of Jimi Hendrix in early 1967; but there was hardly anyone on the planet who wasn't aware of him by 1969. The same is true for many of the artists who appeared at both festivals: Janis Joplin, the Who, the Grateful Dead, Jefferson Airplane, the Butterfield Blues Band, Canned Heat, and Ravi Shankar. The festival also served to launch the careers of several significant new acts, including Crosby, Stills &

Nash, Santana, and the power trio Mountain led by guitarist Leslie West.

This time, however, there were no hassles as to who was going on when. For one thing, the festival was far too chaotic. But also, the rock universe had proven to be vast enough for all of the above-named acts to flourish.

If Monterey had been the coming-out party for the hippie counterculture, Woodstock was more of a farewell fete. A little over a month before Woodstock began, the rock scene was shocked by the drug and alcohol–related death of the Rolling Stones' Brian Jones. His passing was the harbinger of even more grim news. Within a year of the festival, both Hendrix and Joplin would be dead under similar circumstances. The Doors' Jim Morrison followed suit in 1971. Influential rock bands were dying as well. Cream called it quits in 1969, followed by the Beatles in '70.

BUT THERE WAS no stopping the momentum of what these artists had begun. Director Michael Wadleigh's 1970 documentary film of the Woodstock festival was arguably even more influential than the event itself. The film is what really burned the image of Jimi Hendrix playing "The Star-Spangled Banner" indelibly into the culture's collective consciousness. The late-sixties' legacy, as embodied by Woodstock, provided a template for the classic rock seventies' explosion of adventurous new subgenres, among them progressive rock, jazz-rock fusion, glam rock, art rock, Latin rock, heavy metal, country rock, and Southern boogie. These musical permutations brought many exciting new electric guitarists to the fore, including John McLaughlin (Mahavishnu Orchestra), Steve Howe (Yes), Mick Ronson (David Bowie), and Robert Fripp (King Crimson).

The era also saw the advent of professional guitar journalism, starting with the first issues of *Guitar Player* magazine in 1967. This phenomenon gathered considerable momentum in the seventies, with publications offering detailed articles on guitar equipment and playing techniques, not to mention the first reliable sheet music transcriptions of electric guitar rock and other genres.

Electric guitarists enthusiastically welcomed this new source of information, and it fostered a wonderful sense of community among guitar geeks. Ready access to details about guitar technology potentially made a Les Paul or Pete Townshend out of any guitarist. That is, a greater number of players began to think in terms of what was "under the hood" of their instrument, amplifier, and effects. All this would lead to an explosion of hot-rodded, ultra-dialed-in "rock machine" electric guitar gear, not to mention a crop of players with a very high degree of technical accomplishment (although perhaps not always as much in the way of taste).

This phenomenon also spelled the end of rock's "folk music" phase, wherein players were largely self-taught and there were absolutely no rules as to what could or couldn't be done. In this regard, guitar magazines tended to foster a kind of orthodoxy— valorizing certain guitar styles, players, attitudes, and equipment over others.

Meanwhile, rock radio also began to shift in the seventies. It got standardized, as freeform FM radio gave way to the highly structured AOR (album-oriented rock) format. This was the brainchild of Chicago DJ Lee Abrams, who introduced the idea of basing playlist choices on demographic research—the newly created, quasi- (or pseudo-) scientific field of "psychographics." The Abrams format was packaged and sold to radio stations across America, displacing many freeform DJs and programs. The end result was a dramatic narrowing of the range of music heard on rock radio. Lengthy and guitar-intensive album tracks were still favored, but less "accessible," more fringe or radical styles were shunted off the air. No more ragas or warbly voiced folksingers, but listeners could count on hearing a small handful of tracks, such as Led Zeppelin's "Stairway to Heaven" and Pink Floyd's "Dark Side of the Moon," multiple times daily. As the seventies wore on, this narrowcast selection came to be filled by the music of rock bands specifically tailored for the AOR format—Styx, Journey, Boston, Toto, Pablo Cruise, and a host of others who personified what would sometimes be known disparagingly as "corporate rock."

The pushback to all this was punk rock, which gathered momentum in New York and London during the 1976–77 period, soon spreading worldwide. It was a genuine musical revolution. The weapons in the hands of nearly all the punk rock guitarists, though, were the same old Gibsons and Fenders. The only difference was a general indifference to guitar snobbery. Cheap models were just as good, if not better, than expensive ones.

For those who were listening, punk rock issued a loud and clear announcement that the first great era of the guitar hero was over. It had run its course, dead of a corporate infection. There would still be guitar heroes, of course, even within punk. But they would set their sights on virtues other than hot blues licks and histrionic guitar solos. Punk would offer a new kind of challenge, and a new kind of freedom, to guitarists in years to come: you could do anything you want, as long as it wasn't the bombast that had come to typify mainstream rock.

Seminal punk band the Ramones had one cardinal rule, according to the group's guitarist, Johnny Ramone: "No hippie shit. I tried to avoid that as much as I could . . . avoid it to the extreme and to play pure rock and roll and not instill any sort of blues or anything into the music."

But of course not all guitarists were on board with punk's agenda. Some weren't so willing to let go of the old paradigm. This was particularly true for fans of heavy metal, the guitar-centric rock subgenre that had taken shape in the early seventies. Metal hadn't gained much respect from rock critics, nor would it for decades to come. But it would provide a forum for development of the electric guitar—not to mention a brand-new breed of heroes.

*Edward Van Halen and an early
iteration of his "Frankenstrat"*

ERUPTIONS

In his 1976 essay written for *New York* magazine, celebrated American social critic Tom Wolfe defined the seventies as the "Me Decade." He described how U.S. economic prosperity had "pumped money into every class level of the population on a scale without parallel in any country in history," triggering a wave of narcissistic behavior resulting in "the greatest age of individualism in American history." The years immediately preceding Wolfe's piece had marked a grim moment in American history. The early seventies had been dominated by headlines on the Watergate scandal, undermining the average citizen's faith in his or her elected officials; the trial of the Charles Manson family, who had brutally murdered pregnant actress Sharon Tate; and the catastrophic last days of the Vietnam War. The Organization of Arab Petroleum Exporting Countries (OAPEC)'s 1973 embargo of oil to the United States, in response to American involvement in the 1973 Arab-Israeli War, caused the price of oil to soar from $3 per barrel to nearly $12, sending shock waves through Wall Street as the stock market plummeted and inflation skyrocketed.

But after Nixon announced his resignation in 1974 and the

war in Vietnam came to its end in 1975, spirits, it seemed, began
to lift. Escapism prevailed at the box office: *Star Wars, The Rocky
Horror Picture Show, Blazing Saddles, Smokey and the Bandit,* and *Animal
House* were among the top ten grossing films of the decade, and
some of its most remembered. Style veered toward the ostenta-
tious: this was the era, after all, of widened lapels and platform
shoes, as clothing simultaneously became skimpier and more
formfitting. Cocaine took its place as the hyper drug of choice
among young adults, with cocaine initiation rates soaring across
the decade, reaching their peak in the early eighties. Perhaps the
most appropriate emblem of the era was American graphic artist
and ad man Harvey Ball's "smiley face"; its yellow visage could
be seen grinning out from T-shirts, coffee mugs, and underwear.
Though the news continued to bring its daily onslaught of tragedy,
there was still a distinctive, inescapable sense, particularly among
the young, that a corner had been turned.

It was a stark contrast to the mood across the sea, where England continued to struggle economically. Its industrial-based
economy was in a tailspin, unemployment ran rampant, and inflation peaked at over 30 percent. Under these circumstances, it
was no surprise that teens and young adults had become restless,
angry, and cynical, their rage manifested in the punk rock movement that soon ruled Britannia.

American critics loved the anger and raw energy of U.K.
bands such as the Sex Pistols, the Damned, and the Clash. But if
record sales were any indication, most American kids weren't feeling the angst. In 1978, *Never Mind the Bollocks, Here's the Sex Pistols,*
perhaps the most important punk rock album of the era, failed to
dent Billboard's Top 100, while that same year, the soundtrack to
the John Travolta movie *Saturday Night Fever,* featuring the dance
music of the Bee Gees, stayed atop the album charts for twenty-
four straight weeks, selling 15 million units. And if it was rock
and roll you were after, nonthreatening corporate rockers Journey, Foreigner, Boston, and Meat Loaf, whose 1977 *Bat Out of Hell*

album would eventually sell over 43 million copies worldwide, were there to satisfy you.

If you were eighteen and lived in Hollywood, California, you had likely begun hearing of a hard rock band from Pasadena that had recently arrived on the scene, poised to eclipse those more tepid bands. Memorably described by Los Angeles producer Kim Fowley as the musical equivalent of "a six-pack of beer, cruising down the highway with a big-breasted woman while running over animals," Van Halen was the ultimate party band, packing in fans at clubs on the Sunset Strip like the Starwood, the Whisky a Go Go, and Walter Mitty's Rock & Roll Emporium, where 300-capacity rooms were often illegally stretched to accommodate a thousand sweaty kids. Keeping with the spirit of the times, the band could switch at the drop of a dime between playing the classic hard rock of Led Zeppelin and disco hits like "Get Down Tonight" by KC and the Sunshine Band, while somehow retaining their own loose, hip, and happy sound. Their lead singer was a larger-than-life, motormouthed dervish, but the band's main attraction was undoubtedly their young guitarist. For almost five years, word of his otherworldly playing had been burning up West Coast high school hotlines, and his club performances became legendary among local musicians. His approach to the guitar was so radical and exciting, it bordered on magic. Even professional guitarists who went to see him struggled to explain how this kid with the perfect hair and the "What, me worry?" grin was creating the torrent of lightning-fast licks, strange ringing harmonics, and screaming whammy-bar dives. To those who flocked to see him, one thing was clear: he was the real deal—the next Jimi Hendrix or Eric Clapton.

Listeners packed into those Hollywood clubs could only wonder: Who the hell was this remarkable kid, and where on earth did he come from?

•

EDWARD LODEWIJK VAN HALEN moved to Pasadena, California, from his native Nijmegen, Holland, when he was seven, along with his parents and his older brother, Alex. When they arrived in 1962, Ed remembers, the cash-poor family had only "$25 and a Dutch-made Rippen piano," and what little of the former the family had went into teaching the children how to play the latter.

By all accounts, those early years in the United States were not easy. Ed's dad, Jan, was a professional musician who played saxophone and clarinet in wedding bands at night, but kept janitorial day jobs to make ends meet. Life for the boys wasn't much easier.

"When I came to this country I was scared," remembers Eddie. "I couldn't speak the language. I used to get the shit kicked out of me by white people, so to speak. I was a minority. My earliest friends were black kids in the neighborhood. I didn't have to manufacture pain to create."

Alex was the more extroverted of the two boys and worked hard to fit in, while Ed tended to retreat into a world of his own—a world of music. Both boys were trained to play classical piano, but young Edward excelled, winning trophies in local music competitions. Neither particularly enjoyed the music they were being asked to play—they were more attracted to rock bands such as the Dave Clark Five, the Animals, and Cream—but they learned fundamentals that would serve them well in the ensuing years: rhythm, harmony, left and right hand independence, and steely discipline.

Alex eventually drifted toward the guitar, while Ed started banging away at drums. In a cosmic stroke of luck, they decided to trade—or at least Ed was forced to defer when his older brother became more interested in pounding the skins.

"When I first picked up the guitar there was no message from God or anything," Eddie told *Guitar World*. "Some things were easy, some things were hard. But I didn't even think about whether it was easy or hard; it was something I wanted to do, to have fun and feel good about doing it. Whether it took me a week to learn half a song or one day to learn five songs, I never thought of it that way."

Those days and weeks melted into years, as the shy, gifted young man's guitar playing continued to improve. "I used to sit on the edge of my bed with a six-pack of Schlitz Malt talls," he said. "My brother would go out at 7 p.m. to party and get laid, and when he'd come back at 3 a.m., I would still be sitting in the same place, playing guitar. I did that for years."

More than a few of those long practice hours were spent thinking about aspects of the instrument that most simply took for granted. "Since the beginning, everything I picked up off the rack at a music store—even the custom-made stuff—did not do what I wanted it to do," Van Halen said years later. "Either it didn't have enough of something, or it had a bunch of Bozo bells and whistles that I didn't need. A lot of it had to do with the fact that I never took guitar lessons, so I didn't know right from wrong. I didn't know there were rules; I just knew what I liked and wanted to feel and hear."

His tinkering with instruments began early on:

I bought one of my first guitars from Lafayette Electronics, which was like a Radio Shack. They had a 12-string guitar that I really liked, but I didn't want 12 strings; I wanted six. I asked the guy if I could take six off and try it out, and he said, "No." I said, "Why not?" He said, "If you buy it, you can do whatever you want." So I bought it, took six strings off and I loved it! And that was my very, very first successful attempt at changing something that was considered standard to my liking.

Later, Van Halen got more daring with his experiments. After purchasing a rather pricey goldtop Les Paul, he fearlessly took a chisel to the vintage instrument, and replaced the bridge pickup with a louder and more powerful humbucker stolen from one of his other guitars. Then he decided he wasn't a fan of the instrument's gold finish, so he stripped it and repainted it black. The modifications gave Edward more of what he wanted and was a hint of things to come, including the striped paint job that you see on most of his guitars since the band's first album.

Edward destroyed a lot of instruments trying to get them to do what he wanted, but he learned something from every guitar he tore apart, and discovered even more things in the process.

But why did he have to go to so much trouble to create the guitar of his dreams in the first place? Part of the answer was simply Van Halen's idiosyncratic brand of DIY genius; he refused to be constricted by the equipment that was available. But the rest points to a story with implications far beyond Southern California.

LEO FENDER WAS a creative genius and a driven perfectionist, but his run with Fender was coming to an end. A series of strep and sinus infections throughout the fifties and early sixties, along with the stress of running his growing empire, had left him fatigued. Sometime in the mid-sixties, Leo instructed his associates to start looking for someone to buy the company he had built, which had by then expanded to more than five hundred employees occupying twenty-seven buildings in Fullerton.

It didn't take long to find an interested party. In 1965, national and multinational conglomerates had become increasingly significant parts of the American economy. Historians and economists have since identified the fertile period between 1965 and 1969 as the Third Merger Wave, due to a strong economy that gave many firms the resources necessary to acquire other companies. (The conditions were uncommon—the last merger wave had taken place in the twenties.)

Columbia Broadcasting System, Inc. (CBS), the radio and television media giant, was just one of the businesses eager for diversification, and they saw in Fender an opportunity. So, for an impressive $13.5 million (roughly $80 million by today's standards), CBS acquired Fender in early 1965. Considering both companies' ties to the entertainment industry, it seemed like a fine match. And it was—but only for a hot minute.

Within months, CBS started intensifying production and slashing costs. In their first year, they increased Fender's guitar and amplifier output by about 30 percent, and a scant year later they erected an enormous new Fullerton-based facility and increased productivity by an *additional* 45 percent.

The rapid expansion came at a cost. By 1966, CBS was instituting changes that started to negatively impact the feel and quality of Fender instruments and amps. Their most popular guitar—the Stratocaster—was the first to get hit in the twang bar. The guitar's sensuous curves suddenly became less contoured and sleek, and cheaper plastics were used for the pickguards. Indian rosewood supplanted the beautifully figured Brazilian rosewood on the fingerboards, and quality control went out the window.

In 1968 the thin, nitrocellulose lacquer that had been used on every Fender guitar since the early fifties was changed to the cheaper polyurethane. By 1971 the desecration was complete when the Strat was given a three-bolt neck (instead of the conventional four bolts), and bridge saddles fashioned from a cheaper alloy in place of the original pressed steel, all of which contributed to a less lively sound. Eventually CBS started slashing away at product lines; by 1980 they'd eliminated Esquires, Duo-Sonics, Jaguars, Jazzmasters, and thinline Teles, while also purging the majority of Fender's distinctive custom-color options.

To this day among guitar collectors, the term "pre-CBS" is used to describe a utopian world where the just ruled, the righteous prevailed, and all instruments achieved a sort of platonic ideal. "Post-CBS," on the other hand, is a demarcation uttered with the kind of disdain usually reserved for traditional Chinese curses.

Gibson, too, was undergoing extraordinary changes—and

not for the better. In December of 1969, Ecuadorian Company Limited (ECL), a South American beer and cement conglomerate, purchased the Gibson parent company, Chicago Musical Instruments. Perhaps their name was a touch too exotic for U.S. consumers; it was quickly Americanized to "Norlin." The acquisition spelled disaster for the brand.

It would be a stretch to suggest that no great guitars were built during the seventeen-year Norlin era, but it is remembered as a time of missed opportunities, questionable quality control, and downright weird and unpopular products such as the Marauder, an awkward Les Paul/Telecaster hybrid with a Flying V headstock; or the RD, a hideous variation on the Gibson Firebird with electronics designed by synthesizer guru Bob Moog. Among their most egregious acts, however, were the indignities heaped on the once-mighty Les Paul.

The original single-cutaway Les Paul Standard was an instrument that was just slightly ahead of its time. Prematurely discontinued in 1960, it experienced a spectacular revival four or five years later, as we've seen. While any reasonable company would've responded by immediately putting the instrument back into production, Gibson hesitated. When they did finally respond, it was with "the Deluxe," a half-assed variation on the Standard.

Players immediately took offense at the fact that the guitars they were being marketed looked different from the ones their heroes were using. But that was just the beginning. Like the Stratocaster, the Les Paul would be subjected to other detrimental changes, both cosmetically and in construction, and it would take years before the company rectified these injustices.

In the meantime, vintage guitars were all over the pages of music papers, becoming almost as recognizable as the players, and were coveted by musicians the world over.

With the corporate heads at Gibson and Fender turning a tin ear to consumers, a number of manufacturers, big and small, started to see opportunity. As the Japanese were seizing upon weakness in the "Big Three" American automakers, grabbing market share with their sturdy and inexpensive products such as the Honda Civic, something similar was happening to the U.S. guitar industry. Due to a lack of legislation to address patent infringements and restrict import sales, a boatload of high-quality Les Paul and vintage Stratocaster knockoffs, produced by overseas manufacturers, hit the shores in the 1960s and '70s. And players took notice. Japanese manufacturers, including Tokai, Fernandes, Burny, Ibanez, Univox, and Aria, flooded the U.S. market with excellent instruments at reasonable costs. Also sensing gaps in the marketplace were new American companies like Peavey, Music Man, Heritage, and B.C. Rich, who began to take flight themselves.

While these enterprising start-ups posed legitimate threats to the established companies, most players still lusted after the brands their heroes used. And if they couldn't buy those discontinued treasures, maybe they could improve the subpar Strats they already owned.

ONE OF THE inevitable results of the decline of Fender and Gibson in the seventies was the creation of the "aftermarket replacement parts" industry—an unsexy name for a resourceful group of independent tinkerers who started making guitar parts and accessories that improved inferior factory-made instruments.

Leading the charge of this revolution was a young Staten Island, New York, musician and guitar technician named Larry DiMarzio, who built his first Super Distortion pickup as a replacement for factory Gibson humbuckers in 1972.

"I started building my own pickups for the most practical reason," DiMarzio says. "I wanted my guitar to sound better. I wanted to get a bigger sound than what I was getting out of the standard pickups of the day. It turns out others did, too."

Most of DiMarzio's early marketing was by word of mouth

on a local level and via small mail-order-only ads, placed in the back of national music magazines and announcing "The Hottest, Loudest, Longest-Sustaining Pickups Ever Made!" True to his claim, his humbuckers, with their increased output level, made almost any Les Paul roar.

It didn't take long for the word to spread among East Coast guitar cognoscenti. Soon the hottest players in the land, like Kiss's Ace Frehley and jazz virtuoso Al Di Meola, were beating a path to DiMarzio's modest door.

"I worked at the Guitar Lab on 48th Street in Manhattan," he said. "We'd get in a new Les Paul and remove the heavy gauge strings, then grind and polish the frets because the factory hadn't done this properly, and make a total readjustment." Soon he was also adding his own pickups to the mix, trying to extract from inferior instruments the kinds of sounds produced by the classic guitars owned by Eric Clapton and Mountain's Leslie West.

Over the next decade, many other enterprising technicians and luthiers got into the act. After spending time in London and doing repairs for Jimmy Page, George Harrison, Jimi Hendrix, and others, a New Jersey native named Seymour Duncan eventually settled in California and started his own very successful replacement parts company in late 1978.

So did another talented West Coast guitar entrepreneur named Wayne Charvel, who became a local legend in the early seventies for his repair work and stunning custom finishes while employed as an independent contractor for Fender. In 1974, Charvel opened a shop of his own in Azusa, California, and commissions flowed quickly from gigantic bands such as Deep Purple, ZZ Top, and the Who.

Wayne's insider perspective and expertise allowed him to identify common problems and gaps in the market, and he, like DiMarzio, eventually started his own mail-order business that sold guitars as well as his unique inventions, such as a stainless steel tremolo arm for Stratocasters that was four times stronger than the originals. To supplement his business, he enlisted two talented woodworkers—Lynn Ellsworth, who would go on to start Boogie Bodies, and Dave Schecter, who later founded Schecter Guitar Research—to craft bodies and necks with the kind of elegance and precision no longer being offered by the big manufacturers.

But perhaps Charvel's canniest recruit was not an employee but the inquisitive and enthusiastic young musician who regularly haunted his California repair shop, and whom he had taken to mentoring. Eddie Van Halen was still a couple years away from superstardom, and he often visited Wayne's world in the mid-seventies. Sometimes he would boldly pepper Charvel with questions on guitar repair. On other occasions he'd quietly hang out and absorb information that he would use to create his own spectacular innovations—inventions that would eventually put the replacement parts industry on the map for good.

"The first time Ed came in he asked me if I could stop his DiMarzio pickup from squealing," said Charvel.

> I told him I could. I showed him a trick I learned from an electronics genius I knew named Bob Luly, where you soaked the pickup in hot wax, which is now commonly referred to as "potting." To the best of my knowledge, we were the first to "pot" after-market pickups . . .
>
> After that, Eddie would come by the shop a lot, and sometimes he would sit on the floor and play the guitar while I repaired some of his other guitars.

THE STORY OF how Ed built his iconic red, black, and white striped "Frankenstein," or "Frankenstrat," guitar—one of the most famous guitars in rock history—has often been riddled with errors, many perpetuated by the guitarist himself in an attempt to throw copycats off his trail. However, in recent years, he's opened up about his legacy. As Eddie explained to *Guitar World*, the guitar was the product of years of trial and error.

After working on his goldtop Les Paul and getting a taste for guitar modification, Eddie acquired several other guitars that he would put on the operating table, including a 1961 Gibson ES-335 and both 1958 and 1961 Fender Stratocaster guitars. "That 335 used to be my favorite guitar, because it had a thin neck and low action," he said, referring to the close proximity between the guitar's strings and its fretboard. "It was real easy to play, but the guys in the band hated how it looked."

One can only imagine what his group thought after Edward performed some major surgery on the hapless guitar. Frustrated by the fact that the ES-335 would go out of tune every time he depressed the instrument's vibrato arm, he took a hacksaw and cut the tailpiece (which anchors the strings to the guitar's body) in half so only the higher three strings would wiggle when he used his whammy bar. "That way I could always go back to the three lower strings to play chords if the vibrato made the high strings go out of tune," said Van Halen. "People tripped out on that, but I'd try anything to make something work."

As whammy-bar dives became a greater part of his playing style, Van Halen discovered that the Fender Strat's vibrato system was easier to keep in tune. Unfortunately, his picky bandmates considered the Strat's tone too thin. Eddie had a solution to that dilemma: he routed out the body of his '61 Strat and installed a fat-sounding Gibson PAF humbucker in the bridge position.

"I slapped a humbucker in there and figured out how to wire up the rest of the shit," he said. "That got me closer to the sound I wanted, but it still wasn't right. The tone was still too thin, probably because of the wood that the body was made of." After months of experimentation and frustration, Ed decided to start from scratch and build his own guitar, using scraps from previous instruments and cheap parts purchased from his buddies at Charvel.

Modifying a guitar with new or spare parts was a radical idea in the seventies, but it was easy to see where Ed got his inspiration. Southern California was the birthplace of hot-rod culture, where backyard car mechanics, working with junkyard parts, would compete with each other to see who could make the fastest car. His Pasadena hometown was a major center for these DIY mechanics, and custom cars were literally everywhere. Don Blair's legendary Speed Shop, one of the first shops to sell custom parts in Southern California, was located less than two miles from where Ed grew up, and the town's connection to "kustom kar kulture" was caricatured in Jan & Dean's 1964 novelty hit "The Little Old Lady (from Pasadena)," about a granny with a fast car and a lead foot.

At the time, Charvel and Lynn Ellsworth were making replacement guitar bodies and necks and selling them under the Boogie Bodies brand. Van Halen dropped by the factory sometime in 1975 and bought an ash Strat body for $50. It was, he recalls, a "piece-of-shit" body on the bottom of a stack of other bodies. For another $80, he acquired an unfinished maple neck.

Because the body was pre-routed for three narrow, Fender-style pickups, Van Halen chiseled out a larger cavity to install a bigger standard humbucking pickup, nearest to the bridge. He pulled the humbucker from his Gibson ES-335 and mounted it to the new body—a move that enhanced the guitar's bass response, liveliness, and sustain.

Though there were chambers for two more pickups, Van Halen left them empy; he couldn't remember the wiring circuit for installing additional pickups and tone controls ("I never touched the tone controls anyway"). He also installed jumbo Gibson frets on the fretboard, and a brass nut on the neck of the guitar, and salvaged a vibrato tailpiece from one of his vintage Strat guitars to repurpose for this new, homegrown instrument.

To cover the empty pickup holes, he cut a piece of black vinyl and nailed it on, covering the cavity. The final and most distinctive touch was a black-and-white-striped finish. Van Halen applied this by first spraying the body with several coats of black acrylic lacquer paint, then taping it up and spraying several coats of white lacquer paint over it. The tape was removed once the final coat was dry. The result of these modifications was a guitar that combined Van Halen's favorite aspects of his Les Paul Standard, his ES-335, and his Strat.

A Frankenstrat was born.

WHEN VAN HALEN'S self-titled debut album was released in 1978, you could almost hear the resounding thud in the guitar community as jaws hit the ground. Van Halen's debut sounded unlike anything heard before, largely due to Ed's guitar playing. While the opening track "Runnin' with the Devil" offered a taste of his larger-than-life sound, it was the second track that started a revolution.

In a mere 1:42, the solo guitar instrumental "Eruption" changed the way electric guitarists looked at the instrument forever. As the title suggests, the track was an explosion of musical ideas—sounds and techniques that paved the road for guitarists for decades to come.

Using his Frankenstrat guitar, tuned down a half-step to E-flat, through a 1968 Marshall Super Lead tube amp, supplemented by an MXR Phase 90, a Univox echo unit, and the Sunset Sound studio reverb room, Edward offered a brief—but devastating— summary of everything he had been working on in the previous years.

First, there was the tone of his homemade guitar itself, which Van Halen referred to as his "brown sound." He had always admired the rich, liquid textures of Eric Clapton during his Cream era, but Ed's guitar added extra bite to the beauty. His sound was big, round, and majestic when needed, but it could also ring out with sharp clarity during quicker passages. His deft use of reverb and echo contributed to the concert hall vibe.

But what caused the real ruckus was the song's ultra-speedy licks and Eddie's use of two-handed tapping. Employed three decades earlier by Jimmie Webster on his Gretsch guitars, it was still a relatively unused technique wherein the guitarist engages fingers from both hands at once on the fretboard, in order to play intervals and passages that would be impossible using only the fretting hand.

"Tapping is like having a sixth finger on your left hand," Van Halen explained at the time of the album's release. "Instead of picking, you're hitting a note on the fretboard. I was just sitting in my room at home, drinking a beer, and I remembered seeing other players using the technique for one quick note in a solo. I thought, 'Well, nobody is really capitalizing on that idea.' So I started dickin' around and realized the potential. I had never seen anyone take it as far as I did."

Young guitarists completely flipped for Ed's sound, and even the most jaded members of the guitar community were impressed. Led Zeppelin's Jimmy Page, who rarely handed out compliments, said, "For my money, Van Halen is the first significant new kid on the block. Very dazzling. He flies the flag well." Even the curmudgeonly Frank Zappa thanked Eddie for "reinventing the guitar."

After the release of the first Van Halen album, the musical universe shifted. Being a guitar hero was suddenly more fashionable than it had been since the heyday of Hendrix and Clapton. But now the bar had been raised, and the stakes were greater. If you were *really* going to compete with King Edward, you'd better be fast as hell, look cool, have a trove of new ideas, and a guitar nobody had ever seen.

Influenced by the work of eighteenth-century violinist Niccolo Paganini, the fierce Swedish guitar sensation Lars Johan Yngve Lannerbäck, more commonly known as Yngwie Malmsteen, introduced classical scales and arpeggios to the rock world and pioneered the use of sweep picking, a technique in which the guitarist plays single notes on consecutive strings with a sweeping motion of the pick, to produce a lightning-fast series of notes.

The Swede, who often dressed like a flamboyant rock-and-roll Beethoven, preferred to play a traditional Fender Stratocaster, but he radically altered it by scalloping the fretboard, a modification that scoops out some of the wood between the frets and facilitated Malmsteen's tremendous speed and wild vibrato.

A steady stream of shredders were to follow, many with their own signature instruments built to their specifications by up-and-coming guitar companies looking to knock Fender and Gibson off their pedestals. Steve Vai and Joe Satriani, two phenoms from Carle Place, New York, had colorful guitars crafted for them by the Japanese brand Ibanez, both featuring pickups custom-made by Larry DiMarzio. Mick Mars of Mötley Crüe played an angular B.C. Rich Warlock, while Dokken guitarist George Lynch had ESP, another Japanese company, build him an instrument with a "Kamikaze" graphic.

Not since the heyday of bebop in the fifties had so many fast and inventive musicians invaded the pop music market. Most of these flashy young guns played in "hair metal" bands, a hard rock subgenre known for its colorful clothes, androgynous style, crunchy riffs, pop choruses, and incredible guitar solos.

For all the competition, Van Halen would remain one step ahead for years to come. One of his most historically important performances came in 1982 when mega-producer Quincy Jones enlisted Ed to play a solo on Michael Jackson's work in progress, *Thriller*. What eventually became "Beat It" exploded racial barriers on MTV and rock radio. It would contribute to *Thriller*'s claim to being the best-selling album of all time.

Van Halen recalls his role in the song's birth:

I get this call and I said, "Hello?" And I hear a guy on the other end going "Hello? Hello?" We couldn't hear each other, so I hung up. The phone rings again and I hear this voice on the other end asking: "Is this Eddie? It's Quincy, man!" And I'm like, "Who the fuck? What do you want, you fuckin' ass-hole?" So finally he says, "It's Quincy Jones, man!" And I'm goin', "Ohhh, shit! I'm sorry, man . . ." After the record, he wrote me a letter thanking me and signed it "The Fuckin' Asshole."

ED CONTINUED TO tinker with his Frankenstrat across the decades, making it into an even sexier, more formidable monster. In 1979 he had retaped the body of his black and white guitar and painted over it with red Schwinn bicycle paint, creating the guitar look most associated with Van Halen. Additionally, he gave his creation a little "trailer trash" flash by attaching red truck reflectors to the rear of the body and installing large eyehook screws to the horn and back of the guitar—a foolproof method of keeping his strap attached to his instrument.

In addition to revamping the cosmetics, Van Halen would help refine another major guitar innovation: the locking tremolo system. Using a whammy bar was a major part of his playing technique, allowing him to bend notes dramatically. But excessive use often caused his strings to fall hopelessly out of tune. He had developed a number of strategies to minimize the problem, but he was unable to come up with a solution that worked all the time.

Just as Ed's star was rising, a guitarist named Floyd Rose was dealing with the same set of issues. Rose was playing in a rock band and wanted to use his whammy bar the way his hero Jimi Hendrix did, but was frustrated when his guitar wouldn't stay in tune. Using skills acquired from years of jewelry making, he devised an ingenious system of clamps that would lock the strings of the guitar at the nut (where the neck meets the head) and again at the bridge. Together they'd keep the guitar in tune even under extreme duress.

Rose shared his invention with his friend Lynn Ellsworth, who immediately thought of Edward. "So, I went with him to show Eddie the locking system I created," says Rose. "He liked it and gave me a guitar to put one on."

Ed picks up the story from there: "My role in the design and development of the Floyd was adding the fine tuners to the bridge . . . Strings stretch, temperature changes, and depending on how hard you play, your guitar would go out of tune. So, you'd have to unclamp the nut, which involves loosening three screws with an Allen wrench, tune the guitar, and re-clamp the nut down again. There wasn't enough time to do all this in between every song live . . . To put it simply, it was a pain in the ass." So Eddie suggested adding fine tuners to the bridge. This would allow a player to lock down the strings, so they'd essentially stay in tune, but to still make subtle adjustments when needed. And it worked, becoming an essential device for rock players in the eighties and beyond.

It was no surprise that a number of guitar companies started knocking on Van Halen's door. Who wouldn't want to work with the man who had completely revolutionized their business? In the last few decades he has collaborated with Kramer, Music Man, and Peavey, before joining forces with a revived and rejuvenated Fender in 2005. Unlike guitarists who endorse products in name only, Eddie worked tirelessly with each brand he was associated with to improve and refine his ideas in an effort to build better products. One of his latest guitars, the EVH Wolfgang, took over three years to design, and during that time over eighty different pickups alone were tested before one was deemed good enough for the guitar.

When journalists ask Ed who his biggest influences are, he often confounds them by saying Les Paul. Anyone who knows guitar history understands exactly why Van Halen would cite the mighty Wizard from Waukesha. What other figures were equal parts virtuoso and technical innovator? Before Paul passed away in 2009, he and Van Halen had become extremely close friends.

Ed often chuckled at the memories of Les calling him at 3:00 a.m. to discuss some esoteric guitar-related concept, or else to simply bullshit. During those late-night chats, Eddie recalls with pride, Les would often sign off by saying, "There's only been three great electric guitar makers: me, you and Leo [Fender]."

In 2015, Ed promised there would be more new guitars to come. "I don't know if there is such a thing as perfection," the guitarist said, "but the Wolfgang is the best of everything we could find at this moment. I'm always changing, so even 'the best' is a tough word for me to define. I'm going to continue work on building better guitars."

As for his beloved red, black, and white Frankenstrat guitar, Ed still uses it here and there. But lest anyone doubt its lasting significance, in 2011 the Smithsonian National Museum of American History in Washington, D.C., came knocking on Van Halen's door asking to add the prized instrument to its collection. Eddie refused to part with the original, but recognizing the honor, offered up "Frank 2," an exact duplicate made by a master guitar builder at Fender and used during Van Halen's 2007–8 North American tour.

The museum's director, Brent D. Glass, put it solemnly: "The museum collects objects that are multidimensional, and this guitar reflects innovation, talent and influence." Ed would no doubt agree with that assessment, but in his earthy, self-deprecating way he would probably add that it also reflects "a whole lotta dickin' around."

Steve Vai's Ibanez white
JEM7V-EVO, his primary stage
and recording guitar

chapter 10

MADE IN JAPAN

an Halen's massive success meant that Eddie's Frankenstrat would soon be showcased throughout the United States, from arena to arena in the late seventies and eighties. With it came the implied message that the age of Gibson and Fender supremacy had passed, and a new era of guitar-building innovation had arrived. One of the thousands of young, impressionable guitarists who heard Ed's message loud and clear was an earnest, Fender Stratocaster–playing twenty-year-old named Steve Vai, who was attending Boston's prestigious Berklee College of Music.

"It was like a monolith appeared on the planet," remembers Vai.

> Eddie's impact was very sudden. I was in college when his first album came out. My tone sucked, man. I was just interested in chops. I could play fast and pick all sorts of fast notes, but I spent precious little time on my sound. So when I heard Ed, I realized I needed to raise my own bar. It's a very select group of people that have really brought the electric guitar

to a different level. As far as I'm concerned, Jimi Hendrix did it and Edward did it. That's it.

Born in the small town of Carle Place, New York, on June 6, 1960, Vai began playing the guitar at the age of thirteen after hearing Jimmy Page's fast and furious solo in "Heartbreaker" on *Led Zeppelin II.*

"I went wild when I heard that solo," said Vai. "I vowed that I would learn to play it—*I had to learn how to play it.*"

He spent his teens doing just that, taking lessons from another future guitar hero, Joe Satriani, who immediately saw Vai's potential. Satriani taught him the intricacies of music theory and proper playing technique. "I got a kick out of sitting across from a thirteen-year-old Steve Vai and realizing, 'This kid is going to be playing better than me,'" Satriani recalls. "I just instinctively knew it."

While many youngsters would've bridled at the discipline, Vai took to it with the dedication that would become his calling card. "Joe Satriani set an amazingly high standard and pulled me up to it," said Vai. "My lessons were the most important thing in my life. They were treasures."

He was determined to keep pushing the limits of his playing. In 1979, during his stay at Berklee, Vai reached out to the legendary Frank Zappa, perhaps one of the only musicians in the rock world whose standards and workaholism exceeded his own. Zappa, a guitarist and composer of complex, satirical music, had a reputation as a fearsome bandleader who demanded nothing less than perfection from musicians. In an act of sheer chutzpah, Vai mailed Frank a painstakingly accurate transcription he had made of Zappa's "The Black Page," an outrageously complicated drum instrumental, along with a tape of his own guitar playing.

Much to Vai's surprise, Zappa responded. He hired Vai to transcribe a number of the guitar solos that were published in *The Frank Zappa Guitar Book* in 1982. Zappa also enlisted the guitarist to become a full-fledged band member, often referring to Vai admiringly as his "little Italian virtuoso." While the gig didn't exactly make Steve famous—Zappa's music was too bizarre, his following too underground for that—Vai was immediately put on the short list of "musicians to watch" in the guitar community. To be so young and receive praise by someone as discerning and brilliant as Frank Zappa was no small thing, and people began to take notice. It certainly didn't hurt Steve's cause that he was tall, dark, and had the chiseled bone structure of a natural-born rock star.

Big things were in store for Vai, whose chops were beginning to rival anyone's in the rock and jazz world. But like Van Halen before him, Vai grew restless with the limitations of his store-bought Stratocaster. He began to desire an instrument that would offer more tonal flexibility and better accommodate his wizardry, especially in the upper reaches of his fretboard.

"Choosing a guitar was a little bit of a dilemma for me," recalled Vai,

> because I loved the big, humbucking sound of a Les Paul, but at the same time I instinctively understood the potential of a whammy bar. For that reason I had to have a Strat, but I didn't like the way Stratocasters sounded. They never really seemed "rock and roll" to me. They were always a little hard to play, and the single-coil pickups were a little thin-sounding. But that was my main axe. I got a maple Strat when I was fifteen or sixteen, and it didn't sound great, but it had a whammy bar, and I beat that whammy bar to death. I was using this Strat all the way up through my days with Frank.
>
> Then when Van Halen hit the scene and he had a guitar with a whammy bar *and* a humbucker, that changed a lot of things.

Ed's guitar grabbed Vai's attention, but for the next couple of years he persisted with his Fender (despite the fact that Zappa humorously chided his tone as sounding like a "ham sandwich" or "a bunch of buzzing flies"). It wasn't until the young gun left Frank's group to join Alcatrazz, a melodic hard rock band based in Hollywood, that he was forced to really rethink his sound.

Alcatrazz demanded a bigger, beefier sound. The group's keyboardist, Jimmy Waldo, introduced Steve to Grover Jackson, the custom guitar builder who was making guitars for everyone from Ozzy Osbourne's guitarist Randy Rhoads to Jeff Beck. Seeing Vai's potential to become the next big thing, Jackson lent him a brown guitar he had designed for Charvel.

"It was fantastic," said Vai. "It had a humbucker and a whammy bar, and Grover made one of the closest instruments to what I was looking for, but there were still things about it I wasn't crazy about."

Vai recalls having a conversation with Zappa about the Jackson Charvel. What aren't you crazy about? Zappa asked him. The guitarist gave him a laundry list: it didn't have enough frets, the cutaway wasn't right, the body wasn't sexy enough, and so on.

> One of the things I learned, working with Frank—who was the most extraordinary man I ever met—when he would get an idea for something, he would just do it. He would work until he found a solution, whether it was a problem with notation, instrumentation, lyrics, recording techniques, guitars, or guitar effects. So I started experimenting with custom guitar builders, and one of the first ones that I had made was by Valdez Guitar, but it was still more of a Strat. It still didn't fit my needs. When I was asked to play in the David Lee Roth Band in 1985, I decided I'd had enough. I wasn't going to stop until I had the guitar of my dreams.

Joining Roth's group catapulted Vai into the big leagues overnight. The singer had recently shocked the rock world by leaving Van Halen to pursue a solo career, and if Roth was going to form a band that could follow Van Halen, he would need a guitar player brilliant enough to rival Edward, at that time perhaps the most famous guitarist on earth. Vai, whose star had been rising, was an obvious choice. But despite the reverence Vai inspired among musicians, he still didn't own an instrument he truly loved.

"I was still using the borrowed Charvel, which I had taken the liberty of painting fluorescent green, much to Wayne's chagrin," laughed Steve. "It was the main guitar that I used on my first album with Roth, *Eat 'Em and Smile*. But when it came time to tour, I needed some backups and I wanted to have something made. I went to this little guitar shop in Hollywood called Performance Guitar, and I took the Frank approach. I was going to be relentless until I got what I wanted."

This was Vai's chance to really make his mark. Building upon ideas already put in place by Van Halen—a locking-whammy-bar system and humbucking pickups—he expanded the guitar's design in several key areas. Perhaps his most significant and longest-lasting contribution to guitar design was the idea of a "floating tremolo" or "floating bridge" system. In his words:

> I wanted to have a whammy bar that could pull the strings really sharp, not just one tone or half a tone, which is what the conventional systems allowed you to do. I had never seen anything that would do what I wanted, so I just looked at the guitar, looked at it carefully, and I thought, "What's stopping this tremolo from going really sharp?" It was just the wood in the body that the bridge was sitting on, so I took a hammer and a screwdriver and I banged out the wood, pieces flying everywhere. That was it and then I was able to pull way up and notes would go a fifth, a sixth. I could even snap the strings. That was party time for me.

Vai had luthiers do well what he had done crudely. They carved a "lion's claw" cavity behind the bridge of his guitar. He made several other requests, including twenty-four frets on the neck (instead of the standard twenty-two), and a deeper cutaway that would allow him to easily access the upper reaches of his strings.

"I never understood the cutaways on most guitars," said Vai.

> It's pretty uncomfortable to play up high on Strats and Les Pauls. At least with my big hands, you can't get up there and squeeze those notes without having wood in your way.
>
> And there's the shape. I liked Stratocasters, but they were visually a little too pedestrian—they weren't sexy enough. And I couldn't sit with a Les Paul. They were always off to the side or they hung funny. So I had Performance [Guitar shop] sharpen the edges of a Strat-style guitar a bit, and round off certain areas that I thought would feel good, and the finished body looked great to me. It had a real kind of appeal, had some nice shape to it.

Vai also questioned the configuration of traditional electric guitar pickups. He saw the virtues of the double-humbucker sound found in most Gibson guitars, but also enjoyed certain aspects of his Stratocaster's three single-coil pickups, and wondered why he couldn't have the best of both worlds in one guitar. His solution was simple and elegant. He had Performance install two humbuckers, one near the neck and one near the bridge, and a Strat-style single-coil pickup in the middle.

Very little escaped Vai's intense scrutiny, including something as simple as the instrument's input jack. As most players will tell you, one of the great hazards of showing off onstage—posing, jumping, or dancing, for instance—is accidently stepping on your chord and yanking it out of your instrument. Vai, who had developed into quite a showman, decided to solve the problem by designing the input on his guitar to go through the body of the guitar at an angle, from the side, which made it "yank proof."

His coup de grâce, however, was the unorthodox idea of carving a handle, or "monkey grip," into the top of his guitar, near the upper horn. Like Van Halen's striped paint job, it was an eye-grabbing detail that nearly overshadowed all the serious ideas that he packed into his innovative custom design.

Vai asked the luthiers at Performance to make four guitars incorporating all of his wishes, and he had them laminated with risqué images, including nudes clipped from the pages of *Playboy* magazine. As far as Vai was concerned, he had everything he needed.

And it seems he did. *Eat 'Em and Smile,* Vai's debut with David Lee Roth, was a huge success, reaching #4 on the Billboard charts, and after appearing quite prominently in several Roth videos on MTV, the guitarist was on his way to becoming a household name. With the attention came covers on all the major guitar magazines, such as *Guitar World* and *Guitar Player.* So it was hardly surprising when many of the major six-string manufacturers of the day came calling, asking him to endorse one of their instruments. While he entertained all comers, almost every one disappointed.

"What I got back from most companies were basically guitars with a few little modifications," said Vai. He had something singular in mind, and though he had lengthy discussions with a number of builders about what he wanted, they failed to deliver anything that met his exacting standards. All of them except one.

NO HISTORY OF the electric guitar would be complete without some discussion of the wonderful, sometimes bizarre world of Japanese imports. During the sixties and seventies, alongside the rise of Gibson and Fender and their ilk, Asian brands such as Teisco, Kawai, Kent, and Guyatone flooded the United States. They usually came in strange shapes, often festooned with a multitude of glittering knobs and pickups (which rarely did more than make the instrument sound worse). Many also had warped necks and were flimsily constructed, leaving them almost impossible to play. But despite their many faults, they had their virtues too—namely, they looked cool and were cheap as hell. Most were purchased by beginners distracted by their cosmetic bells and whistles, or bought as gifts by well-meaning parents who couldn't differentiate a good guitar from a bad one; but if you ask any guitarist of a certain age, each will likely have a story about an outrageously unplayable Japanese instrument that almost put an end to his or her budding career (both authors of this book included).

That era eventually came to a close in the mid-seventies, when quality Japanese brands such as Yamaha, ESP, and Ibanez emerged. But like the "so bad they're good" sci-fi films of the fifties, the early imported guitars continue to hold a special, nostalgic place in the hearts of players around the world. So who in Japan made these instruments, and how did they evolve into some of the world's leading guitar builders?

Much like in America, the story of the electric guitar in Japan started in the thirties, when the country fell temporarily in the thrall of Hawaiian music played on lap steel guitars. Improbably, during those pre–World War II years, Hawaiian-themed clubs sprang up all over Japan, featuring amateur bands doing their best to replicate the Polynesian sound. They even had their very own lap steel virtuoso, a musician named Buckie Shirakata, who triggered a guitar boom that swept the nation. As the demand for lap steels exploded, craftsmen like Mitsuo Matsuki, nicknamed "Guya-san," or *handyman*, began building them for local musicians. The fad was short-lived, however; when Japan went to war with the United States in 1941, all forms of Western music were banned.

It was more than a decade before American music would again visit the Land of the Rising Sun, most of it brought over by American servicemen stationed across the island in the postwar years. This time, however, it was the electric Spanish guitar that became the rage, and once again, local craftsmen swung into action.

One of the first and most recognizable companies to embrace guitar manufacturing in Japan was the AOI Sound Co., more commonly known in the United States as Teisco. Founded in 1946 by an ex–Buddhist priest named Doryu Matsuda, the Tokyo business initially produced pickups, electronics, and lap steel guitars. In the fifties they began developing both hollow-body and solid-body electrics, and by the end of the decade they'd begun exporting their work internationally. Some of these instruments were quite good, such as the handmade Teisco T-60, which found its way into the hands of the likes of Glen Campbell, one of California's top session musicians.

Mitsuo "Guya-san" Matsuki also started making instruments again, after having crafted Japan's first amplified lap steel guitars in the thirties. Initially he went to work for Teisco as a subcontractor, but soon he left to make his own guitars. By the mid-fifties, "the father of the Japanese electric guitar" had founded Tokyo Sound Laboratory and begun producing his Guyatone instruments, a brand that also became notoriously ubiquitous in the United States in the sixties.

In 1962, Teisco, Guyatone, and newcomer Fujigen manufactured an impressive 20,000 units for the year. Sensing economic opportunity, new guitar companies and factories began sprouting up all over the country, and in 1963 the electric guitar output in Japan soared to roughly 100,000 units, with approximately half of them exported. Japan was just getting started. After the Beatles and the Rolling Stones popularized the notion of the guitar band in 1964, numbers continued to skyrocket. In 1965, 767,000 units were cranked out by twenty-four factories, with 80 percent of them exported.

The Japanese guitar business was on fire, but as sales were peaking so were complaints and returns. Guitar manufacturers, and their often inexperienced designers, were delivering downright shoddy products, which flooded markets all over the world. In a panic, the guitar division of the Japanese National Musical Instruments Manufacturers' Association called an emergency meeting in June of 1965, gathering in Nagoya City to set up strict guidelines for the improvement of guitar quality.

Unfortunately, the damage had already been done—especially in the United States, where Japanese-made instruments had become a punch line. Sales very quickly cooled off, and by 1969 the production of Japanese electric guitars plummeted to approximately 150,000.

Nonetheless, several companies survived and started building instruments that would eventually compete with the very best the United States had to offer. One such manufacturer was the Hoshino Musical Instrument Company, which would become known in the United States as Ibanez. The musical instrument sales division of the Hoshino Shoten bookstore company was founded in 1908, and Ibanez dated back to 1929, when owner Matsujiro Hoshino began importing Salvador Ibanez nylon string guitars from Spain. By 1935, the demand for the guitars outgrew their supply, so the company, now run by Matsujiro's son, Yoshi-taro, began manufacturing their own.

However, in March 1944, a bombing raid destroyed the Hoshino factory, forcing Yoshitaro to start from scratch. Miraculously, among the few items spared from obliteration was a list of Hoshino's export customer contracts. To help get the company running again, Hoshino exported tortoiseshell picks. While most companies made picks that replicated the look of tortoiseshell, Hoshino's were created from the real deal, making them immensely popular. The demand for the picks gave the company enough capital to once again build instruments.

Yoshitaro's sons picked up the baton and began manufacturing electric guitars around 1957 in response to the success of companies like Teisco and Guyatone. However, unlike many of their competitors, Ibanez adhered to a strict level of quality, and their copies of Gibson, Fender, and Rickenbacker models in the sixties often equaled or exceeded the originals. Spurred on by Philadelphia businessman Harry Rosenbloom, whose Elger Company became the sole U.S. distributor of Ibanez guitars in 1972, the brand continued to improve, creating imaginative original designs like the Iceman and the Roadstar, while picking up an impressive roster of superstar endorsers such as Paul Stanley of Kiss, the Grateful Dead's Jerry Garcia, and jazz legend George Benson.

The U.S. division of Ibanez, led by Rosenbloom, also hired a team of smart, aggressive young executives. And it was a good thing, too, because by 1977 Gibson had finally had enough of Ibanez's nearly identical copies of its Flying V and Les Paul instruments, and filed a suit against Elger/Hoshino that forced them to abandon the strategy of copying now-classic American guitar designs.

Among the sharp Americans enlisted to help Ibanez move forward in the United States was a hustling adman named Jeff Hasselberger, whose tenacity helped Ibanez procure many of their early key endorsers, including Steve Miller, Garcia, and Benson. Another key acquisition was marketer Bill Reim, whose spiky hair and flamboyant punk rock style announced to the world that he was going to keep the company on the cutting edge.

"When I came on board in the early eighties, there was this idea that not only did we need a great guitar aimed at the hard rock community, but it would also need an identity," said Reim.

We decided the quickest way to build our name in that world was to procure a marquee endorser. We weren't necessarily looking for the biggest rock star—we wanted the best one. We wanted the most skilled, smartest, and most adventurous guitarist we could find. Executive Director Joe Hoshino came over from Japan and he reinforced the idea of finding a player's player—someone that would give us not only brand recognition, but also credibility. We all looked at each other and our team almost simultaneously said, "Well, it's gotta be Steve Vai." Steve was a little bit under the radar at the time because he was still in Alcatrazz, who were not that popular, but we had admired his playing with Frank Zappa and saw his star potential. Steve was the right guy, at least in our minds.

All that was left was to actually snag him, which wasn't as easy as it sounded. Vai was being actively courted by some of the biggest guitar companies in the business, many of which had deep pockets. To make matters worse, the Japanese main office of Ibanez was not particularly supportive of their distant American outpost. They liked to do things their own way, and they were very reluctant to take suggestions or shell out money to develop a new guitar.

"[At present] there are no Americans involved in development or design," said Reim. "The Americans have been completely excluded from the picture because the Hoshino Corporation wants Ibanez to be a Japanese thing. But what made us successful during the eighties was when you had a few smart people like Joe [Hoshino] who had some interest in collaborating."

The American team was woefully underfunded and lacking in even the most basic tools to build a prototype worthy of a perfectionist like Vai, but they were determined to give it their best shot. Despite the challenges going it alone presented, in some ways Reim and his coworkers, Rich Lasner, Bill Cummiskey, and Mace Bailey, felt they might actually be better off working without the assistance of Japan. Corporate, they rationalized, would never sign off on some of Vai's more outlandish ideas.

"It gave us kind of an opportunity to see what we could do with the crappy tools that we had at the time," laughed Reim. "We really didn't have anything to work with. It was just stuff we bought at Sears. It was almost a joke. I just remember Lasner saying, 'Oh, it's got to be as ugly as possible, too, because that's what Steve likes.' So after we finished building a prototype, we painted it to look like green and pink snakeskin."

Somehow the ragtag team finished an instrument close to

Vai's specs in an astounding three weeks and convinced Vai's family to put the finished product under their tree for Christmas as a surprise. It was such a crass move—Reim wasn't sure whether it was going to backfire and piss Steve off or endear them to him. But luckily it worked in their favor. Steve loved the guitar and gave Ibanez the green light to develop a production model.

But before Vai signed off and the Japanese could embrace their new star, there was one remaining matter of diplomacy. Lasner suspected that Ibanez brand pickups were not going to cut it for Steve, and he was right. Vai insisted that he wanted to work with custom pickup designer Larry DiMarzio, leaving little room for the Japanese to argue.

"They didn't like the idea," said Reim, who eventually rose to CEO of Hoshino USA. "They wanted to make the pickups themselves, but I often argued that the company you keep can help elevate. In this case partnering with DiMarzio lifted Ibanez a little bit, because his pickups had a pretty good reputation."

The first Steve Vai guitar, called the JEM, rolled off the assembly line in 1987 and was available in three eye-popping colors: Loch Ness Green, Flamingo Pink, and Desert Yellow. Each featured green and pink pyramid-shaped inlays on the fretboard, light pink pickups, multicolored tone knobs, plus a floating bridge and all the design idiosyncrasies the guitarist demanded (including his distinctive "monkey grip" handle). From our modern perspective, the JEMs appear almost absurdly garish, but in the mid-eighties they were the epitome of cool to kids being fed a steady diet of sticky-sweet hair metal bands like Poison, Cinderella, and Quiet Riot. In many ways, Vai's JEMs were the apotheosis of a guitar trend that had been building throughout a very experimental and extroverted moment in music.

"I picked those colors because they fit the David Lee Roth show, which was completely like a circus," said Vai. "Anything else seemed wimpy to me. People mock the eighties for being so outlandish, but it was a really exciting time to be a successful rock musician. The decade was just excess to the bone, man, and we took advantage of everything we could. The clothes were ridiculous and stage shows were gigantic. The groupies, the parties . . . it was nonstop, over-the-top fun."

ARGUABLY THE MOST significant musical event of the eighties, and the catalyst for many of the wild fashions of the day, was the August 1, 1981, launch of MTV, a revolutionary twenty-four-hour cable and satellite television channel devoted to playing nothing but music videos. Just as the 1979 hit song by the Buggles eerily predicted, video did indeed "kill the radio star." Within months, record stores were selling music by newly minted MTV stars like Bow Wow Wow, Stray Cats, and the Human League by the boatload, whether the local FM station played them or not.

Video-oriented pop acts such as Madonna, Duran Duran, Michael Jackson, Culture Club, and Prince ruled the eighties. But so did a number of hard rock and heavy metal bands like Twisted Sister and Mötley Crüe, who shamelessly mugged for the camera in mascara and clothes made of colorful leather and spandex. The dominance of MTV forced most bands to completely rethink how they presented themselves, and for many, that included their instruments.

If Van Halen was the primary reason many guitarists began reconsidering their old guard instruments—those made by Fender, Gibson, and Gretsch—MTV was a close second. If you wanted to stand out and be noticed, a tasteful sunburst Stratocaster or an understated black Les Paul wasn't going to cut it. Soon players were looking to up-and-coming guitar companies to create something outrageous and new.

One of the earliest and most significant guitar manufacturers to capture the spirit of the time was B.C. Rich. Even though the company was founded back in 1969, they hit their stride in the early eighties when they introduced their over-the-top Warlock series. Looking more like a medieval weapon than a musical instrument, the Warlock expanded on the trend toward pointy guitar shapes that had been initiated with Gibson's Flying V in 1958 but had become all the rage in the metal community in the eighties. The brand was immediately embraced by Blackie Lawless of W.A.S.P., Mick Mars of Mötley Crüe, Slayer's Kerry King, and countless other bad boys determined to make an impression when the video cameras swiveled their way.

Wayne Charvel and Grover Jackson also became key players in the eighties. The duo had become partners in the late seventies and hit pay dirt when Charvel became closely associated with Van Halen's early Frankenstrat guitars, and Jackson collaborated with Ozzy Osbourne guitarist Randy Rhoads on his iconic Concorde Flying V guitars. Soon every guitarist on the West Coast came running to them, and together they created a series of colorful instruments with unforgettable custom paint jobs like the pink and black bull's-eye guitar for Twisted Sister's Eddie Ojeda or the elaborate crossed-swords graphics found on Ratt's lead guitarist Warren DeMartini's instruments.

While these designers were steering the electric guitar toward the outrageous, there were others taking the opposite tack. In the eighties, Ned Steinberger built and marketed his startlingly minimal, headless Steinberger guitars and basses. Unlike Charvel or B.C. Rich, Steinberger thought the best way forward for the guitar was to completely jettison the past, with its useless tradition and ornamental clutter. He'd begun his career designing office and hospital furniture, and his instruments had the same antiseptic feel. "Functional and clean," he remarked. "That's my thing." His spare, rectangular black guitars made from graphite and carbon fiber were masterpieces of eighties postmodern minimalism. They were undeniably cool in conception and execution, but if hard rock musicians were clamoring for bright, bold, and audacious instruments, who was Steinberger's target market?

Not every band in the MTV era puked glitter and spandex.

Post-punk bands such as Joy Division, Siouxsie and the Banshees, Gang of Four, Devo, Sonic Youth, and Talking Heads—bands that drew inspiration from punk, funk, dub, electronic music, and even disco—rejected the aesthetics of traditional rock. Their ideas, both musically and visually, were often derived from modernist art and literature. In that sense, Ned's inventions were of a kind with their musical innovations.

A non-musician, Steinberger became aware of the guitar's design shortcomings when he shared a woodworking space with luthier Stuart Spector. Steinberger was particularly interested in improving electric bass instruments. As he explained:

> Traditional basses were neck-heavy, awkward to hold, and had dead spots on them, tonally. And one day it just dawned on me, if I took the tuning machines and put them on the body instead of at the end of the neck, the balance problems would be over. But if you take a bass guitar and chop off its head off, you can't stop there. It was such a radical move that you had to come up with a whole new concept. So once the head came off, the body pretty much came off too.

Soon top bassists such as Sting of the Police, reggae session legend Robbie Shakespeare, and King Crimson's Tony Levin were sporting Steinbergers—the perfect "axe" for a new moment in music: a de-mythologized, de-eroticized bass guitar. No phallic headstock. No "womanly" curves. All that was left was tone. The Steinberger guitar and bass were iconoclastic and, in a real way, as visually groundbreaking as any of Steve Vai's fluorescent JEM guitars.

AS THE DECADE wound down and the nineties began to make subversive plans of their own, Vai had one more significant bit of innovation to offer the guitar world. In 1989, Vai convinced Ibanez to add a seventh string to his JEM. It might've seemed like an innocent request, but it was truly a monumental gesture, defying a convention that stretched back to the eighteenth century, when six strings became the guitar norm.

"I just had the thought that it would be cool to have a seventh string on my guitar—an extra lower string for darker rhythms and bigger chord voicings," said Vai. "I had a very quick conversation with Ibanez about it. Basically, I said, 'Can you make me a JEM with a seventh string and without the handle?'" Given the success of Vai's guitars, who was Ibanez to argue?

Seven-string guitars weren't completely unheard-of. They had appeared briefly in Russia in the early nineteenth century, and again in Brazil in the late nineteenth century. In the United States, jazz guitarist George Van Eps had had a seven-string guitar built for him by Epiphone in the late thirties, and several other jazz players such as Howard Alden, John Pizzarelli, and Lenny Breau experimented with the idea. But Vai's newly christened Universe was one of the very few production-model seven-string electric ever manufactured.

When it was introduced to the public in 1990, most guitarists saw the Universe as more of a curiosity than a necessity. It was expensive, roughly $1,700, and more than a little intimidating to play. But there were perhaps other reasons the Universe didn't exactly fly off the shelves. As the effervescent eighties were coming to an end, there was evidence that guitarists and music fans were tiring of all the garish colors, flashy costumes, and blistering solos. After binging on too much frosted cake, audiences started pining for music with more substance. The rise of gritty, tattooed bands like Guns N' Roses and Metallica in the late eighties, and flannel-wearing indie bands such as Seattle's Soundgarden and Nirvana, was a sign that pop music was undergoing a dramatic sea change.

Within that context, a seven-string guitar painted like an Easter egg felt out of place. The Universe was discontinued in 1994 due to poor sales, and all the wonderfully exciting, innovative instruments created during the MTV era were being sold, shoved under beds, and burned in fireplaces. It looked as though the party was over. But reports of the death of Steve Vai's seven-stringed guitars would prove premature.

Carlos Santana and his Paul Reed
Smith guitar

THE REVENGE
OF THE NERDS

In 1975, the Detroit-based guitarist Ted Nugent was on fire. He had just released his first solo album, and it was screaming up the charts thanks to FM hits like "Stranglehold" and "Hey Baby." Although Nugent didn't drink or do drugs, he was widely acknowledged as one of rock's most outrageous characters. Like a modern Tarzan, he often performed his hard rock anthems in a loincloth, and was known to whip out a bow and arrow for a little target practice onstage when he grew tired of soloing on his '62 Gibson Byrdland. In other words, the self-proclaimed "Motor City Madman" was a wild and formidable presence.

The only thing more outlandish than Nugent, however, was the sheer audacity of a geeky nineteen-year-old named Paul Reed Smith, who bluffed his way backstage at a concert in Baltimore to show the rocker a guitar he'd built by hand.

"I remember meeting Paul vividly," said Nugent many years later with a laugh.

He was a classic nerd—a gawky, snot-nosed kid with glasses. I let him backstage because I knew that some of the greatest amplifiers and guitars came from mad scientists in their basement.

What really got my attention was the neck on his guitar, which was spectacular; it beckoned you to explore and play. However, at the time, I was so addicted to my Gibson Byrdland it would've taken a miracle to make me switch, but I commissioned him to make me a guitar anyway.

As for Smith, he had tried his best to put on a good show for Nugent, but later admitted the whole time his knees were knocking:

> I mean, how would you feel if you were a teenager trying to talk to a wild man like Ted Nugent? I was totally intimidated, but rock stars were the only guys with enough money to buy my early guitars. I didn't have any other choice but to pound on their doors. I was charging two thousand dollars for guitars, which at the time was crazy.
>
> Without their support, I had nothing. So I made a deal with Ted. If he didn't completely fall in love with the guitar that I built, he didn't have to buy it and he would get his deposit back. That's how I got him, and many others, to talk to me.

It was a promising beginning for what would be a long, hard road to creating one of the most successful American guitar companies since the heyday of Fender and Gibson. Over the next decade, the nervous youngster would rise up and be the guitar industry's David, hurtling rocks at the establishment and shaming them back into respectability.

"It was Paul Reed *fucking* Smith that forced Gibson and Fender to get back into the game," said Nugent.

Yes, Paul's guitars were wonderful, and yes, the guitar playing community now has a wonderful spiritual relationship with Paul and his creations, but more importantly he was an American alarm to Gibson and Fender, that they were dropping the ball. And here's the beauty of it—they responded. In the late eighties, they realized that this kid was kicking their ass, and they finally started making really good guitars again.

LIKE MANY GIANT slayers, Smith heard destiny calling early. At sixteen he started tinkering with guitar building in high school woodshop, but by his senior year it had become something of a full-blown obsession, when he landed part-time work as an instrument repairman at Washington Music Center in Maryland.

During his employment, he was often shocked by what he saw. It was one thing to fix an older instrument that had fallen into a state of disrepair, but more often than not he was being asked to fix up brand-new instruments that had been shipped directly from factories.

"There were immense quality problems," remembers Smith, echoing sentiments expressed by many guitarists of the era. "Often frets weren't properly finished or leveled, necks weren't straight, and polyester was slopped everywhere. To me, the pre-CBS Fender versus CBS Fender wasn't anywhere near as big a deal as the quality nightmare going on in 1974. Even though I was pretty young, I saw an opportunity. I didn't see myself as somebody who was going to change the guitar industry, but I could see how I could make a difference by doing things right."

After graduating high school, Smith went to St. Mary's College to become a mathematician, but after eighteen months he knew it wasn't for him. In his last semester on campus, he made a deal with a resident music professor: in return for four academic credits, Smith would buy wood from a violin maker and make a guitar. "I built my first 'real' guitar in the basement of the art building." The single-cutaway Les Paul Junior–style guitar, now on display in the entrance hall of the present PRS factory, was a promising start, but Smith knew it wasn't going to set the world on fire.

He had a vision, though. He dropped out of college, moved back in with his parents, and began building and repairing guitars in his bedroom. He quickly outgrew the space and began scouring the historic area of Annapolis. He dreamed of renting a hippie palace where people could watch him build guitars. Instead, his lack of funds led to a minuscule garret apartment over the top of a bar called the Happy Buzzard, a place so small he had to wipe wood chips off the bed before he went to sleep at night. And there was one other major problem.

"I was so mad," said Smith. "I called my landlord and screamed, 'You rented me a haunted room and didn't tell me!' He innocently replied, 'Oh, don't worry, it's never hurt anybody.'"

The place wasn't ideal, but it was a start. And now that he was officially a guitar maker by trade, Smith began to deeply consider what he had seen as a repairman. Not only had he witnessed a drastic decline in the production of modern electric guitars, but he had also seen his share of beautiful vintage instruments from the golden era of the fifties, and wondered how he could improve upon their greatness. His overarching dream was to create a guitar that could provide the tones of both a Stratocaster and a Les Paul, and have a look, feel, and playability that would compete with those classic instruments.

"I would say very early on I had a theory that an electric guitar was an acoustic guitar with a magnetic microphone on it, and that the acoustic sound of solid-body guitar made a huge difference to the electric sound. You can put the same pickups on a '69 Telecaster as on a '53 Telecaster and they'll sound different, therefore the acoustic sound must have some impact. Everybody seemed to miss that point."

From there, Smith, a former math student and son of two professional mathematicians, started doing what came naturally: rigorously analyzing every aspect of how electric guitars past and present were constructed. He began questioning every design decision made over the last thirty years. What were the tuning pegs and nuts made of? How was the truss rod installed? How was the bridge anchored? How much water was in the wood of the body? The intensely intellectual young man studied all the instruments he repaired for clues—what made them tick and what made some ring out with glorious clarity while others sounded dead as the dodo. If the tone of a great electric guitar started with its inherent acoustic sound, he reasoned, there must be a code he could crack to make his instruments among the best ever made.

"I learned I could test a good electric guitar with a stopwatch," explained Smith. "A solid-body guitar that rings for ten seconds without an amp is simply not as good as a guitar that rings for forty-two seconds."

As Smith was sorting these and other puzzles, he continued to relentlessly pursue famous musicians to try out his guitars. Emboldened by his success with Nugent, in 1976 the young builder finagled his way backstage once again, this time convincing Peter Frampton to commission a guitar. Frampton was perhaps the biggest rock star on the planet at the time, due to his smash live album *Frampton Comes Alive!,* which sold six million copies in less than a year. Selling him a guitar was a coup that would generate Smith an immense amount of publicity and credibility. Realizing the magnitude of the commission, Smith worked doggedly to fashion his greatest instrument yet, a beautiful mahogany guitar that would be "the seed from which all subsequent production PRS instruments would grow." In addition to its lightly arched top, double-cutaway, and ornate headstock with Smith's now famous eagle logo, the fingerboard would also feature the logo as inlays, becoming his signature feature.

Before he handed over the instrument to Frampton in May of 1976, he took the finished guitar to a show at the Capital Centre in Landover, Maryland, featuring a double bill of the jazz-fusion band Return to Forever and his personal hero, Carlos Santana.

After showing some roadies his creation, they introduced Smith to Return to Forever's guitarist Al Di Meola. Impressed, Di Meola immediately ordered an electric twelve-string with a built-in phase shifter (a device that alters an electric guitar's signal to create a dramatic "whooshing" sound, often compared to a jet plane in flight), a guitar he would use on the title track of his commercially successful 1977 solo album, *Elegant Gypsy*. Smith was also introduced to Santana, who also played the Frampton guitar but, much to Smith's disappointment, was less enthusiastic.

Santana, however, recognized that there was something different, and perhaps exceptional, about Smith and his guitar. "His bright eyes were filled with hope, possibilities and opportunities," said Santana.

He had this beautiful cherry red guitar, but it had a different cherry finish than anything that I'd ever seen. He was very gentle, but persistent. At that time I was with Yamaha guitars, and I had some very disappointing experiences with Gibson, so I wasn't really as receptive as I should have been, but nevertheless he persevered. His tenacity made me realize that he was invested in something that he believed in. For me, even more than the guitars, it was his vision. How can you describe the intangible? Well, you could say, "It's a man's dream." And he had this vision about what he wanted to do that was very contagious. What I remember about that first guitar is that it sounded like a tenor. It had a very rich, low, masculine tone; a belly tone, like the great Italian opera singer, Pavarotti.

The guitarist was intrigued, but he stopped short of ordering an instrument. This was both a crushing blow and a motivation for Smith to redouble his efforts to make something so classic and undeniable that even Carlos Santana, the guitarist with one of the most gorgeous tones in music, could not resist.

Over the next few years, Smith continued to improve and collect a high-profile clientele that included Nancy Wilson and Howard Leese of the rock band Heart, but he often struggled to make ends meet, regularly returning to repair work so he had enough money to put food on the table. Up to that point his guitars were made primarily of mahogany, a functional but unremarkable wood. It sounded great and was fine for the working guitarist, but it lacked the visual impact he desired. Smith longed to create something that evoked the greatest electrics ever constructed—the Gibson Les Paul models made between 1958 and 1960. Part of the appeal of those instruments was their elaborate curly-maple sunburst arched tops. But prime maple was neither cheap nor easy to come by.

As if by providence, Smith discovered that a friend owned an antique dresser with curly maple drawer fronts, and, seizing the opportunity, he asked his pal if he could have the wood. His friend shrugged, and Smith went to work stripping the furniture. The first guitar made from the dresser was stunning.

In the fall of 1980, Smith once again went to a Santana show and slithered his way backstage armed with one of his mahogany guitars, this time featuring a fanciful dragon inlay and P-90 pickups. At first Carlos refused to see the guitar maker, but after a sympathetic roadie insisted on showing Santana Smith's latest creation, the guitarist had a change of heart and let Smith in.

"When I walked backstage, Carlos was already playing my guitar," remembered Smith. "Every note was feeding back in a completely controlled way. That was his test. He looked at me and asked if he could play it onstage that night, and I certainly wasn't going to say no. Then he started looking through a scrapbook I had with me. He came across the first curly-maple-top guitar I had made for Heart's Howard Leese and his eyes lit up and he said, 'That's the kind I want.'"

A commission from Santana was a major victory for Smith, but when he returned to his workshop he had a dilemma. He wanted to get a guitar to Carlos as quickly as possible in case the rock star changed his mind, but he knew it would take him at least a few weeks to make a new one from scratch. Suddenly, he had a brainstorm. Leese was due to send his maple PRS back for some maintenance, so Smith persuaded him to send it to Santana, who had just started to record his *Zebop!* album.

"Carlos got the guitar and plugged it in and immediately started recording the album with it," said Smith. "When I called his people to see how he liked it, they said I couldn't have it back. I had to explain to them that it was Howard's guitar, but they could borrow it until I could make a new one. However, while discussing the specifications of his new guitar, Santana insisted on an improvement. He wanted me to add a vibrato arm that stayed in tune. I agreed, but as soon as I hung up I thought, 'How in the *fuck* am I going to do that?'"

Santana was adamant that he didn't want a complicated locking system, like the Floyd Rose tremolo made popular by Edward Van Halen, so Smith had to quickly figure out an alternative. He came up with a solution that included the installation of a nut that used miniature rollers on each string to reduce friction, locking tuning pegs, and a brass bridge. Together they worked like a charm.

Santana was impressed, calling it "an accident of God." Carlos then dared Smith to make him another that was equally good. Four guitars later, each of them brilliant in its own way, Santana finally acknowledged Smith's superior skill as a luthier, admitting sheepishly, "Well, I guess they weren't accidents of God."

"Carlos made me earn his respect," said Smith. "He was in the position where he could play anything he wanted to. Nobody could tell Carlos Santana what to like."

WITH SEVERAL OF the world's most respected guitarists endorsing his instruments, Smith's reputation began to spread. Magazines such as *Guitar Player* and *Musician* were beginning to take note, and with momentum on his side it was time for him to finally step up and realize his earliest ambition: building a game-changing guitar that could provide the tones of both a Stratocaster and a Les Paul without copying either.

While his guitars from this period still had the Gibson Les Paul Special double-cutaway shape, they featured a few significant changes that were Smith's own innovations, most notably the guitar's fretboard length. Most Gibson electrics had 24¾-inch scale necks, while Fender Stratocasters and Telecasters have 25½-inch scale necks. Smith opted for a 25-inch scale to make a guitar that felt comfortable in the hands of Les Paul and Fender players alike. He was shooting for the middle, because he felt "guitar players wished there was something in the middle."

"You had your Gibson players and your Fender players," recalled Smith. "Fifty percent played one and 50 percent played the other. If you only made the Gibson guys happy, and if only one of two of those guys liked the guitar, you still only had 25 percent of the market. I knew if I didn't draw the line down the middle and combine the best features of the Fender and Gibson, I was dead."

And the middle was what Smith continued to aim for when he finally got around to designing a new and distinctive body shape for his instruments. In 1984, he thought long and hard on what he wanted. As a starting point he took a Fender Strat shape and a Gibson Les Paul Junior shape and drew them on top of each other and averaged the lines. Everyone agreed the result was aesthetically horrible, so he spent the next two years revising the shape until finally arriving at the modern PRS at 3:00 a.m. one morning after a long and wearying evening of sanding.

The double-cutaway body shape with an elongated horn on the upper bout became the foundation for the PRS Custom. It was a triumph of long hours, hard work, persistence, and design.

But Smith was at a crossroads. He realized that in order to make a living as a guitar builder, he needed to either sell his designs to a major manufacturer or start his own company to manufacture them. In 1985 Smith was ready to go national, and with the help of an investor he formed a limited partnership, raising $500,000 in capital. PRS Guitars was born.

AT THIS POINT in the story it certainly would be fair to wonder how a traditionalist like Smith was getting so much attention. After all, wasn't this the eighties—the era of MTV, garish colors, Frankenstein contraptions, and instruments made out of synthetic materials? It would seem that a guy who wanted nothing more than to make an instrument worthy of Leo Fender or Ted McCarty would be all too easily overlooked.

Well, yes and no.

As the electric guitar matured and gained in popularity, it was only natural that styles, tastes, and trends would diversify. For every iconoclast like Steve Vai or Ned Steinberger, there were large numbers of conservatives that loved every last thing about classic Telecasters from the fifties, or old Gretsch White Penguins. Pointy guitar merchants like B.C. Rich may have been grabbing the attention, but there was also a groundswell of craftsmen like Smith, and West Coast builders such as Tom Anderson in Newberry Park, California, and Valley Arts Guitar in North Hollywood, who more closely identified with the aesthetics of founding fathers like Ted McCarty and Leo Fender.

And guitar makers weren't the only ones suspicious of the newfangled instruments being produced by Ibanez or Jackson. There was a whole new crop of players who also felt more comfortable playing either vintage instruments or new ones that felt vintage. In 1983, blues sensation Stevie Ray Vaughan recorded his debut with a battered and bruised 1963 Stratocaster. Brian Setzer of the Stray Cats—a true darling of MTV—appeared in his videos with a 1959 Gretsch Chet Atkins 6120 model. And most punk rockers, like Joe Strummer of the Clash, who played old Telecasters, had zero interest in a new guitar with a fancy paint job or a locking whammy bar.

While most agreed that Gibson and Fender had hit the skids, there were different ideas on what to do about it. Builders and dreamers such as Paul Reed Smith and Edward Van Halen had opted to make new instruments, but many players simply started digging through garages and yard sales and under their dad's bed for older instruments that were made when the companies truly cared. And, thus, the vintage guitar market was born.

Before the vintage guitar market caught fire in the eighties, it had been the domain of a small handful of guitar geeks. Some of these obsessives went on to become famous musicians themselves. Rock and Roll Hall of Famers Billy Gibbons of ZZ Top, Cheap Trick's Rick Nielsen, and Joe Walsh were just a few of the young kids that figured out, way before anyone else, that these older guitars possessed something today's guitars lacked, and they would buy them and often resell them as a way to make money and make friends with the musicians they regarded as heroes.

Nielsen told journalist Tom Beaujour that when he started buying guitars from the fifties and early sixties, most people didn't understand why. "They were just 'used' guitars, not 'vintage,' and it was a great time to start a collection if you knew where to look . . . You could go out to the country and maybe a farmer would have a Gibson Firebird under the bed. He'd say, 'Well, I don't know what it is, but I don't want it anymore because it only has five strings left on it.' "

Gibson Les Pauls were an area of particular interest. He recalled selling one to Jeff Beck in 1968. "I had gone to see the Jeff Beck Group play in Chicago. After the set, I saw Beck's roadie pick up a Les Paul . . . The guy grabbed the guitar by the body, dropped it, and the headstock snapped off. I pushed my way backstage and told the band's road manager, 'Jeff probably doesn't know it yet, but his roadie just accidentally broke his guitar. I'm a guitar collector, so please take my number and give it to Jeff in case he needs something.' "

Soon enough Nielsen's phone rang and he was on a flight to

Philadelphia with six guitars. "[Jeff] picked out a 1960 Les Paul with a Bigsby on it, and gave me $350, which was the going rate for those at that time. And then Jeff and I stayed up late into the night and played guitar, which for me, of course, was worth more than anything."

Joe Walsh, who would later become a superstar as a solo artist and lead guitarist with the Eagles, was another early collector who recognized the value of guitars made in the fifties, and made it his mission to search high and low for spectacular used instruments long before it was fashionable. Like Nielsen, he gained a reputation as a go-to guy for hard-to-get instruments, and soon some of the biggest names in rock and roll came knocking on his door when they were in need of something special.

It was Walsh who provided Led Zeppelin's Jimmy Page with his '59 sunburst Les Paul, one of the most iconic instruments in rock-and-roll history.

In April of 1969, Walsh's early band, the James Gang, was touring with Led Zeppelin when he heard Page was looking for a new instrument. "Jimmy was still playing the Telecaster that he played in the Yardbirds," said Walsh.

> He was looking for a Les Paul and asked if I knew of any, because he couldn't find one that he liked. It turned out I had just acquired two of them, so I kept the one I liked the most and sold him the other one. I gave him a really good deal, about 1,200 bucks. I had to hand-carry it and fly out to New York to give it to him. So whatever my expenses were, that's what I charged him . . . but again, I just thought he should have a Les Paul for godsakes!

But the man perhaps most responsible for spreading the gospel of vintage was George Gruhn, owner of the world-famous Gruhn Guitars in Nashville, Tennessee. Had the course of his life run just a little differently, Gruhn might well have been a professor of herpetology (the academic study of reptiles). As it was, he became the undisputed dean of the vintage guitar trade, an expert whose opinion is often sought and cited, and whose vintage guitar shop at 400 Broadway in Nashville became a mecca for rock stars, well-heeled collectors, and guitar aficionados of every stripe. Among these pilgrims, *Gruhn's Guide to Vintage Guitars*—cowritten with Walter Carter and now in its third edition—is still revered as the collectors' bible.

"I could joke about it and say that my specialization in reptile behavior has helped me deal with certain dealers or musicians," Gruhn said.

> But that's not really true. What my zoological background did was give me a systematic way of looking at guitars, which I view very much as being alive. And they fit very nicely in a taxonomic system, which is what I've developed in my books. I look at guitars in the same way a herpetologist studies reptiles and amphibians. You look at their structural features and you study them in their environment. Guitars evolve over time in their design as they adapt to an environment that includes social, demographic and technological changes, not to mention musical and economic trends.

Although his Nashville shop was often populated with snakes, lizards, and a parrot, Gruhn's pets never kept guitar collectors from his door:

> Billy Gibbons has bought over 100 guitars from me since 1970. Rick Nielsen has bought over 100 guitars from me, also going back to '70. I have other customers who have been buying from me ever since the mid-Sixties, before I even had a store. They keep coming back for more. Basically I only lose customers when they get senile or die. My basic business plan for the future is to outlive them all. My

uncle Otto lived to be 105 and I'm just 65 now. So that gives me another 40 years of sales. I don't have a retirement plan. How do you retire from a hobby?

Gruhn traced today's lucrative market for vintage American guitars back to the folk music boom of the late fifties and early sixties. It makes sense that devotees of old-time musical traditions would also value instruments with a past. Folk is what first got Gruhn hooked on guitars in 1963 while he was an undergraduate at the University of Chicago. Searching for a guitar he could use to play traditional music in the style of the Carter Family, he went through a Conde Hermanos classical from Madrid, a circa-1920 Gibson Style O, and a 1937 Martin F7 archtop before lighting on a Gibson L-5 signed and dated by Lloyd Loar. For this, he paid the princely sum of $400 at Sid Sherman's music store on Wabash Avenue in Chicago.

"On a college student's income, that was a lot of money," he said. "But that guitar today would be worth 50 or 60 thousand dollars."

In essence, Gruhn began dealing to support his growing vintage guitar addiction. "I have never been an electric player," he said. "I'm only interested in acoustics. But I found that, for every guitar I wanted personally to collect I'd turn up 50 more that were terrific deals even though I didn't want them for myself."

In those pre-Internet days, Gruhn would source guitars through classified newspaper ads, college bulletin boards, and a few Chicago stores, such as the Fret Shop, that sold used and vintage instruments. "I don't claim that I created the vintage guitar market," he said. "There were folks like John Lundberg in California who were already dealing to some extent, as well as Harry West in New York and Tom Morgan in Tennessee. But I was certainly one of the first to write about it extensively. When I started in '63, you couldn't get as much as a Martin serial number list. There were no articles. No books."

Gruhn's early vintage guitar articles appeared in small blue-grass publications such as *Muleskinner News* and *Bluegrass Unlimited*. But with the advent of professional guitar journalism in the late sixties, his name became ubiquitous. During the same period he moved on to graduate studies at the University of Tennessee in Knoxville by which point he was dealing heavily. On summer breaks, he'd make the round of folk festivals down south, selling vintage guitars. It was around then that he made the sad discovery that one day dawns upon many an earnest grad student: there just aren't a lot of jobs, academic or otherwise, for people with advanced degrees in specialized fields like herpetology.

Then one day he received a phone call that shaped his destiny. As Gruhn recalled:

At the end of 1968, probably in December, I got a call from Hank Williams Jr. at my apartment in Knoxville. He'd heard from Sonny Osborne, of the bluegrass group the Osborne Brothers, that I had a bunch of old Martins, and he was looking for those. I told him a bit about what I had. He said, "I'll be there in four hours." Well, there was no interstate between Nashville and Knoxville in '68. It was all winding, two-lane mountain roads. Normally you couldn't do it in four hours. But Hank did. He was driving a Jaguar E, which doesn't have much hauling capacity. So he bought three guitars. He didn't have room in the car for more. But he said he could be back the next day with a bigger car. He came back with a Cadillac Eldorado and bought as many guitars as that car could hold.

He said he didn't know of anybody who had the sort of stuff that I had. And if I ever wanted to come to Nashville and set up in business, he'd have an apartment waiting for me and help me get started. It seemed like a good idea. I dropped out of school and moved to Nashville. For a couple of years, Hank Williams Jr. was the best customer I had. To

a considerable extent, he was supporting me just by buying guitars that he personally wanted. But I was also still
actively wheeling and dealing. I remember selling a Dobro
[brand guitar] to Duane Allman in 1969. At that time, a
fancy Dobro was only $350. And Duane paid me at the rate
of $50 every other week. Music was not a lucrative career for
him at that time. The part of his career where he had any
money was very brief.

In 1970 Gruhn opened his first shop, at 111 Fourth Avenue
North in Nashville, near the corner of Fourth and Broadway,
about a hundred yards from Gruhn's current location and right
behind Ryman Auditorium, then home of the Grand Ole Opry
and country icon Johnny Cash's influential network TV variety
show. "All the performers who played the Johnny Cash TV show
came into our store," said Gruhn. "We had vintage stuff they
found fascinating. Back then there weren't any stores nearby that
were selling vintage instruments. And serious musicians weren't
interested in new stuff because it was crap; 1970 was a low, low
point for new instrument quality. So we met Crosby, Stills, Nash &
Young, Bob Dylan, Merle Haggard, Joni Mitchell, Derek and the
Dominos, you name it."

Gruhn has always been notoriously underwhelmed by rock
stars, and is famous for failing to recognize even worldwide musical icons when they walk into his shop. "I could care less about
them," he shrugged. "For instance, Metallica comes in here anytime they're in town. They buy. Do I know the guys? Not really.
My employees know who they are. If James Hetfield walked
through the door, would I know who he is? No."

In a way, however, Gruhn's indifference to musical trends was
his strength. He's never catered to any one genre or style of musical instrument. "I'd starve to death if I had to rely on country
players alone," he said. "If you walk in my shop, you'd never know
what kind of music I was into."

Gruhn has flourished down through the decades, moving to a bigger shop in '76. At the dawn of the nineties he brought guitar historian Walter Carter into the fold to assist in the creation of the first *Gruhn's Guide*. "It's organized like a zoological field guide," Gruhn explained. "One of the most influential books in my life was the Schmidt and Davis field guide to snakes, which was published in 1941. The identification keys used for guitars in the *Gruhn's Guide* were very much modeled on the Schmidt and Davis field guide to snakes identification keys."

Gruhn's Guide to Vintage Guitars was first published in 1991, and recently went into its third edition. "It's very much changed," said Gruhn. "It not only expands on the first and second editions; there's also reorganization."

The store moved to its third and present location in '93. Gruhn Guitars now resides in a 13,000-square-foot, four-story building at 400 Broadway in Nashville. The showroom occupies only about a quarter of the total space. Gruhn needed a good deal of room for storage and also an extensive repair shop where newly acquired guitars are painstakingly but unobtrusively restored to pristine condition prior to sale.

"In nature, almost all the most successful animals have a body that's quite a bit bigger than their head," Gruhn philosophized. "Characters in political cartoons are the other way around—the head is bigger than the body. A business that's built like a political cartoon will fail, whereas one that's built like a real live animal will thrive."

Which Gruhn has done. His single largest sale, of which he's quite proud, was a guitar belonging to pioneering country guitarist Maybelle Carter, which sold for $575,000 and now resides in the Country Music Hall of Fame.

THE FIRST MODELS mass-produced by Paul Reed Smith Guitars in 1985 were the Standard, Custom, and Metal, none of which was cheap. The mahogany Standard sold for $1,150, while the Custom, with its curly-maple top, and the Metal, with its custom graphic finish, went for $1,350. (By comparison, that same year a Fender U.S.-made Vintage listed at $750, and a Gibson Les Paul Standard sold for $999.) Despite the expense, the guitar community quickly embraced Smith's instruments, enthralled with their attention to detail and handiwork.

The timing for the company couldn't have been better. By the end of the eighties, several factors had paved the way for PRS Guitars' success. To begin with, many of the kids who started playing in the sixties and seventies had grown up, finished college, and had well-paying jobs that gave them enough disposable income to indulge in their rock-and-roll fantasies. Even if they were never going to play Madison Square Garden, they could buy a custom-quality instrument worthy of such a gig, and Paul's handsome instruments fit that bill perfectly. Their beauty and stellar craftsmanship were so evident, you could display one in your living room like a piece of fine art, and many players did. It was a signifier.

The general guitar consumer had also become much better educated, primarily due to the rise of monthly magazines such as *Guitar World, Guitar Player,* and *Musician,* which breathlessly covered the most recent trends in the musical instrument industry. Smith became the poster boy for those publications—the shining beacon for integrity and commitment to excellence. And, while he could've gotten cocky, instead he doubled down on his reputation as a white knight.

In the early eighties, Smith's restless and inquisitive mind led him to the U.S. Patent and Trademark Office in Virginia, where he pored over the classic designs of Gibson's early electrics. While attempting to unlock the secrets to those instruments, he kept stumbling on the name Ted McCarty.

"I thought, who's Ted McCarty?" Smith laughed, marveling at his own ignorance.

Then I realized he was the guy behind most of the instruments I loved and respected . . . We first met in 1986, and I wanted to know *everything*. I asked him what glues he used, how he leveled fretboards, how he dried them, why he made the Explorer and the ES-335. Instead of being annoyed, Ted got a little emotional and said nobody had asked him those questions in years. It was unbelievable, so we hired him as a consultant and I tried to download as much of his vast knowledge as I could before he passed away in 2001.

McCarty had faded into obscurity, and Smith was determined to change that in a very public way. McCarty had never had a guitar with his name on it, so in 1994 Smith decided to honor his mentor with a special instrument that incorporated everything that McCarty had shared into a standard PRS instrument. Although the former Gibson president did not contribute any specific designs—his eyesight was too poor by then—his fingerprints were all over it.

The 1994 McCarty guitar became a defining moment in the ongoing growth and success of Smith's company, and in many ways is a milestone in the history of the electric guitar. By channeling the spirit of one of the great pioneers into a modern design, PRS Guitars showed the guitar world a way to move forward without tossing out all that was good about the past. He also demonstrated, once again, that you could create a quality, mass-produced product and still turn a profit. As Nugent noted earlier, the once-gangly youth raised the bar for American guitar makers with a vengeance, and woke them from their stupor.

Still, you can't please everyone.

Many modern rock and rollers were derisive of Smith and his squeaky-clean guitars, dismissing them as slick and expensive instruments for yuppies and lawyers. "I'm no guitar snob, I'll play anything. But you'd never catch me dead playing a Paul Reed Smith," Green Day's Billie Joe Armstrong once spat.

If you were a humble rock musician who couldn't relate to a gleaming PRS or to the garish instruments created for hair metal musicians, or couldn't afford a skyrocketing vintage guitar, what were your options? Some started to double back to Fender and Gibson, who were making better instruments than they had in recent years. But for many others, there was yet another option.

*Jack White and his thrift-shop
1964 Montgomery Ward Airline*

chapter 12

PLASTIC FANTASTIC

Billed as "Music's Biggest Night," the annual Grammy Awards ceremony is a time-honored pop music ritual—and it is indeed big in every way. Because the show features multiple live performances by many of the music industry's top-grossing acts, it is the largest physical production of any awards ceremony. Many millions of dollars are spent on sound, lighting, and broadcast equipment, special effects, fog machines, wardrobe, limousines, lavish record company after-parties, and every other pop-star extravagance imaginable.

The 2004 Grammy Awards ceremony was no exception—an evening of over-the-top production numbers teaming many of the highest-earning stars of popular music. In a Dolce & Gabbana evening gown, Beyoncé Knowles set the tone for the night, singing her hit ballad "Dangerously in Love" amid a *tableau vivant* consisting of a dozen or more dancers and models garbed in early-twentieth-century attire, enclosed by a massive gilt frame, like something out of Louis XIV's palace at Versailles. She returned later on to duet with Prince on a medley from *Purple Rain*, midway down a grand staircase on a stage set that wouldn't have been out of place in Fritz Lang's cinematic sci-fi epic *Metropolis*. They were accompanied by a full band, a black-clad string section, and a troupe of backup dancers. This time Knowles was resplendent in a skimpy pink Roberto Cavalli frock. Prince sported one of his trademark purple "Love Symbol" guitars, designed by German luthier Jerry Auerswald—a consummately flashy axe if ever there was one.

Among the evening's other attractions, it was a pretty good night for great guitarists and high-end guitars. Dave Matthews strummed a beautiful Martin acoustic, and Vince Gill played lead on a nice Epiphone thinline as they joined Sting and Pharrell Williams in a tribute to the Beatles. Dave Grohl played one of his vintage Gibson Trini Lopez models as his band, the Foo Fighters, was somewhat incongruously paired with jazz piano great Chick Corea. And gospel steel guitar ace Robert Randolph wowed the crowd in a tribute to funk music also featuring George Clinton, OutKast, and members of Earth, Wind & Fire. Album of the Year winners that year, hip-hop favorite OutKast was making a grand display of its musical roots.

But amid all this carefully choreographed mainstream entertainment, the '04 Grammy audience was also shocked out of its comfortable seating by a raw and raucous garage band from Detroit called the White Stripes. There were only two of them onstage, and they certainly weren't wearing Dolce & Gabbana.

The White Stripes had been nominated for a slew of awards that year and would walk away with Best Rock Song honors for their single "Seven Nation Army." It was something of a left-field choice for the Grammys. More typical were the honors doled out that year to pop idols—and former Disney *Mickey Mouse Club* stars—Justin Timberlake and Christina Aguilera. But then, the Grammys' rock categories have often skewed somewhat rough-and-ready.

For the big show, the Stripes played "Seven Nation Army," then segued into a frenzied, amped-up rendition of "Death Let-

PLASTIC FANTASTIC · 301

ter," an old blues song by the singer and slide guitarist Son House, based on a mortality-charged motif that dates back to the 1930s, if not earlier. Their performance was everything the evening's other musical turns weren't—wild, noisy, disruptive, barely controlled. A megawatt lighting backdrop was the only concession to Grammy production values. Otherwise the White Stripes did exactly what they'd been doing in tiny, grimy alt-rock clubs for years.

Pounding her candy-striped red-and-white drum kit, dark hair flying, Meg White exuded a tough yet vulnerable sense of cool. Looking every bit the tortured outsider in a black T-shirt and skinny red jeans, Jack White coaxed an ungodly deluge of squeals, squawks, belches, and primordial blues riffs from a battered, budget-line 1950s Kay hollow-body electric guitar with a cheap sunburst finish. It was plugged into two Sears-brand Silvertone amps from the 1960s.

To put these instruments in context, the thrift-shop guitar rig that White chose to play at the Grammys was one that might have embarrassed a kid in a mid-sixties garage band performing at a high school talent show. Like the White Stripes' music itself, it was defiantly out of step with the Grammy aesthetic of conspicuous consumption. This was simply and honestly the equipment White liked to play in this period. But it's hard not to regard it as a gesture as well—a righteous blow struck not only against soulless commercial pop music but also against the baby boomer hegemony of high-end, ultra-dialed-in musical equipment.

The White Stripes were at the vanguard of what was hailed as the neo-garage-rock movement, a stylistic phenomenon that also included groups such as the Strokes, the Hives, the Vines, and, slightly later, the Black Keys. It was hardly the first revival of mid-sixties garage rock. But it was arguably the first to garner Grammy recognition and other mainstream accolades.

The neo-garage bands were seen as the antithesis of the nu-metal/rap-metal sounds that had dominated the rock market through the late nineties and early 2000s. The Neanderthal aggression of nu-metal acts such as Korn and Limp Bizkit had been critically regarded as a new nadir for rock music. A back-to-basics movement is generally what's required to blast any musical idiom out of stagnant waters, and garage rock provided just that— exactly as punk rock had done at the tail end of the seventies. The parallel is hardly surprising, as neo-garage stands firmly rooted in the post-punk tradition.

Neo-garage was one of the first great musical statements by the generation known as millennials. Like all things millennial, it was largely Internet-enabled. By the early years of the twenty-first century, music fans had instant access not only to just about any piece of music ever recorded but also to unlimited information on obscure guitars and amps of yesteryear, via a host of guitar-geek blogs. While abundant, as we all know, Internet information is completely unfiltered by any kind of critical or historical per-spective. Music recorded in 2012 is heard right alongside songs recorded in 1942, with little or no sense of which came first, or how the two things might be related.

So old hierarchies were broken down. Who's to say Jack White's beat-up Kay was a lesser guitar than a '59 Les Paul? While the Kay was a favorite of White's in this period, the guitar he was most closely associated with during the White Stripes' rise to fame was equally modest: a Montgomery Ward Airline guitar made in 1964. The instrument's angular body was fashioned from bright red plastic, not unlike a mid-twentieth-century children's toy. The Airline originally retailed for under $100 (not much money for an electric guitar, even back then) and was sold through the Mont-gomery Ward mail-order catalog and department store chain. Playing this guitar was a defiant statement on White's part.

"The idea behind using the Ward's Airline in the White Stripes," he told *Guitar Player* magazine, "was to prove that you don't need a brand new guitar to have character, to have tone and to be able to play what you want to play."

While certainly a declaration of independence, White's selection of the guitar was also in keeping with garage rock tradition. He'd purchased the instrument in 1999 from Jack Yarber (aka Jack Oblivian), the guitarist in nineties garage bands the Compulsive Gamblers and the Oblivians, who had been influential for the White Stripes. Yarber himself had bought the guitar secondhand for $200 five years earlier. Along with its raunchy tone, the guitar's red color must have been a major selling point for White. In this period, everything about the White Stripes—including stage clothing and musical instruments—adhered to a strict red and white, candy-swirl color scheme. A gifted guitarist, White was certainly aware of the instrument's limitations. But these too seemed to suit the White Stripes' minimalist garage aesthetic.

"It's obviously harder for me to work with a 1964 plastic guitar, compared to a brand new one right off the factory line, perfectly intonated and all that stuff," he admitted. "Sometimes you say to yourself, 'God, does anyone even realize how much harder this is? Why do I even bother?' But I'm not doing it to prove something to 'them.' I'm doing it to prove something to myself. And if someone says 'good show' or 'good album' I know I can be proud of it because of the conditions it was made under."

The sound of White's struggle with the guitar is one of the things that made the White Stripes' music so compelling. Electric guitars and guitar playing had become a little too slick by the end of the twentieth century. Gone were the squealing, random tonal accidents; the sense of danger and desperate urgency that had informed the work of early pioneers like Elmore James or Link Wray. Even distortion and feedback had been reduced to a science by the century's end. Young players could find YouTube tutorials explaining the precise order in which harmonic intervals manifest themselves as a guitar starts to feed back, and why they do so. Where's the fun in that?

The Airline guitar was manufactured for Montgomery Ward by Valco, a company launched in 1942 by Victor Smith, Al Frost, and Louis Dopyera—the first initials of their given names spelling out the V-A-L in Valco. All three men had been part of the National and/or Rickenbacker companies back in the 1930s when these firms brought the first commercially produced electric guitars to the market.

So the wheel had come full circle. One of the hippest guitars of the early-twenty-first century was designed by men who had played a role in first bringing the electric guitar into the world some seven decades earlier.

Valco had risen from the ashes of the National Dobro Corporation in the aftermath of World War II. Louis Dopyera had bought out his brothers' interest in National and had tried to forge ahead in the new paradigm of postwar electric guitar making. And for a few decades, at least, he and his colleagues had succeeded. The Valco company went under in 1968, but some of its guitars lived on to define a new era of retro-chic.

While it is generally described as plastic, the Airline guitar's body is actually fashioned from Res-O-Glas, a form of fiberglass—a plastic reinforced with glass fibers. Fiberglass was one of the miracle materials of the mid-twentieth-century modernist design movement. Two of the most iconic examples of modernist automotive design—the Chevrolet Corvette and the Studebaker Avanti—were made with molded fiberglass bodies, a design innovation that was considered quite futuristic at the time.

So Res-O-Glas was more than just inexpensive. It was also state-of-the-art. In essence, the Montgomery Ward Airline comes out of the same design aesthetic that gave rise to the Fender Stratocaster and Gibson Flying V. Valco just took it a step further by employing a nontraditional material as well as a nontraditional body shape. This, moreover, was entirely in keeping with Dopyera, Frost, and Smith's National/Rickenbacker legacy. Back in the thirties, Rickenbacker had revolutionized electric guitar design by using another modernist plastic—Bakelite—to fashion electric guitar bodies.

Nor was the budget-priced Airline guitar the only instrument that Valco manufactured from Res-O-Glas. They employed the same material for some of their higher-priced models, marketed under the Supro and National brand names.

Valco's top-of-the-line Res-O-Glas instrument was the National Glenwood. At the time it was introduced, in 1962, it was priced comparably with the Fender Stratocaster and Gibson SG, all selling for just under $300 retail. For this kind of money, a customer could get a Glenwood equipped with high-quality appointments such as a Bigsby tailpiece and the same Grover "Rotomatic" tuning machines Gibson used on some of their Les Pauls. On top of that, the body was shaped like a somewhat abstracted map of the United States.

Malleability was another of Res-O-Glas's cardinal virtues. The guitar bodies were fabricated by pouring the molten polymer into a mold, and the mold could be virtually any shape. You could do more with it than you could with a hunk of wood and a band saw. The instrument's color could be mixed into the molten substance as well, eliminating the need for a separate manufacturing process either to paint the guitar or to apply a fine wood finish. An added benefit of this method is that, unlike conventional guitar finishes, Res-O-Glas colors never fade. The vintage Res-O-Glas Airline or National you buy today—probably for anywhere between $1,500 and $3,000—has exactly the same vibrant mid-century color it did when it first left the factory. So Res-O-Glas offered Valco the dual advantages of a cool new look and a more streamlined manufacturing process.

"We found that, with the electrics, you didn't need all that resonance," Al Frost recalled. "So we tried making the bodies out of polyester resin and fiberglass. We would take a mold, spray the finish in, then the fiberglass, pull it out of there, and the finish would already be on it. Oh, it was beautiful. We made Res-O-Glas guitars in reds and blues and whites and all sorts of colors. They were really something."

"Beautiful" is an adjective quite appropriate to the Airline guitar and its Res-O-Glas Valco counterparts. The angular Airline body is both innovative and handsomely proportioned. So why do guitar journalists and historians invariably use dismissive language to describe these instruments? Typical of the phenomenon is a 2013 article on the Airline in *Guitar Player* magazine that bears the headline "Whack Job." In it the writer Terry Carlton uses terms such as "weirdo" and "rinky-dink" to describe the guitar, grudgingly admitting that while the Airline "looks almost ridiculous," it "plays quite well" and has "a very unique sound."

Part of the derision stems from the fact that, unlike Stratocasters and Flying Vs, Res-O-Glas guitars pretty much fell out of use after the sixties. The Airline, Glenwood, and other Res-O-Glas shapes didn't stick around long enough to become "iconic," and thus are disassociated in people's minds with any particular time period.

Also, a great deal of electric guitar history has been written by baby boomers, who tend to see in these instruments the cheap, crummy guitars they played as adolescents, before moving up to Fenders, Gibsons, and other more prestigious brands. For them, guitars of the Valco breed are embarrassing memories of awkward youth.

But to millennial eyes, guitars like the Airline look quite different. Millennial fascination with these instruments is very much of a piece with the recent hipster preference for vinyl records, manual typewriters, and other artifacts of a time before the advent of personal computers. To them, it all seems quite romantic.

Of course the Airline doesn't *sound* anything like a 335, a Les Paul, or Stratocaster, particularly when overdriven to distortion. Nor does it sound anything like an Ibanez JEM or PRS guitar. That's the real point here. The Airline possesses less sustain than any of the aforementioned guitars, but more lower midrange "honk." Which places it outside the normative definition of what a great guitar should sound like. But this is also the very thing that makes it interesting and appealing to ears thirsting for a new sound and a new aesthetic.

Up through the nineties, you were more likely to encounter an Airline guitar at a modernist antique show than at a vintage guitar show or shop. That began to change with the mainstream breakthrough of the White Stripes, and again with the Black Keys. One of the common nicknames for the Montgomery Ward Airline is the "Jetsons" guitar, a reference to the early-sixties animated sitcom that depicted a stylish, sci-fi future where life was made easy by an endless array of streamlined, mechanized devices. The first program to be broadcast in color on ABC-TV, *The Jetsons* originally ran from 1962 to '63, just when the guitars under discussion were coming onto the market. If Judy Jetson—the series' quintessential teenage girl of the future—were to play an electric guitar, it would look something like an Airline.

But if the twenty-first-century revival of interest in guitars like the Airline represents a revolution in taste, a movement away from baby boomer aesthetics, it also has a very practical side. Prices for vintage Fenders, Gibsons, Gretsches, and other more well-known guitar brands skyrocketed in the nineties, to the point where the most desirable Les Pauls and Stratocasters from the fifties were commanding six-figure prices, making them inaccessible to most rank-and-file guitarists or young musicians just starting out. High-visibility auctions of vintage guitars by celebrity collectors sparked widespread public interest in these instruments, touching off a veritable feeding frenzy. Eric Clapton's Crossroads guitar auctions in 1998, 2004, and 2011 netted $5.1 million, $7.4 million, and $2.2 million respectively. Actor and guitar collector Richard Gere's auction in 2011 fetched nearly a million. Proceeds from all these sales went to charity. As the head of the Fine Musical Instruments department at Christie's auction house in New York, an *Antiques Roadshow* appraiser, and a vintage guitar expert, Kerry Keane was right at the center of much of the action.

"The foundation of the vintage guitar market is certainly Americans buying the guitars of their youth," Keane said.

> The demographic is postwar baby boomers who want to buy the guitars they couldn't afford when they were sixteen years old. And on top of that, buying the guitars that were their heroes' guitars. It's that desire to purchase those iconic objects from their youth. The most likely vintage guitar buyer is a banker, attorney, orthodontist, or someone who owns a string of car dealerships—someone who has the money and happens to be a guitar player, maybe playing with a band every Thursday night for relaxation. And the Clapton sale of 2004 certainly revved up that market to a degree where you suddenly had people buying guitars for investment purposes.

The stock market crash and Great Recession of 2008 brought the high-end vintage guitar market down a few notches. But the instruments still remained largely out of the reach of those who made less than, say, half a million dollars a year. So if you were an aspiring young Jack White and you wanted a vintage guitar, something like an Airline made an attractive option. Even at a premium price of $3,000, it was still a lot more accessible than a guitar priced at $30,000 or more. Besides, what young player covets the same kind of guitar owned by orthodontists and stockbrokers? Who among them wants a "dad" guitar?

Valco's Airline, Supro, and National Res-O-Glas guitars represented just the tip of a veritable iceberg of affordable electric guitars that were available in the early to mid-sixties. The Harmony and Kay companies produced an abundance of budget electrics under their own brand names and also manufactured guitars and amps that were marketed by Sears, Roebuck & Company bearing the Silvertone brand name. Valco, Danelectro, and Teisco also supplied Sears with Silvertone instruments.

Much like Valco, both Harmony and Kay were American companies with roots in the very earliest days of the electric guitar. While both certainly sought to attract professional players, the bulk of their marketing and manufacturing efforts were aimed at the vast number of guitarists at the semipro and amateur levels— the garage band players, working-class parents looking to buy their kid a Christmas present, and really just about any guitar player without a whole lot of money to spend. In this regard, companies such as these were even more populist than Fender. But, somehow, they haven't been mythologized in quite the same way.

Nor was America the only country in this game. The mid-sixties also witnessed an explosion of affordable guitars from Italy—instruments manufactured by Eko, Crucianelli, Avanti, Wandre, Goya, Polverini, Meazzi, Gemelli, and many others. The home of Stradivari, Guarneri, Amati, Fabricatore, and Cavelli, Italy has a long and proud tradition of both violin and guitar luthiery. And in the mid-sixties, Italy was very much one of the world's style capitals. Italian sports cars and couture were very much in demand. The slender outlines, narrow lapels, and iridescent fabrics of Continental men's tailoring were very much an Italian inspiration.

Not surprisingly, Italian electric guitars from this period are big on mid-sixties bling. Many of the makers were accordion manufacturers eager to cash in on the rock-and-roll craze. So they began incorporating the brightly colored, textured, sparkly plastics of accordion making into their guitar designs. Futuristic body contours bedizened with pickups, knobs, and switches were the rule rather than the exception. But there's more to these guitars than just novelty value or retro garage rock appeal. The celebrated alt-country guitarist Buddy Miller, for example, is a longtime devotee of Wandre guitars. His association with the brand has helped raise its status substantially, with some vintage Wandres selling for as much as $40,000.

Mid-sixties Italian electrics, in turn, are just part of an overall

European boom in electric guitar making in this period. Guitars such as Hagstroms from Sweden and Musimas from East Germany made their way into the U.S. and U.K. at the time. Eventually, though, nearly all these guitars were eclipsed by affordable electrics coming out of Japan, and perhaps best symbolized by that ultimate garage band guitar, the Teisco Del Rey.

It all amounts to a literal world of sixties guitars that few guitarists had ever heard of—up until recently. This opened up the classic sixties period in electric guitar music to a new generation in a whole new way. Much like the recent garage rock movement itself, it has been a multicultural phenomenon. Just as garage rock CD compilations spotlight obscure bands from Southeast Asia, Latin America, and other geographic regions hitherto neglected by Western rock fans, a more internationalist perspective has crept into the appreciation of electric guitars as well.

THERE'S A SECOND nickname for the Montgomery Ward Airline guitar that illuminates another key factor in the plastic guitar resurgence. It is also known as the "J. B. Hutto" model in honor of bluesman Joseph Benjamin Hutto, who was active from the fifties through the eighties and played the Airline model prominently. While Jack White and the Black Keys' Dan Auerbach have often been rivals, and have certainly spoken unkindly of one another, one thing they are united in is a deeply felt love of the blues. But not necessarily the same blues venerated by the baby boomer generation. Not the blues of virtuosic guitar soloing or shared stages with Eric Clapton at his Crossroads festival. The millennial take on the blues is something else again—a primordial sound generated largely by lone performers wrenching wildly distorted tones from cheap electric guitars.

"I like raw, really stripped-down blues," Auerbach said in 2014. "So much so that I didn't even really listen to Muddy Waters or Howlin' Wolf much. Not the Chicago recordings, because it was almost too big of a band. I like that Memphis stuff—Joe Hill Lewis, Pat Hare, and Willie Johnson. And I really loved T-Model Ford's album *Pee-Wee Get My Gun* when that came out when I was seventeen [in 1997]. And that's when I started playing with Pat [Carney, the Black Keys drummer]. We started recording and I was listening to T-Model and R. L. Burnside, having grown up playing blues and bluegrass."

T-Model Ford and R. L. Burnside are two artists who recorded for the Fat Possum record label, based in Oxford, Mississippi. The label was launched in 1991, with an initial mission to seek out and record obscure Mississippi blues artists who had hitherto received little or no exposure. These included men like Ford, Burnside, and Junior Kimbrough—raw-edged performers still working the local juke joints at the time, just as legendary bluesmen of the twenties and thirties such as Robert Johnson and Charley Patton once had done.

For decades, blues guitarists from the rural, impoverished South had been obtaining their instruments from mail-order catalogs such as those circulated by Sears and Montgomery Ward. The guitars were affordable, and in more remote areas catalogs would have been the only source from which a musician of humble means could purchase a new instrument. Even the mighty Howlin' Wolf started out on a modest Kay Thin Twin model in the fifties before moving on to larger audiences and fancier guitars. But for every Wolf, there were dozens of blues artists who didn't get a chance to move to Chicago as Wolf and Muddy Waters had done, let alone go on to enjoy the adulation of the baby boomer generation. For them, a catalog guitar wasn't just a starter instrument, but a viable and lifelong musical tool.

With its early-nineties launch, the Fat Possum label was able to capture the tail end of this generation of largely forgotten bluesmen—those who had stayed closer to their rural roots while still embracing the raw timbres of distorted electric guitars. As such, Fat Possum built a kind of bridge between the blues and punk rock. The original punk rockers of the seventies had rejected blues licks as a baby boomer affectation. But Fat Possum artists were something different. Their attitude was very much summed up by the title of a well-received series of Fat Possum compilation albums: *Not the Same Old Blues Crap.*

And this was music to the ears of aspiring garage rockers, particularly Dan Auerbach. Growing up, his guitar-playing father and uncles had turned him on to more well-known bluesmen such as T-Bone Walker and Slim Harpo. Through parental and avuncular tutelage and record collections, he'd pretty much absorbed the baby boomer perspective on folk and blues tradition by his teen years. But the Fat Possum artists seemed to him to take all this into another dimension.

Like any aspiring guitarist, Auerbach paid close attention to the kinds of instruments his newfound blues heroes were playing. "I usually use off-brand guitars," he said,

> because the guys I was listening to when I started playing were playing those guitars. Hound Dog Taylor, J. B. Hutto, and all that weird Fat Possum stuff—they were using weird guitars. I just liked it. My first guitar was a Stratocaster that my mom bought me without sort of asking me what I wanted. And I immediately took it to a guitar shop in Cleveland and I traded it for a Silvertone. The guy told me that it was a great deal and I said, "OK, sure." And I got a Silvertone. It's like a Teisco Del Rey, really, but it's Silvertone branded. Green sunburst body, four pickups with all the switches and stuff. I was just a kid, fifteen years old, obsessed with Hound Dog Taylor. I did *not* want to play a Strat.

Auerbach was still in his teen years when he began traveling down south to Memphis and Mississippi to seek out some of his Fat Possum blues heroes:

I went down to Greenville, Mississippi, on one trip and tracked down T-Model Ford. My friend and I hung out with him for a few days and I spent a night on the linoleum-tile floor of his trailer home. I was in a sleeping bag. And just playing guitar with him . . . People would hire him to play parties and then we played a juke joint at night. His son was playing drums and I'd play guitar and he'd play guitar. He kept me safe down there. I'm sure it was a pretty dangerous part of town we were in. But he kept me and my buddy safe.

The Black Keys would go on to release several low-budget albums on the Fat Possum imprint before landing a major label deal with Nonesuch Records in 2006. This would result in major hit records such as "Tighten Up" and "Lonely Boy" and multiple Grammy Awards. They were hailed as a keynote group in the second wave of the neo-garage revival of the twenty-first century's second decade.

By this point, garage rock had become an institution almost as venerable as the blues. Both are essentially outsider musical genres that have come to impact the course of popular music in different ways. While the garage influence hasn't been as pervasive as that of the blues—the genre never produced an Eric Clapton or Stevie Ray Vaughan—it has nonetheless been a prime mover in less mainstream genres.

The original sixties garage bands provided a key source of inspiration for the rise of punk rock in the mid-seventies. One major catalyst was the 1972 *Nuggets* compilation album, a sampling of 1960s garage rock tracks compiled by the music critic Lenny Kaye, who went on to become the guitarist for one of the seminal punk rock bands, the Patti Smith Group. Many of the most important first-wave punk bands covered or referenced the sixties' garage band repertoire. Smith peppered her own compositions with canny quotations from the Shadows of Knight/Them classic "Gloria" and Chris Kenner's "Land of a Thousand Dances," which had been a mid-sixties hit for Cannibal and the Headhunters. Similarly, the Sex Pistols covered the Paul Revere & the Raiders/Monkees garage rock standard "(I'm Not Your) Steppin' Stone," and the Ramones performed "Surfin' Bird" by the Trashmen and "California Sun" by the Rivieras.

Ramones guitarist Johnny Ramone's choice of a Mosrite Ventures II model was a fairly overt sixties garage reference, although the instrument's affordable price was the main thing that appealed to the notoriously parsimonious guitarist. Prominent use of the Fender Jazzmaster by Elvis Costello and Television's Tom Verlaine helped to bring that model out from under the shadow of Stratocasters and Telecasters, where it had languished for decades. As such, the Jazzmaster and Jaguar models served the needs of players looking for guitars that weren't associated with the classic rock/AOR radio era.

Patti Smith's adoption of the inexpensive Fender Duo-Sonic as her guitar of choice was also a quintessentially garage rock gesture, although legend has it that the instrument originally belonged to Jimi Hendrix. Smith mainly deployed her Duo-Sonic to generate waves of disruptive, atonal noise in concert.

"I wanted to open up and immediately make use of the sonic aspects of the electric guitar and amplifier," she said. "So I really explored the electric guitar as deeply and committedly in my own way, I feel, as anyone else who did. I just wasn't really interested in playing leads or chording or playing songs. I was basically interested in achieving some kind of communication with the gods through sound."

The atonal and nontraditional aspects of Smith's approach were of particular interest to avant-garde composer and guitarist Glenn Branca, who landed in New York in 1976, just as punk rock was getting under way.

"I was impressed with Patti Smith, Richard Hell, Television, the Ramones, all those people," Branca recalled.

I put together this sort of performance-art/rock band called Theoretical Girl. To be honest, I wasn't taking it seriously, I just wanted to do it. We started out as pretty much a straight punk band with noise breaks in the middle, but it sounded good. And in New York, it got people's interest, which might not have happened anywhere else. There was just this tremendous audience interest. I decided I wanted to make it bigger than just a rock band. So we decided to push the music towards composers we liked, like [German composer Karlheinz] Stockhausen. They were all writing music that was as extreme as heavy metal, except they weren't using guitars. As we went off in that direction, the further we got from the center, the more successful the band became. In 1979, I took it outside the band and wrote an instrumental piece for six guitars.

Branca began writing compositions for increasingly large guitar ensembles—or "guitar armies," as they came to be known. The culmination of this would be compositions such as Branca's *Symphony No. 13: Hallucination City*, written for an orchestra comprising no less than a hundred electric guitars. Branca often used cheap, thrift-shop guitars, or even instruments he found in the street, to make up these electric guitar orchestras. Such humble instruments were useful to him because he wasn't interested in conventional electric guitar tonalities or even tunings. He placed the guitars in alternate tunings, which allowed him to exploit the harmonic overtones generated by electric guitars en masse in ways that hadn't been done before. Eventually he began to build guitar-like instruments of his own design. Some were as simple as a single guitar string and a pickup mounted on a piece of wood (an echo of George Beauchamp's earliest experiments at the dawn of the electric guitar). Others were more complex, with multiple bridges. Still others were designed for the strings to be struck with drumsticks rather than played in the conventional manner.

The seventies intersection of New York's punk rock and down-town music communities contributed much to a renewed interest in what had once been thought of as off-brand electric guitars. Another brilliant product of this hybrid is the guitarist Marc Ribot. His approach combines more traditional electric guitars, such as a 1957 Fender Telecaster and 1963 Jaguar, with more garage-level instruments, such as a 1952 Harmony Stratotone. He has often employed these in conjunction with a wide range of nontraditional playing techniques that trace back to avant-garde composer John Cage and his prepared piano compositions. In this spirit, Ribot has been known to attack his guitar strings with inflated balloons, massage vibrators, cappuccino frothers, and electric fans. In such applications, obviously, using a guitar that can create a conventional rock, blues, or jazz tone is of absolutely no importance.

"I'm bored with most things on guitar," Ribot told *Guitar Player* magazine.

Eight zillion people have tried to play as fast as they can, and so what? The sounds we're talking about are not part of the tempered scale, but are part of the established language of free improvisers and downtown New York City noisemakers. They're not part of what most kids learn in music school. It goes back to one of the oldest understandings of why people make music at all, and that's because music is mimetic of nature. That theory bored me too until I understood what composers like [John] Zorn, Elliott Sharp, and Arto Lindsay are doing, which is creating the mimesis of the absence or death of nature, and our connection to it. Understanding ideas like that will get you a lot further than going to Berklee.

By drafting some of this thinking into their own musical approaches, New York's punk and post-punk bands were able to reassert rock music's outsider status—something that had become lost with the music's codification and enshrinement as "classic rock." Glenn Branca's guitar ensembles included many guitarists from New York's underground rock community, including members of Sonic Youth and Swans. As these guitarists got their own bands going, they began incorporating some of Branca's ideas about alternate tunings and atonality into more of a rock-oriented presentation.

"It was completely inside, atonal guitar music," Sonic Youth guitarist Thurston Moore said of Branca's work. "But I wanted to tie that in with the high-energy rock of the MC5 and Stooges. Which wasn't something that people like Glenn Branca were really that interested in at all."

In its early career particularly, Sonic Youth employed a range of thrift-shop electric guitars in both live performances and on recordings. Some of the band's alternate tunings originated on guitars in such poor shape that they couldn't hold a conventional guitar tuning. So they were tuned to whatever intervals would remain relatively stable for the length of a song.

Sonic Youth, in turn, became a key influence on the Seattle grunge scene of the nineties, which brought Nirvana to the fore as one of the era's most influential rock bands. Nirvana leader Kurt Cobain's embrace of budget Fender models such as the Mustang was partially born of necessity. He often smashed his guitar at the end of a performance, so he frequently needed to find affordable replacements. Thrift shops held the answer (while also providing him with much of his wardrobe). His enormous popularity certainly contributed to rock guitarists' thinking outside the box.

The nineties U.K. counterpart to grunge was the dream pop genre spearheaded by bands such as My Bloody Valentine, Lush, and the Cocteau Twins. Several of these groups also employed alternate tunings and layers of grainy distortion created by hooking together multiple fuzz pedals and other effects devices. As in all the music styles under discussion in this chapter, unconventional playing techniques were eagerly embraced. One of the most influential dream pop artists, Kevin Shields of My Bloody Valentine, achieved an otherworldly "wobbling" tonality by leaving the vibrato arm of his Fender Jazzmaster and Jaguar guitars only partially screwed in to its socket and keeping it in more or less perpetual motion as he strummed chords.

But amid all these guitar-centric alternative rock styles—part of what music historian Jon Savage has termed the post-punk diaspora—garage rock has remained a constant. The late seventies and early eighties saw a garage rock revival that included the Fuzztones, the Pandoras, and the Chesterfield Kings. Several of these groups played on sixties period instruments. The Pandoras were notable for their Vox gear (including Italian-made guitars for the Vox brand). Chesterfield Kings bassist Andy Babiuk would go on to become a leading historian of sixties guitars. By the late eighties, these bands had been joined by seminal garage rockers such as Thee Headcoats, Thee Mighty Caesars, and the Gories.

Along with being very much a multicultural phenomenon, as noted above, the garage rock genre has always been especially welcoming to female performers. This goes all the way back to the music's mid-sixties origins, a period that spawned all-girl groups such as Goldie & the Gingerbreads, the Pleasure Seekers, the Luv'd Ones, and the Liverbirds. This tradition has been reflected in the various garage rock revivals, in which all-female groups such as the Pandoras and Thee Headcoatees—and their leader, Holly Golightly—have been just as highly regarded as their male counterparts. All-girl bands are particularly prevalent on the most recent garage scene, with groups such as the 5.6.7.8's, Thee Tsunamis, the She's, and Summer Twins attracting significant underground followings. Sporting a red, mid-sixties Teisco Del Rey, guitarist Yoshiko "Ronnie" Fujiyama of Japan's 5.6.7.8's is highly emblematic of the current garage scene.

Punk and alternative rock in general have typically been cultures that empower women musicians, and this can be seen as one more legacy derived from punk's roots, the original mid-sixties garage rock explosion. Nor has it been only a matter of all-girl groups. Mixed gender bands have been common in all the garage/punk genres and subgenres. In this regard, the White Stripes' gender-equal lineup is very much in keeping with garage rock values.

GARAGE ROCK HAS also always been very much a regional phenomenon. The White Stripes emerged in the late nineties from a wave of Detroit garage bands that included the Von Bondies, the Dirtbombs, the Detroit Cobras, and Bantam Rooster. But a few factors set the White Stripes apart. One was their radically minimal lineup, with just two members, Jack and Meg White, playing electric guitar and drum kit, respectively. Alternative rock had spawned several two-piece groups previously, notably the Flat Duo Jets from Athens, Georgia. But the White Stripes would become the first to break through to the mainstream.

Second, there was Jack White's profound sense of identification with the blues. As a form of rock music, all garage rock is of course blues-based, but White made the connection more explicit, specifically through actions such as bringing a Son House song onto the Grammy stage in 2004. His retro-futurist approach to blues guitar playing brought new life to an idiom that had hitherto seemed played out. From a traditionalist standpoint, he broke the rules—for example, by combining slide guitar with relatively modern devices such as the DigiTech Whammy pedal. Digitally enabling guitarists to execute dramatic pitch transpositions of an octave or more, the Whammy allowed White to turbocharge the kind of dramatic glissandos that have long been a key element of slide playing. It's nontraditional, certainly. But Son House or Elmore James themselves probably would have loved having a Whammy pedal of their own.

Guitar magazines began ranking Jack White highly in their polls of the best electric guitarists. Music critics were quick to take note too—particularly won over by White's high-concept take on garage rock. The White Stripes' distinctive color scheme was just one aspect of the band's conceptual framework. Song lyrics, album art, video clips, and every other aspect of the band's presentation were deeply imbued with White's almost obsessive use of symbols and recurring leitmotifs. One would have to go back to the era of Bob Dylan's ascendancy to find something comparable. White proved that high-concept and lo-fi need not be mutually exclusive.

The revival of interest in thrift-shop guitars, and attendant mainstreaming of what had hitherto been regarded as oddball, was just one small aspect of the garage rock phenomenon. But its role in bringing some fresh thinking into the arts of electric guitar playing and design has been an important one. More widespread use of these instruments, however, quickly brought some of their limitations to the fore. While they look and sound incredibly cool—particularly to postmodern eyes and ears—many of these instruments are difficult to play for one reason or another. Typically, they don't intonate properly or are hard to keep in tune, or both. Switches, knobs, and other components can be crackly and cantankerous.

As a result, the Black Keys' Dan Auerbach, for example, employs a full-time guitar tech, Dan Johnson, to refurbish his collection of Silvertone, Harmony, Kay, Teisco, Supro, and other thrift-shop vintage guitars—refretting them, retrofitting them with better bridges and electronics. White has moved to more conventional Gretsches, Fenders, and other guitars in his post–White Stripes work. Auerbach, for his part, employs a combination of thrift-shop vintage guitars and more mainstream instruments.

Recent years have also seen the rise of guitar makers who create high-quality instruments with a retro-garage, mid-twentieth-century look and feel. These include Deusenberg guitars designed by German luthier Dieter Golsdörf, and Italia guitars created by the British luthier Trev Wilkinson. Both makers take mid-twentieth-century European guitar design as a jumping-off point for creating stylish, often quite ornate instruments. Not surprisingly, Deusenberg tends to draw more from German design in this period, while Italia, as its name implies, takes a major cue from blingy Italian instruments from the age of *La Dolce Vita*. Both brands have been very well received. Deusenbergs in particular have attracted attention in the hands of high-profile players such as Keith Richards, Ron Wood, Elvis Costello, Paul McCartney, Billy Gibbons, and many others.

Eastwood Guitars, a Canadian company, was launched in 2001 with a line of guitars that copied Valco's Airline instruments. From there the company has grown to offer a full line of retro-style guitars under both the Eastwood and Airline brand names. Many of these guitars have found favor with alternative rock and alt-country artists such as Neko Case, Calexico, the Decemberists, and Yo La Tengo.

But Eastwood, Deusenberg, and Italia are just three out of hundreds of smaller guitar brands and boutique luthiers currently in operation. Long gone are the days when the electric guitar market was dominated by a handful of companies. Today's electric guitarist can choose from a vast and sometimes daunting field of options. That applies not only to guitars, but also to amps, effects pedals, and replacement parts such as pickups, bridges, nuts, and more. At this point in musical history, every single aspect of classic electric guitar design has been analyzed down to the millimeter. Computer technology has assisted in both the measurement and the reproduction of the most desirable qualities. And designers are always coming up with new refinements, as the Internet keeps a new generation of super-informed guitarists up to date on each new development.

In a sense, the most recent garage rock revival is a reaction against all this—a willful and well-considered embrace of primitivism. But then garage rock itself is just one out of hundreds of guitar-driven musical subgenres that owe their existence to fan bases garnered and maintained through websites and social media.

At the opposite end of the stylistic spectrum from garage rock, one might cite a guitarist like Tosin Abasi, the Nigerian American leader of the progressive metal band Animals as Leaders. He's known for his technically advanced playing style—frenetic bursts of abstract melodic and rhythmic phrasing that he executes with dazzling precision on seven- and eight-string electric guitars. For Abasi and other guitarists in his genre, the golden age isn't the garage rock sixties or even the Hendrix/Clapton classic rock era, but rather the shred metal eighties, when guitars were pointy and had more than six strings.

Then again, there's guitarist Gemma Thompson with the critically acclaimed Anglo-French band Savages, who bases her approach on the post-punk sounds of bands such as the Birthday Party, Swans, and Siouxsie and the Banshees. In the true matriarchal tradition of punk rock, she plays the Fender Duo-Sonic model once favored by Patti Smith. But rather than just imitate the styles of a bygone decade, Thompson takes this music as a point of departure, in much the same way that Abasi doesn't imitate Steve Vai, but rather creates something new based on the direction that Vai and his compatriots outlined.

Another guitarist who has become a phenomenon is Annie Clark, who performs under the stage name St. Vincent. A highly accomplished player, she grew up under the tutelage of her uncle, jazz guitarist Tuck Andress, and attended the prestigious Berklee College of Music. This kind of background can doom a guitarist to a life playing jazz-fusion that can only be appreciated by other guitarists. But Clark has instead focused her talents on creating arty, witty meta-pop and collaborating with highly regarded art rockers such as former Talking Head David Byrne. Clark has also brought her own take on the retro-modernist aesthetic to a signature model Ernie Ball brand guitar she designed in 2016.

"My particular guitar," she said, "is based a lot on ['80s synthpop performance artist] Klaus Nomi's aesthetic, the Memphis design movement—which was an ['80s] Italian design movement—and those '60s and '70s Japanese-designed guitars like the Teiscos. And then I went for classic car colors."

Like a few other recent electric guitar designers and manufacturers—notably entrepreneur Tish Ciravolo's Daisy Rock Girl Guitars—Clark has tailored her signature model instrument to be a better fit for the female anatomy than conventional designs. Specifically, she crafted an instrument with a lighter weight and narrower waist.

"I can't even play a '60s Strat or '70s Les Paul," she said. "I would need to travel with a chiropractor on tour in order to play those guitars." As for the instrument's narrow waist, she said, "I wanted to make something that looked good not just on a woman, but any person."

As the work of recent artists such as Abasi, Thompson, and Clark clearly indicates, the electric guitar has entered a new era of diversity, offering a wider array of talents and styles than any previous era in the instrument's history. But there is no one predominant style, as there has been in bygone decades, nor is there likely to be. Web platforms such as YouTube, SoundCloud, Bandcamp, and ReverbNation have created an environment in which virtually anyone can have two hundred fans, but very few indeed can have twenty million, or even two million.

The impact of the Internet on both the art and business of music has been immense, and its end result is yet to be seen. While it has created a climate in which anyone's music can be heard, it has also fostered an economic environment in which most artists, musical and otherwise, can no longer earn a living from their art. Piracy and online streaming have catastrophically reduced revenues that artists receive from music sales. An increasing number of highly gifted artists are finding that music making has been downgraded from a profession to a hobby.

"The inevitable result," wrote David Byrne in a 2013 article for *The Guardian,* "would seem to be that the internet will suck the creative content out of the whole world until nothing is left."

One can only hope that Byrne's prediction is wrong. But at the time of this writing, the only new, young musical artists whose livelihoods aren't imperiled by the Internet are the small handful that rise to the top of highly commercial, formulaic genres, such as corporate pop and mainstream R&B. "A culture of blockbusters is sad, and ultimately it's bad for business," Byrne wrote. "That's not the world that inspired me when I was younger. Many a fan (myself included) has said that 'music saved my life,' so there must be some incentive to keep that lifesaver available for future generations."

AMID THE RADICAL transformation currently taking place in the music business, and in the entire culture of music consumption and appreciation, it becomes very difficult to predict what the future of the electric guitar might be. But it's a safe bet that the instrument isn't about to disappear anytime soon. Ever since the seventies, analysts have agonized over the imminent demise of the electric guitar at the hands of one electronic music form or other—disco, rap, hip-hop, synthpop, techno, or EDM (electronic dance music). All these musical genres have been hugely influential, and the electric guitar indeed no longer dominates popular music the way it once did. But still, the instrument persists.

It is true that most popular music today is created on personal computers, which can be used not only to record music but also to generate sounds on their own. But computer technology has yet to create anything that can replace the tactile satisfaction of both playing and hearing an electric guitar—all the subtle and expressive tonal variations that come from human flesh pressing against metal strings. In fact, many of the most widely used music software programs are plug-ins that provide digital emulations of the classic tube guitar amps and analog effects pedals of the classic rock era. These can be used in tandem with other plug-ins that emulate vintage analog recording equipment and old-school analog synthesizers. It's telling that, given the theoretically endless possibilities afforded by software programming, what many have chosen to do with software is evoke the past.

Which means that today's electric guitarist has ready access to a credible simulation of all the gear that Hendrix, Townshend, Link Wray, B. B. King, Van Halen, Steve Vai, or any other legendary guitarist once commanded. While these emulations don't sound exactly like the real thing, they're close enough to make it easy for any producer or songwriter to incorporate a bit of that classic rock, blues, funk, or jazz guitar sound into their productions.

And musical artists are still doing this to a significant degree. The sound of the electric guitar has become a sort of instant signifier of rock-and-roll rebellion and wild, unbridled freedom. It has also become a signifier of honesty, of "realness." Speaking with *Rolling Stone* magazine in early 2016 to promote his *Black Market* album, the rapper Rick Ross said, "I made this album a little more soulful and sophisticated by adding live guitars and shit like that."

Those who do take up the electric guitar today are in a very different position than someone who picked up the instrument during the crucible years of the fifties and sixties. The field is less wide open. The electric guitar is now a mature instrument. It may not be as old as the violin or even the saxophone, but the electric guitar's basic form and lineaments have been firmly established. There's a lot of history and tradition there—not to mention a lot of rebellion against history and tradition.

For the past six decades or so, rock music has been the predominant driving force in the electric guitar's evolution, and vice versa. That may not be the case in the future, as rock increasingly becomes a heritage genre like bluegrass, for example, or baroque—a period music played on period instruments. Similarly, while America and Great Britain have traditionally played a leading role in electric guitar design innovation, that too is rapidly changing. The electric guitar is already well on its way toward globalization. But will there ever be another mass musical phenomenon like rock and roll—itself a uniquely Anglo-American cultural phenomenon—that is as inherently amenable to the electric guitar's tonality and playing techniques?

No one can predict the future. Not in this case, anyway. But the electric guitar's versatility and adaptability make it a highly likely candidate for survival in the Darwinian mechanics of musical evolution. All musical instruments mutate over time. Through a series of tiny developmental steps, the harpsichord became the piano, the rebec became the violin, and the shawm became the oboe. The mutation of any instrument tends to cease—or at least become temporarily arrested for long periods of time—when people stop creating new music on that instrument. In the case of the electric guitar, that eventuality still seems quite distant.

The greatest practitioners in all art forms are often those who break the rules. But the electric guitar seems particularly welcoming to iconoclasts. It seems happiest when you try to turn it up to 11, to push any of its parameters a little further than they were designed to go. All of the instrument's great innovators have done so—not by discarding the electric guitar's past, but by finding new ways to contextualize it. A creative spirit can always manage that. And, if nothing else, the electric guitar has always proven a friend of creative outsiders.

TIMELINE

September 4, 1882: The nation's first electricity-generating power station opens its doors in Manhattan.

September 2, 1890: The first patent for an electric guitar design is given to inventor George Breed. The instrument is small and extremely heavy, and it produces an unusual, continuously sustained sound.

Nineteenth Century

1900s–1920s

October 10, 1902: The Gibson Mandolin-Guitar Manufacturing Company is founded.

January 29, 1907: Lee De Forest patents the first electronic amplification device, the triode vacuum tube.

1921: The first paper-cone loudspeaker is developed by Chester W. Rice and Edward W. Kellogg.

1928/29: The Stromberg-Voisinet Electro, the first commercial electric guitar, is introduced to general indifference.

1932: The production model of the Ro-Pat-In Electro A-25 "Frying Pan" hits the market. It is hailed as the first successful commercially produced electric guitar.

October 31, 1932: Guitarist Gage Brewer gives what is regarded as the first public electric guitar performance at the Shadowland Pavilion in Wichita, Kansas.

1933: Electric guitar models are introduced by Gibson, Vivi-Tone, and Dobro.

1935: Electric guitar models are introduced by Audiovox, Epiphone, and Volu-tone.

1930s

November 20, 1936: Gibson delivers the first ES-150, which achieves unprecedented notoriety due in large part to its endorsement by prominent guitar players of the day, such as Eddie Durham and Floyd Smith.

March 31, 1938: American swing guitarist George Barnes makes the first commercial recording of an electric guitar, in sessions with blues artist Big Bill Broonzy.

August 16, 1939: Charlie Christian is invited to play in Benny Goodman's sextet. By February 1940, Christian and his Gibson ES-150 dominate jazz and swing polls, as he becomes the first widely acclaimed electric guitar hero.

ca. 1939: Les Paul begins work on the "Log" solid-body electric guitar.

1930s

1940s

1945: "It's Been a Long, Long Time," Bing Crosby's first record with the Les Paul Trio, becomes a hit.

1946: The Fender Electric Instrument Company is launched.

1947: The single release "Lover" debuts Les Paul's "New Sound." It is recorded on a revolutionary multitrack device invented by the guitarist, and features a staggering eight electric guitar parts, all played by Paul.

April 1948: Muddy Waters creates his two landmark blues recordings, "I Can't Be Satisfied" and "I Feel Like Going Home," featuring his bottleneck slide on an amplified guitar.

May 25, 1948: Work is completed on the Travis-Bigsby solid-body electric guitar.

1950: The Fender Broadcaster solid-body electric guitar is introduced; it is renamed the Telecaster the following year.

1951: The Fender Precision Bass is introduced. It is the first electric bass to earn widespread attention.

1952: The Gibson Les Paul solid-body electric guitar is introduced.

1953: The Gretsch Duo Jet is introduced.

1954: The Fender Stratocaster is introduced.

1955: The Gretsch Chet Atkins 6120 is introduced.

January 27, 1956: Elvis Presley releases "Heartbreak Hotel," arranged by guitarist Atkins. It is the first song to top pop, country, and R&B charts simultaneously.

January 6, 1958: Chuck Berry records the ultimate guitar anthem, "Johnny B. Goode," using his Gibson ES-350T. It's a major hit with both black and white audiences.

1950s

1960s

1962: Gibson is first to market with a mass-produced consumer fuzzbox, the Maestro Fuzz-Tone (FZ-1).

February 9, 1964: The Beatles make their U.S. television debut on *The Ed Sullivan Show.* George Harrison performs on a Gretsch Country Gentleman and John Lennon plays a Rickenbacker 325.

Autumn 1964: Pete Townshend of the Who smashes his guitar for the first time, onstage at the Railway Hotel, London.

1965: Cashing in on the guitar band fad sweeping America, Japan floods the U.S. market with hundreds of thousands of cheap guitars.

January 1965: CBS acquires Fender Musical Instruments.

1960s

July 25, 1965: Folk musician Bob Dylan embraces the electric guitar at the Newport Folk Festival, and sets off a firestorm of controversy. He is accompanied by electric guitarist Mike Bloomfield, who becomes one of the archetypal guitar heroes of the rock era.

July 1966: *Blues Breakers: John Mayall with Eric Clapton*, aka the "Beano" album, is released. Clapton's virtuosity and larger-than-life sound—a Les Paul through an early Marshall amp—play a major role in ushering in the era of the guitar hero.

November 1966: The first wah-wah pedal is created by Warwick Electronics Inc./ Thomas Organ Company.

1967: *Guitar Player*, a popular magazine for guitarists, is founded.

May 12, 1967: *Are You Experienced*, the debut album by the Jimi Hendrix Experience, is released. Hendrix is eventually widely acknowledged as the greatest electric guitar player of all time.

August 15–18, 1969: Jimi Hendrix closes the Woodstock Music and Art Fair with a set that includes "The Star-Spangled Banner," a solo piece showcasing modern guitar innovations such as feedback and distortion.

January 2, 1970: Gruhn Guitars opens in Nashville, Tennessee. It becomes the flagship for the burgeoning vintage guitar market, attracting the likes of Duane Allman, Hank Williams Jr., and Eric Clapton.

1972: Larry DiMarzio builds and markets his first Super Distortion pickup, kicking off the replacement parts revolution.

1975: A nineteen-year-old Paul Reed Smith sells one of his first handmade instruments to hard rock guitarist Ted Nugent.

1970s

ca. 1975: Edward Van Halen constructs his first "Frankenstrat" guitar, using parts from a Gibson ES-335 and replacement guitar bodies and necks made by Boogie Bodies.

October 28, 1977: *Never Mind the Bollocks, Here's the Sex Pistols* is released.

1979: The first "headless" Steinberger bass, made entirely out of a graphite and carbon fiber mix, is introduced.

1970s

1980s

1980: *Guitar World,* a popular magazine for guitarists, is founded.

August 1, 1981: MTV debuts on cable television, programming pop music videos twenty-four hours a day, seven days a week.

February 13, 1983: The single "Beat It," written and performed by Michael Jackson, featuring Edward Van Halen on lead guitar, is released. The video of the song is often credited as paving the way for black artists on MTV.

1985: Paul Reed Smith produces his first factory-built PRS Custom.

1987: Ibanez introduces the Steve Vai JEM series. It is followed in 1990 with the Universe series, a seven-string version of the JEM.

March 21, 1991: Leo Fender dies at age eighty-one.

1998: Billionaire Paul Allen purchases the Hendrix Woodstock Strat for a reported $2 million.

1999: Jack White of the White Stripes purchases a vintage 1966 Montgomery Ward Airline guitar from Detroit musician Jack Yarber (aka Jack Oblivian). White's eventual success revives interest in what many had considered "junk" guitars from the fifties and sixties.

1990s

Twenty-first Century

2001: Canada's Eastwood Guitars launches a line of Valco Airline copy guitars.

June 13, 2001: Glenn Branca conducts his *Symphony No. 13: Hallucination City* for a hundred electric guitars at the base of the World Trade Center in New York.

August 12, 2009: Les Paul dies at age ninety-four.

2016: The Ernie Ball St. Vincent signature model guitar is introduced. Annie Clark (St. Vincent) designed the guitar such that, among its many features, it better accommodates female players.

ACKNOWLEDGMENTS

For guidance throughout, both authors are deeply indebted to our editor at Doubleday, Yaniv Soha. His enthusiasm for the project has been unflagging and his insights have helped shape the narrative at every turn. Kudos are also due to Yaniv's assistant, the detail-oriented and diplomatic Margo Shickmanter. And, of course, the whole thing might never have happened at all without the dedication and good faith of our literary agent, David Dunton at Harvey Klinger.

I would like to thank all my former colleagues at *Guitar World* magazine, where I served as editor in chief for close to twenty-five years. It was during those decades I learned most of what I have to share in this book. The careful guitar scholarship of Chris Gill, Paul Riario, and Harold Steinblatt were particularly instructional.

I'd also like to acknowledge the late musicologist Robert Palmer, whose books *Deep Blues* and *Rock & Roll: An Unruly History* served as inspiration. I am also indebted to Robert's daughter, the very talented Augusta Palmer, for sharing the raw transcripts of his interviews with blues legend Muddy Waters, conducted for *Deep Blues*. They were particularly helpful in writing about Waters's early years in Chicago.

This book wouldn't exist without great musicians and talented luthiers, and I'd like to thank several that spoke with me at length. Steve Vai, Larry DiMarzio, Bill Reim, and Paul Reed Smith helped fill in the missing blanks on the very fertile recent past. Speaking with them not only thoroughly illuminated the last thirty years of electric guitar history, but renewed my optimism about the instrument's future.

On a more personal note, my gratitude goes out to the fabulous Izzy Zay, who suffered through many long and boring weekends while I brought *Play It Loud* to fruition. And thank you to my writing partner, Alan di Perna, whose excellent and insightful work kept me sharp, focused, and moving in the right direction (especially on those evenings when all I wanted to do was eat cereal and watch CNN).

When I really consider the genesis of *Play It Loud*, perhaps the most important people were the Lauerman brothers: Rudy, Ray, and Rob. Ray and Rob were Rudy's older brothers. Both taught me the secrets of how to play electric guitar, years before magazines and YouTube made mysteries such as barre chords and finger vibratos common-day and accessible. Rudy, a fine keyboardist, was perhaps more crucial. He and bassist Jeff Rozany were my best buddies in high school, and it was our shared obsession with playing and listening to music that set me on my path to being a musician and a writer.

—BRAD TOLINSKI

The first chapter of this book, and indeed many other parts, could not have come about without the assistance of my good friend the organologist and electric guitar historian Matthew Hill, who kindly let me read his doctoral dissertation on George Beauchamp prior to its publication. Those who are interested in this fascinating, and often overlooked, chapter of electric guitar history will want to check out Dr. Hill's forthcoming book, *The Rise of the Electric Guitar, 1740–1939.*

Another early electric guitar historian, collector and friend Lynn Wheelwright, offered vital and generous assistance, fielding naive questions and helping me get inside the mind-set of early-twentieth-century guitar makers. John Hall, president of Rickenbacker guitars, furnished a wealth of information, images, and intriguing anecdotes. And Gretsch historian Ed Ball kindly provided production statistics not obtainable elsewhere.

For many years, the musical instrument appraiser and expert Kerry Keane has been one of my most reliable and cordial go-to sources for information on the guitar auction market. His insights were also essential to the preparation of this book. Pioneering electric guitar historian Andre Duchossoir graciously provided a pristine scan of the vintage Fender Telecaster ad on page 70.

It goes without saying—but I'll say it anyway—that I owe a huge debt of gratitude to the many legendary guitarists, guitar makers, and others who have patiently and generously sat for interviews with me over the years. Their words have been an education and an inspiration; their contributions to this book are acknowledged throughout the endnotes.

Another person without whom my share in this project would never have seen completion is my beloved wife, Robin—confidante, research assistant, proofreader, sternest critic, and all around muse. An ocean of thanks also goes out to my coauthor, colleague, and friend of many years, Brad Tolinski, whose abundant talent shines beautifully throughout these pages, and whose generosity and good humor have seen me through many a dark moment.

—ALAN DI PERNA

NOTES

CHAPTER I BROTHER MUSICIAN, LISTEN TO A MIRACLE!

4   Beauchamp's friend: André Millard, ed., *The Electric Guitar: A History of an American Icon* (Baltimore: Johns Hopkins University Press, 2004), 43.

10   "Adolph was a real": Author interview with John C. Hall, December 15, 2005 (Alan di Perna Archive).

10   Known as "Rick" to his friends: Ibid.

12   The Great Depression would: Robert S. McElvaine, *The Great Depression: America, 1929–1941* (New York: Times Books, 1984), 75.

13   De Forest himself: Ritchie Fliegler, *Amps! The Other Half of Rock 'N' Roll* (Milwaukee: Hal Leonard Publishing, 1993), 12.

16   "If you can amplify": Millard, *The Electric Guitar,* 47.

16   A small number: Matthew Hill, *George Beauchamp and the Rise of the Electric Guitar up to 1939* (unpublished doctoral dissertation, University of Edinburgh, 2013), 35–41.

19   There's a legend: Ibid., 76.

20   While primarily designed: Ibid., 90–91.

23   "In the orchestra": Collection of the Wichita-Sedgwick County Historical Museum.

26   "When everybody started": Richard R. Smith, *The Complete History of Rickenbacker Guitars* (Fullerton, Calif.: Centerstream Publishing, 1987), 20.

CHAPTER 2 THE CHRISTIAN CRUSADE

31 Goodman would later: John S. Wilson, "Benny Goodman, King of Swing, Is Dead," *New York Times* (June 14, 1986).

33 "To bring recognition": John Hammond with Irving Townsend, *John Hammond on Record* (New York: Penguin Books, 1977), 68.

34 The bandleader, who: Ibid., 223.

35 Locating a job: Wayne Goins and Craig McKinney, *A Biography of Charlie Christian, Jazz Guitar's King of Swing* (Lewiston, N.Y.: Edwin Mellen Press, 2005).

35 "You couldn't escape": John Perry, "Deep Second Still Lives in Dreams," *The Oklahoman* (January 8, 1993): http://newsok.com/deep-second-still-lives-in-dreams/article/2417719.

36 "We was really dropouts": Jim O'Neal and Amy van Singel, *The Voice of the Blues: Classic Interviews from* Living Blues *Magazine* (Abingdon, U.K.: Routledge, 2002), 142.

38 "For a while it was": Robert Gottlieb, *Reading Jazz: A Gathering of Autobiography, Reportage, and Criticism from 1919 to Now* (New York: Vintage Books, 1996), 108.

42 Two anxious weeks: Goins and McKinney, *A Biography of Charlie Christian*, 150.

44 "Benny didn't have to": Gottlieb, *Reading Jazz*, 128.

45 "I wasn't worried": Ibid., 128

CHAPTER 3 THE WIZARD FROM WAUKESHA

51 "We enjoyed sharing": Andy Babiuk, *The Story of Paul Bigsby: The Father of the Modern Electric Solidbody Guitar* (Savannah, Ga.: FG Publishing, 2008), 33.

53 "Looking back over": Author interview with Les Paul, September 8, 1999 (Alan di Perna Archive).

53 "They were short on hats": Ibid.

53 Hillbilly and western: Bob Millard, *Country Music: 70 Years of America's Favorite Music* (New York: HarperCollins Publishers, 1993), 9–16.

55 "In 1934 the Cumberland": Author interview with Les Paul, September 8, 1999.

57 "In the daytime": Ibid.

59 "When I started fooling": Ibid.

59 And so, starting: Alan di Perna, Michael Molenda, Art Thompson, and Walter Carter, *The Guitar Collection: Stories* (Bellevue, Wash.: Epic Ink, 2011), 62.

60 "I took it to": Dave Hunter, *The Gibson Les Paul: The Illustrated History of the Guitar That Changed Rock* (Minneapolis: Voyageur Press, 2014), 20.

62 "Epi looked at me": Author interview with Les Paul, September 8, 1999.

62 "The guy told me": Ibid.

64   "Bing just loved": Ibid.

66   "She said, 'Lester'": Ibid.

67   "I remember the sound": Chris Gill, "Jeff Beck Pays Tribute on *Rock 'N'*
      Roll Party Honoring Les Paul" (*Guitar World,* April 2011).

68   "She was a very": Author interview with Les Paul, September 8, 1999.

68   "That wouldn't have fell": Ibid.

CHAPTER 4 THE MODEL T

73   "Ozzie said, 'I know'": Author interview with James Burton, Febru-
      ary 4, 2010 (Alan di Perna Archive).

76   "Leo wanted to move": Author interview with George Fullerton, July 14,
      1999 (Alan di Perna Archive).

77   "Leo said that": Forrest White, *Fender: The Inside Story* (San Francisco:
      Miller Freeman Books, 1994), 13.

77   "former shipping clerk": Ibid., 15.

77   "Those years were absolute": Ibid., 15.

79   Exposure to the instruments: Andy Babiuk, *The Story of Paul Bigsby: The*
      Father of the Modern Electric Solidbody Guitar (Savannah, Ga.: FG Publish-
      ing, 2008), 19.

80   "I kept wondering why": Merle Travis, "Recollections of Merle Travis
      1944–1955," *JEMF Quarterly* (Los Angeles: John Edwards Memorial
      Foundation, 1979). Quoted in Babiuk, *The Story of Paul Bigsby,* 44.

82   In later years: White, *Fender,* 39.

83   "We used to draw": Author interview with George Fullerton, July 14,
      1999.

85   "YOUR USE OF TRADEMARK": Richard Rayhill Smith, *Fender: The Sound*
      Heard 'Round the World (Milwaukee: Hal Leonard Publishing, 2003), 86.

85   Reluctantly, Randall: Ibid.

86   "It is a shame": Ibid.

88   "The idea was": Charles and Ray Eames, *An Eames Anthology* (New
      Haven: Yale University Press, 2015), 315.

88   His goals were identical: Charles and Ray Eames, "The Best for the
      Most for the Least," Eames official site, eamesoffice.com.

92   "The guitar should": Tony Bacon and Paul Day, *The Fender Book* (San
      Francisco: Miller Freeman, Inc., 1992), 21.

93   "Two is good": Ibid.

95   "I went to him and said": Author interview with Dick Dale, March 13,
      2009 (Alan di Perna Archive).

96   "I'm interested in": Ibid.

96   "When I plugged that": Ibid.

98   "The teenage market": Robert Perine, "How I Helped Leo Fender"
      (*Vintage Guitar,* September 1997).

99   "[Leo] said, 'Sit down'": White, *Fender,* 145.

99   "Monday evening, January 4": Ibid., 146.

CHAPTER 5 THE BLUES (AND COUNTRY) HAD A BABY

103 It was hard for him: From the raw transcript of an interview with Muddy Waters conducted by Robert Palmer for his book *Deep Blues: A Musical and Cultural History of the Mississippi* (New York: Penguin Books, 1982), courtesy of Amanda Palmer.

104 "I'd be hittin'": Ibid.

104 "It was the fastest": Ibid.

106 "The country sounds": Ibid.

106 "Muddy had a Gretsch": Robert Gordon, *Can't Be Satisfied: The Life and Times of Muddy Waters* (New York: Back Bay Books, 2003), 74.

109 "He had a bass": Ilene Melish, "The Man Who Shaped a Sound," *Melody Maker* (October 6, 1979).

109 Little Walter knew: John Anthony Brisbin, "Jimmy Rogers: I'm Havin' Fun Right Today," *Living Blues* (September/October, 1997).

112 "He was traveling": Author interview with Fred Gretsch III, n.d. (Alan di Perna Archive).

114 In a 1992 interview: Tony Bacon, *The Gretsch Electric Guitar Book* (New York: Backbeat Books, 2015), 16.

116 "At the time I": Ibid.

117 "The colored folk been": Nicholas Dawidoff, *In the Country of Country: A Journey to the Roots of American Music* (New York: Vintage, 2011).

119 "We took the twang": Gerald W. Haslam, Alexandra Russell Haslam, and Richard Chon, *Workin' Man Blues: Country Music in California* (Berkeley and Los Angeles: University of California Press, 1999), 135.

119 "Hoochie Coochie Man": Jas Obrecht, *Rollin' and Tumblin': The Postwar Blues Guitarists* (San Francisco: Miller Freeman Books, 2000), 107.

120 "The music played": Chuck Berry, *Chuck Berry: The Autobiography* (New York: Faber & Faber, 2001), 3.

121 "It was the feeling": Ibid., 98.

CHAPTER 6 THE SOLID-BODY STRADIVARIUS

128 "There were several stores": Eric Clapton, *Clapton: The Autobiography* (New York: Broadway Books, 2007) 52–53.

128 "It was almost brand new": Michael Leonard, "Touched by the Hand of God," *Guitarist Icons* (n.d.), 15.

129 "The result": Clapton, *Clapton*, 72–73.

132 "As is well known": Author interview with Billy Gibbons, May 29, 2007 (Alan di Perna Archive).

134 "He was a Golden": Author interview with Paul Reed Smith, 2009 (Alan di Perna Archive).

135 "Their attitude was": Tony Bacon and Paul Day, *The Gibson Les Paul Book: A Complete History of Les Paul Guitars* (San Francisco: GPI Books, 1993), 13.

137   "I said, 'What about Les Paul?'": Willie G. Moseley, "Ted McCarty: I'm Not a Musician," *Vintage Guitar* (April 1999).

137   McCarty vehemently denied: Bacon and Day, *The Gibson Les Paul Book*, 16.

138   Les claimed credit: Author interview with Les Paul, September 9, 1999 (Alan di Perna Archive).

144   "I preferred the tone": Moseley, "Ted McCarty."

144   "Fender was talking": Ibid.

CHAPTER 7   THE FAB TWELVE

157   On January 2, 1964: Richard Smith, *The Complete History of Rickenbacker Guitars* (Fullerton, Calif.: Centerstream Publishing, 1987), 69.

157   "Watch out for": Ibid.

157   "I have a definite": Andy Babiuk, *Beatles Gear: All the Fab Four's Instruments from Stage to Studio* (San Francisco: Backbeat Books, 2001), 108.

160   Sitting in bed in: Smith, *The Complete History*, 77.

168   "Roger certainly had": Author interview with John C. Hall, December 15, 2005 (Alan di Perna Archive).

168   He and his wife: Ibid.

168   "He became the father": Ibid.

168   The twelve-string guitar produces: Michael Simmons, "12-String Power," *Acoustic Guitar* (November 1997), 51.

169   It's a subtle difference: Bjorn Eriksson, "The Beatles and Their Rickenbacker Guitars," rickbeat.com (website).

169   The Beatles' prominent use: Author interview with Gretsch historian Edward Ball, June 3, 2015 (Alan di Perna Archive).

173   In the vivid language: Ritchie Fliegler, *Amps! The Other Half of Rock 'N' Roll* (Milwaukee: Hal Leonard Publishing, 1993), 31.

174   Clarke phoned his boss: Babiuk, *Beatles Gear*, 67.

176   "When we started playing": Author interview with Keith Richards, July 25, 1997 (Alan di Perna Archive).

177   "British R&B bands": Author interview with Giorgio Gomelsky, 1983 (Alan di Perna Archive).

177   "The very little budding": Ibid.

178   "We were a blues band": Author interview with Keith Richards, July 25, 1997.

178   "The Stones weren't really": Author interview with Gomelsky, 1983.

180   "Brian was always searching": Author interview with Keith Richards, July 10, 2002 (Alan di Perna Archive).

181   "It was my first touch": Ibid.

CHAPTER 8   THE REVOLUTION WILL BE AMPLIFIED

187   "The Star-Spangled": Author interview with Michael Lang, October 9, 2013 (Alan di Perna Archive).

189 "On that song": Author interview with Billy Cox, January 22, 2013 (Alan di Perna Archive).

190 "The rain really": Author interview with Jack Casady, April 21, 2009 (Alan di Perna Archive).

190 "Jimi looked out": Author interview with Billy Cox, January 22, 2013.

191 Hendrix backpedaled: Charles Cross, *Room Full of Mirrors: A Biography of Jimi Hendrix* (New York: Hyperion Books, 2005), 271.

191 "He would never raise": Author interview with Jeff Beck, January 11, 1999 (Alan di Perna Archive).

194 One report has claimed: Sy and Barbara Ribakove, *Folk-Rock: The Bob Dylan Story* (New York: Dell Publishing, 1966), 61.

195 "The electric guitar represented": Howard Sounes, *Down the Highway: The Life of Bob Dylan* (New York, Grove Press, 2001), 200.

195 "I was absolutely screaming": Ibid., 182.

196 "He played all kinds": Jan Mark Wolkin and Bill Keenom, eds., *Michael Bloomfield: If You Love These Blues* (New York: Backbeat Books, 2000), 99.

197 "I remember going to": Author interview with Jorma Kaukonen, May 22, 2013 (Alan di Perna Archive).

197 "I saw him at a few": Jann Wenner, "The Rolling Stone Interview: Mike Bloomfield," *Rolling Stone* (April 6, 1968).

197 "It was never like": Wolkin and Keenom, *Michael Bloomfield*, 101.

198 "Dylan just got a hair": Sounes, *Down the Highway*, 180–81.

203 "Bill hired B.B.": Wolkin and Keenom, *Michael Bloomfield*, 124.

204 "Prior to Bloomfield": Author interview with George Gruhn, October 20, 2010 (Alan di Perna Archive).

204 "When Bloomfield was playing": Ibid.

205 Bob Dylan himself: John Anderson, director, *Born in Chicago* (documentary film, Anderson Productions, 2013).

206 "I had a terrible": Author interview with Jeff Beck, January 11, 1999.

207 "It was totally magical": Ibid.

209 "Auto-destructive art": Peter Selz and Kristine Stiles, eds., *Theories and Documents of Contemporary Art: A Sourcebook of Artists' Writings* (Berkeley: University of California Press, 1996), 401–4.

209 "The toggle switch": Author interview with Pete Townshend, July 6, 1994 (Alan di Perna Archive).

211 "I started to knock": Richard Barnes, *The Who: Maximum R&B* (New York: St. Martin's Press, 1982), 37.

212 "Pete was one of": Author interview with Jim Marshall, June 11, 2002 (Alan di Perna Archive).

213 "They came to me": Ibid.

214 "When Pete started to": Ibid.

214 "I bought some": Author interview with John Entwistle, July 5, 1994 (Alan di Perna Archive).

216 "Hendrix came to": Author interview with Pete Townshend, July 6, 1994.

216 "Jimi was covered": Author interview with Pete Townshend, April 26, 1996 (Alan di Perna Archive).

218 "I was the hotshot": Jerry Hopkins, *Hit and Run: The Jimi Hendrix Story* (New York: Perigee Books, 1983), 81.

218 Bloomfield introduced himself: Ibid., 81.

219 As a musician: Author interview with Al Marks, January 18, 2013 (Alan di Perna Archive).

219 "I shared with Eric": Author interview with Pete Townshend, April 26, 1996.

221 "I thought it was incredible": Eric Clapton, *Clapton: The Autobiography* (New York: Broadway Books, 2007), 80.

221 "Even if it had been crap": Author interview with Jeff Beck, January 11, 1999.

225 The idea of putting: Author interview with Lou Adler, August 8, 2007 (Alan di Perna Archive).

226 "Jimi was on acid": Author interview with Pete Townshend, July 6, 1994.

228 "Monterey was predominantly": Peter Neal, ed., *Jimi Hendrix: Starting at Zero* (New York: Bloomsbury, 2013), 88.

228 "That was something that I couldn't": Author interview with Michelle Phillips, August 10, 2007 (Alan di Perna Archive).

231 "He couldn't see a market": Author interview with Jeff Beck, January 11, 1999.

231 "I also knew that stereo": Marc Meyers, "The Making of 'Whole Lotta Love,'" *Wall Street Journal*, May 29, 2014.

232 "From 1966 onwards": Michael Doyle, *The History of Marshall* (Milwaukee: Hal Leonard Publishing, 1993), 16.

235 Seminal punk band: Author interview with Johnny Ramone, March 8, 1995 (Alan di Perna Archive).

CHAPTER 9 ERUPTIONS

238 Cocaine took its place: Office of Applied Studies, Substance Abuse and Mental Health Services Administration, *Preliminary Results from the 1997 National Household Survey on Drug Abuse* (Rockville, Md.: U.S. Department of Health and Human Services, 1998), 66.

239 Memorably described by: Ian Christe, *Everybody Wants Some: The Van Halen Saga* (Hoboken: John Wiley & Sons, Inc., 2007), 33.

240 When they arrived: Ibid.

240 "When I came to": Chris Gill, "Of Wolf and Man," *Guitar World* (February 2009).

240 "When I first picked": Steven Rosen, "The Life and Times of Van Halen," *Guitar World* (July 1985).

241   "I bought one": Gill, "Of Wolf and Man."

245   "I started building": Chris Butler, "Fathers of Invention," *Guitar World Buyer's Guide 1990–91* (New York: Stanley R. Harris, 1990), 133.

247   "The first time Ed": Wayne Charvel, www.wayneguitars.com.

248   "That 335 used": Gill, "Of Wolf and Man."

248   "I slapped a humbucker": Ibid.

251   "Tapping is like": Steven Rosen, "California Dreamin'," in *Guitar World Presents Van Halen* (Milwaukee: Backbeat Books, 2010), 36.

251   "For my money": Author interview with Jimmy Page, October 1999 (Brad Tolinski Archive).

252   "I get this call": Joseph Bosso, "The Monster of Rock," in *Guitar World Presents Van Halen* (Milwaukee: Backbeat Books, 2010), 190.

255   "I don't know": Gill, "Of Wolf and Man."

255   "The museum collects": "National Museum of American History Receives Van Halen's 'Frankenstein Replica' Guitar," National Museum of American History, press release, February 6, 2011, http://american history.si.edu.

CHAPTER 10   MADE IN JAPAN

257   "It was like a monolith": Author interview with Steve Vai, September 30, 2015 (Brad Tolinski Archive).

265   In 1962, Teisco: Frank Meyers, *History of Japanese Electric Guitars* (Anaheim, Calif.: Centerstream Publishing, 2015).

266   founded in 1908: Joe Bosso, "How the West Was Won," in *The Wild & Weird History of the Electric Guitar* (single-issue magazine from *Guitar One* and *Guitar World*, 2012).

267   "When I came on": Author interview with Bill Reim, September 21, 2015 (Brad Tolinski Archive).

270   Within months, record stores: Simon Reynolds, *Rip It Up and Start Again: Postpunk 1978–1984* (Penguin Books, 2006), 340, 342–43.

271   "Functional and clean": Author interview with Ned Steinberger (Alan di Perna Archive).

272   "Traditional basses were": Ibid.

CHAPTER 11   THE REVENGE OF THE NERDS

277   "I remember meeting Paul": Author interview with Ted Nugent, December 9, 2015 (Brad Tolinski Archive).

278   "It was Paul Reed": Ibid.

279   "There were immense": Author interview with Paul Reed Smith, November 23, 2015 (Brad Tolinski Archive).

281   Realizing the magnitude: Dave Burrluck, *The PRS Guitar Book: A Complete History of Paul Reed Smith Guitars* (New York: Backbeat Books, 1999).

282 "His bright eyes": Author interview with Carlos Santana, May 23, 2008 (Alan di Perna Archive).

285 While his guitars: Burrluck, *The PRS Guitar Book*, 30.

285 "You had your Gibson": Chris Gill, "Building the Perfect Beast," in *The Wild & Weird History of the Electric Guitar* (single-issue magazine from *Guitar One* and *Guitar World*, 2012).

287 "They were just": Tom Beaujour, *Guitar Aficionado, The Collections: The Most Famous, Rare and Valuable Guitars in the World* (New York: Time Home Entertainment Inc., 2013), 147.

288 "Jimmy was still playing": Author interview with Joe Walsh, October 10, 2012 (Brad Tolinski Archive).

289 "I could joke": Alan di Perna, "George Gruhn: Nashville's Vintage Guru," *Guitar Aficionado* (Winter 2011).

294 "I thought, who's Ted McCarty?": Author interview with Paul Reed Smith, November 23, 2015 (Brad Tolinski Archive).

295 McCarty had faded: Burrluck, *The PRS Guitar Book*.

295 "I'm no guitar snob": Author interview with Billie Joe Armstrong, 2004 (Alan di Perna Archive).

CHAPTER 12 PLASTIC FANTASTIC

302 "The idea behind": Jimmy Leslie, "Jack White Mega Sonic on the Sounds That Drive the White Stripes, Raconteurs and Dead Weather," *Guitar Player* (September 9, 2010).

303 "It's obviously harder": Author interview with Jack White, April 13, 2007 (Alan di Perna Archive).

305 "We found that": Tom Wheeler, *American Guitars: An Illustrated History* (New York: HarperCollins, 1990), 310.

306 In it the writer: Terry Carlton, "Whack Job: 1964 Montgomery Ward Airline," *Guitar Player* (June 4, 2013).

308 "The foundation of": Author interview with Kerry Keane, September 15, 2015 (Alan di Perna Archive).

310 "I like raw": Author interview with Dan Auerbach, June 11, 2014 (Alan di Perna Archive).

312 "I usually use off-brand": Ibid.

312 Auerbach was still: Ibid.

314 "I wanted to open up": Author interview with Patti Smith, October 9, 1997 (Alan di Perna Archive).

314 "I was impressed": H. P. Newquist, "Glenn Branca Interview: The Devil's Choirmaster," *Guitar Magazine* (March 1996).

316 "I'm bored with": Anil Prasad, "Marc Ribot," *Guitar Player* (October 17, 2008).

317 "It was completely inside": Author interview with Thurston Moore, May 19, 2000 (Alan di Perna Archive).

322 "My particular guitar": Corbin Reiff, "St. Vincent Discusses Her New

Signature Ernie Ball Music Man Guitar," *Guitar World* website, posted February 14, 2016.

323 "I can't even play": Ibid.

323 "The inevitable result": David Byrne, "The Internet Will Suck All Creative Content Out of the World," *The Guardian* (October 11, 2013).

324 "A culture of blockbusters": Ibid.

325 Speaking with *Rolling Stone*: Simon Vozick-Levinson, "Q&A: Rick Ross," *Rolling Stone* (January 28, 2016).

BIBLIOGRAPHY

Babiuk, Andy. *Beatles Gear: All the Fab Four's Instruments from Stage to Studio.* San Francisco: Backbeat Books, 2001.

Babiuk, Andy. *The Story of Paul Bigsby: The Father of the Modern Electric Solidbody Guitar.* Savannah, Ga.: FG Publishing, 2008.

Babiuk, Andy, and Greg Prevost. *Rolling Stones Gear: All the Stones' Instruments from Stage to Studio.* Milwaukee: Backbeat Books, 2013.

Bacon, Tony. *The Gretsch Electric Guitar Book.* New York: Backbeat Books, 2015.

Bacon, Tony, and Paul Day. *The Fender Book.* San Francisco: Miller Freeman, Inc., 1992.

Bacon, Tony, and Paul Day. *The Gibson Les Paul Book: A Complete History of Les Paul Guitars.* San Francisco: GPI Books, 1993.

Barnes, Richard. *The Who: Maximum R&B.* New York: St. Martin's Press, 1982.

Berry, Chuck. *Chuck Berry: The Autobiography.* New York: Faber & Faber, 2001.

Bosso, Joseph. "The Monster of Rock," in *Guitar World Presents Van Halen.* Milwaukee: Backbeat Books, 2010.

Burrluck, Dave. *The PRS Guitar Book: A Complete History of Paul Reed Smith Guitars.* New York: Backbeat Books, 1999.

Carson, Annette. *Jeff Beck: Crazy Fingers.* San Francisco: Backbeat Books, 2001.

Carter, Walter. *The Gibson Electric Guitar Book: Seventy Years of Classic Guitars.* New York: Backbeat Books, 2007.

Christe, Ian. *Everybody Wants Some: The Van Halen Saga.* Hoboken: John Wiley & Sons, Inc., 2007.

Clapton, Eric. *Clapton: The Autobiography.* New York: Broadway Books, 2007.

Cross, Charles. *Room Full of Mirrors: A Biography of Jimi Hendrix*. New York: Hyperion Books, 2005.

Dawidoff, Nicholas. *In the Country of Country: A Journey to the Roots of American Music*. New York: Vintage Books, 2011.

di Perna, Alan, Michael Molenda, Art Thompson, and Walter Carter. *The Guitar Collection: Stories*. Bellevue, Wash.: Epic Ink, 2011.

Doyle, Michael. *The History of Marshall*. Milwaukee: Hal Leonard Publishing, 1993.

Eames, Charles and Ray. *An Eames Anthology*. London: Yale University Press, 2015.

Fliegler, Ritchie. *Amps! The Other Half of Rock 'N' Roll*. Milwaukee: Hal Leonard Publishing, 1993.

Goins, Wayne, and Craig McKinney. *A Biography of Charlie Christian, Jazz Guitar's King of Swing*. Lewiston, N.Y.: Edwin Mellen Press, 2005.

Gordon, Robert. *Can't Be Satisfied: The Life and Times of Muddy Waters*. New York: Little, Brown, 2002.

Gottlieb, Robert. *Reading Jazz: A Gathering of Autobiography, Reportage, and Criticism from 1919 to Now*. New York: Vintage Books, 1996.

Hammond, John, with Irving Townsend. *John Hammond on Record*. New York: Penguin Books, 1977.

Haslam, Gerald W., Alexandra Russell Haslam, and Richard Chon. *Workin' Man Blues: Country Music in California*. Berkeley: University of California Press, 1999.

Hill, Matthew. *George Beauchamp and the Rise of the Electric Guitar up to 1939*. Edinburgh: University of Edinburgh Press, 2013.

Hopkins, Jerry. *Hit and Run: The Jimi Hendrix Story*. New York: Perigee Books, 1983.

Hunter, Dave. *The Gibson Les Paul: The Illustrated History of the Guitar That Changed Rock*. Minneapolis: Voyageur Press, 2014.

McDermott, John, with Eddie Kramer. *Hendrix: Setting the Record Straight*. New York: Warner Books, 1992.

McElvaine, Robert S. *The Great Depression*. New York: Times Books, 1993.

Meyers, Frank. *History of Japanese Electric Guitars*. Anaheim, Calif.: Centerstream Publishing, 2015.

Millard, André, ed. *The Electric Guitar: A History of an American Icon*. Baltimore: Johns Hopkins University Press, 2004.

Millard, Bob. *Country Music: 70 Years of America's Favorite Music*. New York: HarperCollins Publishers, 1993.

Neal, Peter, ed. *Jimi Hendrix: Starting at Zero*. New York: Bloomsbury, 2013.

Norman, Philip. *Shout! The Beatles in Their Generation*. New York: Simon & Schuster, 1981.

Obrecht, Jas. *Rollin' and Tumblin': The Postwar Blues Guitarists*. San Francisco: Miller Freeman Books, 2000.

O'Neal, Jim, and Amy van Singel. *The Voice of the Blues: Classic Interviews from Living Blues Magazine*. Abingdon, U.K.: Routledge, 2002.

Palmer, Robert. *Deep Blues: A Musical and Cultural History of the Mississippi Delta to Chicago's South Side to the World*. New York: Penguin Books, 1982.

Reynolds, Simon. *Rip It Up and Start Again: Postpunk 1978–1984*. New York: Penguin Books, 2006.

Ribakove, Sy and Barbara. *Folk-Rock: The Bob Dylan Story*. New York: Dell Publishing, 1966.

Rosen, Steven. "California Dreamin'," in *Guitar World Presents Van Halen*. Milwaukee: Backbeat Books, 2010.

Smith, Richard R. *The Complete History of Rickenbacker Guitars*. Fullerton, Calif.: Centerstream Publishing, 1987.

Sounes, Howard. *Down the Highway: The Life of Bob Dylan*. New York: Grove Press, 2001.

Thurber, James. *The Thurber Carnival*. New York: Harper & Row, 1945.

Wheeler, Tom. *American Guitars: An Illustrated History*. New York: Harper Perennial, 1990.

White, Forrest. *Fender: The Inside Story*. San Francisco: Miller Freeman Books, 1994.

Wolkin, Jan Mark, and Bill Keenom, eds. *Michael Bloomfield: If You Love These Blues*. New York: Backbeat Books, 2000.

INDEX

Page numbers in *italics* refer to illustrations.

ILLUSTRATION CREDITS

Page 2   George D. Beauchamp. United States Patent Office Application,
            "Electrical String Musical Instrument." June 2, 1934.
Page 21   Courtesy of John Hall, Rickenbacker
Page 30   Courtesy of JP Jazz Archive/Redferns
Page 48   Courtesy of Michael Ochs Archive/Getty Images
Page 70   Courtesy of Andre Duchossoir
Page 102   Courtesy of Michael Ochs Archive/Getty Images
Page 126   Courtesy of Michael Ochs Archive/Getty Images
Page 152   Courtesy of K & K Ulf Kruger OHG/Redferns
Page 186   Courtesy of Barry Z. Levine/Getty Images
Page 236   Courtesy of Ross Halfin
Page 256   Courtesy of Jesse Wild/Guitarist Magazine via Getty Images
Page 276   Courtesy of Robert Knight Archives/Redferns
Page 298   Courtesy of Ross Halfin_Idols